A West Ham season ticket holder, who also follows Torquay United, Peter Caton has watched over 1,400 matches at 110 different grounds. In 2004 he set up the campaign Stand Up Sit Down, which aimed to allow the choice for all supporters to either sit or stand as they watch football. This was merged with the Football Supporters' Federation in 2009 and Peter remains an active member of their Safe Standing Group.

The author's first book Essex Coast Walk was published in 2009 and describes a walk along the entire length of the Essex coast. His second book, No Boat Required was published in 2011 and describes his travels to the 43 tidal islands which can be walked to from the UK mainland.

www.petercatonbooks.co.uk

STAND UP
SIT DOWN

A choice to watch football

PETER CATON

Matador
9 Priory Business Park,
Wistow Road, Kibworth Beauchamp,
Leicestershire. LE8 0RX
Tel: (+44) 116 279 2299
Fax: (+44) 116 279 2277
Email: books@troubador.co.uk
Web: www.troubador.co.uk/matador

ISBN 978 1780881 775

British Library Cataloguing in Publication Data.
A catalogue record for this book is available from the British Library.

Typeset in 11pt Sabon MT by Troubador Publishing Ltd, Leicester, UK
Printed and bound in the UK by TJ International, Padstow, Cornwall

Matador is an imprint of Troubador Publishing Ltd

CONTENTS

More photographs of the football grounds visited, and information on the author's other books can be seen at:

www.petercatonbooks.co.uk

INTRODUCTION

How often do we hear commentators refer to fans on the terraces, when these have been banned from our top grounds for over fifteen years? How often do we hear debate about a 'return to standing', when almost half our lower league grounds still have terraces and many supporters at all-seated stadia stand in front of their seats?

For more than a hundred years most supporters stood up to watch football and to many this remains the natural way to be part of an exciting sporting event. The tragic loss of 96 lives at Hillsborough, the ongoing problem of hooliganism and the state of many of our grounds, meant that something had to be done. A report by Lord Justice Taylor recommended that stadia should be all-seated and by the mid 1990s terraces had disappeared from our top grounds.

Despite Lord Taylor's prediction, many supporters neither got used to or accepted sitting, and there are repeated calls for standing to be permitted once more. The Government, safety and football authorities however resolutely rebuff attempts by supporters for the regulations to be changed. It is an often emotive argument that is far more complex that many realise.

In Stand Up Sit Down I have set out to document and consider the arguments for and against permitting the choice to stand at all football grounds. I've looked in depth at the background that led to all-seating and at some of the myths that prevail, particularly regarding the appalling events at and in the aftermath of Hillsborough. The current situation, legal position and various solutions which have been put forward to allow the choice to stand, are considered in detail.

In order to find out how well our terraces work and whether there were plans for redevelopment, I visited the 23 English clubs where they remain, talking to supporters, safety officers and club management. At some I watched matches, observing whether standing caused any problems and how popular it was with supporters. My travels also took me to Yorkshire to watch a rugby league match and to Germany to stand on a brand new convertible standing/seating area.

Campaigns by supporters' organisations for the choice to stand are examined, providing much insight into the arguments and background behind them.

By seeking information from the various bodies that oppose the reintroduction of standing at Premier League and Championship grounds, I have been able to set out the arguments in favour of retaining all-seating. These I have considered in detail and drawn together as conclusions in what I originally thought would be then last chapter. My final chapter perhaps raises more questions than the rest of the book answers.

I have tried to include as many photographs as possible of the terraces that remain in England, partly as a record, and partly to help the reader consider whether they appear safe.

At this point I should tell you about myself and my background. As a West Ham supporter, who also follows Torquay United, plus occasionally AFC Hornchurch and England, I've watched over 1,400 matches at 110 different grounds. Perhaps I've chosen the wrong clubs, as not counting play-offs, in 35 years I've seen just three trophies won – one FA Cup courtesy of Sir Trevor Brooking, one (old) Division Two Championship and, on a very enjoyable evening in Metz, the egg cup sized Intertoto Cup.

My interest in football has always extended to the supporters who watch it, whether it be the songs they sing, the numbers who travel away, the way we are policed, or the choice to stand. I was involved in the anti Bond Scheme protests at West Ham, the campaign for supporters to be consulted about the move to Stratford and have been an active member of various supporters' organisations.

In 2004 I set up the campaign Stand Up Sit Down, which sought choice for how supporters watched the game. I have used the same name for this book, because like the campaign it is looking at choice for all, not simply the right to stand. Having worked closely with the Football Supporters' Federation's Safe Standing campaign, in 2009 the two were merged, and I became part of the FSF's Safe Standing Group. My main role on this has been 'Protection of Existing Terraces', as we sought to prevent further loss of standing areas.

In my visits to clubs I have worn two hats, as both author and FSF representative. I must stress however that this book is my own initiative and that is has not been written on behalf of the Football Supporters' Federation, whose views it may not necessarily represent.

A great deal of research has been carried out in writing the book, with information obtained from numerous sources. I've researched information as much as reasonably possible and made every effort to ensure that all facts are accurate, but will be happy to be corrected if otherwise.

I should make it clear that some opinions shown are those of the individual and may not represent those of the organisation to which they belong. There are many comments that I would like to have included but have had to leave out in order not to break confidences or harm relationships.

I have often referred to the Football Licensing Authority (FLA) who changed their name to the Sports Grounds Safety Authority shortly before the book was completed. To save confusion I have however referred to them throughout as the FLA.

Although I started writing the book already holding firm views, I wanted to show and consider all the arguments. I was however willing to be swayed or conclude that the argument may be finely balanced. I have made my own conclusions, but aimed to present the evidence so that readers may form their own views. I hope that those reading will put aside any pre-conceived opinions and come to a reasoned conclusion based on the facts I have presented.

ACKNOWLEDGEMENTS

I am grateful for the help of many people in the researching and writing of this book. In particular:

David Ayris
Michael Brunskill
David Caton
Debbie Caton
Margaret Caton
Michael Caton
Malcolm Clarke
Jon Darch
Peter Daykin
Phill Gatenby
Jon Keen
Amanda Matthews
Chris Nash
Steve Powell
Dean Purkis
Ruth Shaw
Mark Willis
Stuart Wood

Also all the contacts at the clubs I visited, who provided information, showed me round grounds and allowed me to photograph their terraces.

PART ONE

BACKGROUND TO ALL-SEATING

CHAPTER ONE

A SERIES OF DISASTERS

It's normal to stand to enjoy a rock concert. A church congregation sits down for the sermon but stands to sing hymns. A theatre audience sits for the show but often stands at the end to applaud. Spectators sit to watch cricket, maybe jumping up when a wicket is taken, but during a horse race most stand. The difference perhaps – we sit to be entertained, but stand to be a more active part of an event.

Many football supporters don't go just to be entertained – if this were the case some of us would be disappointed more often than not! Supporters want to be part of the event – to make the atmosphere, encourage their team, banter with opposition fans, berate the referee and perhaps goad the other team's star player. Hence it is natural to want to stand. Some fans prefer to sit, but many wish to stand, a choice that is being taken away from us. Polls consistently show that a majority of fans believe there should be a choice to stand or sit.

Traditionally the majority of supporters stood on terraces and gate money formed the bulk of clubs' income, but the game has changed. No longer is it just a sport but now a business. The paying customer is often taken for granted, their views ignored and the agenda set by TV, police, politicians, self interest and money. We were told that all-seated grounds are the way forward, that we'd get used to sitting and this is the civilised way to watch football. 'Watch' being the key word. One sits to watch, one stands to participate in the event. Many supporters however have refused to accept all-seating. Tens of thousands stand up in front of seats every week and campaigners seeking the choice to stand continue to work on their behalf.

It is generally accepted that for political, if not necessarily safety reasons, we will not again see the likes of Aston Villa's Holte End terrace, which held 22,600 prior to being replaced with an all-seated stand in 1995. Irrespective of whether they meet safety regulations, terraces such as Liverpool's Kop, Manchester United's Stretford End and Arsenal's North Bank have gone forever. Many supporters however see no logical reason why we cannot have smaller safe standing areas at all grounds, not just those in the lower divisions.

Ironically it was to get round a safety regulation that the first British football ground went all-seated. Clydebank's promotion to the Scottish Premier Division in 1977 meant that if their ground capacity was over 10,000 it would have to comply with the Safety of Sports Grounds Act. Faced with a large bill to ensure compliance of Kilbowie Park, the club opted to bolt wooden bench seats onto open terraces, cutting capacity to 9,950. Aberdeen followed suit in 1979, putting benches onto the South Terrace, and when the following year a cantilevered roof was added, Pittodrie became the first British covered all-seater football ground.

Highfield Road, England's first all-seated ground, proved to be an unsuccessful experiment. Conversion was pushed through against the wishes of fans by Coventry's controversial chairman, the ex Fulham player and TV pundit Jimmy Hill, who was convinced that this was the way to stop hooliganism. However within months Leeds fans proved him wrong, ripping up 400 seats as missiles after their team lost 4.0. Conversion cut capacity from 36,500 to 20,600 and with every game all-ticket, attendances dropped. Four years after they had been installed, seats were taken out of the East 'Kop' Terrace and Hill's all-seater dream had failed.

Hooliganism, a problem from the 1960s, peaked from the mid 70s to early 80s, with all-seating often suggested as a solution. The practice of 'taking' home ends sometimes caused problems inside grounds, with away fans attempting to occupy home strongholds. Serious fighting was however less common than generally perceived, probably as the majority of those involved, whilst gaining a tribal thrill from taking the territory, didn't actually want to throw a punch. Contrary to popular belief, serious trouble in grounds was mostly restricted to certain fixtures, such as local derbies. Fans could usually predict games where problems would occur and knew that most would pass off without incident. By the mid 80s 'taking' home ends was largely out of fashion and hooliganism, although still a problem, was calming down. Whilst still having standing areas, grounds were becoming less confrontational and violence rare.

However, perhaps the most infamous football 'riot' in England occurred in February 1985, when Millwall played at Luton in an FA Cup 6th round match. Knowing they would have a large following Millwall had requested that the game be made all-ticket, but the home club declined. The away terrace was full well before kick off and fans scaled fences, some to escape overcrowding, but others intent on causing trouble. Home stands were attacked, with seats used as missiles, and the match halted twice. With TV news showing dramatic film of Millwall followers invading the pitch and hurling seats at police, the nation was shocked. Margaret Thatcher, a Prime Minster known neither for her love of football or understanding of society's problems, vowed to deal with hooliganism.

Responding to the Millwall riot, Luton Town brought in a membership scheme, banning all visiting supporters from Kenilworth Road and forcing home fans to carry identity cards. The club were barred entry to the League Cup for breaching its rules on away allocations, but Chairman David Evans, himself a Conservative MP, stood firm. They didn't however stop some determined visiting fans (including me!) from getting into Kenilworth Road.

Outbreaks of violence though were becoming increasingly isolated.

Arrest rates in 1984/5 were just 0.034% and the combined arrest / ejection rate 0.072%. The following season these fell by 51% and 33% respectively, yet the common perception, fuelled by media hysteria, was that fighting took place at almost every match.

Despite reducing hooliganism, football was at a low by the mid 1980s. Attendances had fallen, ageing stadia often lacked more than basic facilities, and with tragic consequences, there was woefully inadequate concern for safety. Three disasters rocked the world of football and shocked the country.

Before considering these however, we should look back to 1971 when 66 fans died on a misty winter afternoon in Glasgow. On 2nd January, a Rangers v Celtic match that had been goalless and unusually uneventful, sprang to life when Jimmy Johnstone scored a header in the final minute. As Celtic fans celebrated, Rangers won a free kick from which Colin Stein steered home the equaliser. At the final whistle the home fans turned to leave, but on Stairway 13 someone slipped and in an instant a massive chain reaction saw people pile up on top of each other. As more supporters continued to set off down the stairs there was no escape, with fans crushed and suffocated. Bodies heaped six foot high. Of the 66 dead, 31 were aged less than twenty, the youngest just eight years old. Five young classmates from the town of Markinch in Fife died together on the stairs.

This was not the first incident on Stairway 13. In 1961 two men had died and in 1969 twenty four were injured in another crush. Little had been done to improve safety and on that foggy January afternoon, once the barriers buckled under the weight of people, heavy loss of life was inevitable.

A public inquiry headed by Lord Wheatley refuted initial suggestions that the crush was caused by Rangers fans, who had left after Celtic scored, attempting to return to the terrace when they heard the cheer for the equaliser. This myth is however still commonly believed today. Wheatley concluded that the cause was simply the downward force of so many supporters leaving at the same time, with the momentum of the crowd meaning that once people started to fall there was no way of holding back the mass of bodies.

Following the inquiry, the Government passed the Safety of Sports Ground Act 1975, which required that 'designated grounds' possessed a safety certificate. Improvements were made, notably that zig zags were put into exits to avoid long continious stairway descents. Sadly though, another 191 football supporters would die and more than 1,600 be injured, before the combined dangers of inadeqaute stadia and poorly regulated crowds was finally grasped.

On 11th May 1985 Bradford City were playing Lincoln City in what should have been a celebration of Bradford's promotion. When smoke was seen in the antiquated wooden stand few were initially concerned, but within four minutes the whole stand was a horrifying inferno, with burning bitumen falling from the roof. Many supporters escaped onto the pitch. Others headed for the exits under the stand, but found that most were shut, with no stewards to open them. Despite many heroic and selfless acts of bravery (over fifty people were credited with saving at least one life), 56 fans died and 265 were injured.

An inquiry headed by Sir Oliver Popplewell found that the cause was a lighted match or cigarette igniting accumulated rubbish under the stand. There were no risers between the wooden steps and litter had built up for years. A police officer searching the remains found a 1968 copy of the local *Telegraph and Argus* newspaper. It seems hard to believe that smoking was permitted in a wooden grandstand, but attitudes then to both smoking and safety were very different from those of today.

The inquiry learned that West Yorkshire Metropolitan County

Council, the body responsible for football ground and fire safety, had written to the club less than a year earlier, specifically warning about the main stand – *'The timber construction is a fire hazard and in particular, there is a build-up of combustible materials in the voids beneath the seats. A carelessly discarded cigarette could give rise to a fire risk.'* The club however failed to act on the warning, or even reply to the letter. Vice chairman Jack Tordoff told Popplewell, and the subsequent legal action by the bereaved and injured, that he believed the letter referred to surface litter, not to rubbish under the stands. Interviewed by *The Guardian* twenty five years after the tragedy he said they were operating, *'in the culture of those days'*, when the authorities had a less rigorous approach to health and safety. If the council considered the fire risk *'a big issue'*, he argued, it had the power to close the ground, which it did not do.

Popplewell noted that between 1977 and 1983 there had been no fewer than 86 fires in grandstands and 200 fires elsewhere in sports grounds. As the home of a third division club, Valley Parade did not come under the jurisdiction of the 'Guide to Safety at Sports Grounds', commonly known as the 'Green Guide' and introduced under the Safety at Sport Grounds Act, which had resulted from Ibrox. Popplewell stated that, *'Had the Green Guide been complied with this tragedy would not have occurred'*. With sad irony Bradford's promotion to the second division meant that the ground would then be 'designated', so this was the last match under which it would not apply. Metal girders for a new roof already lay outside the ground waiting to be fitted in the summer.

Popplewell made many recommendations, which led to new legislation. With an omission that was to have tragic consequences four years later, the legislation however did not take proper heed of his recommendation that, *'The importance of allowing full access to the pitch where this is likely to be used as a place of safety in an emergency should be made plain.'* Had there had been fences in front of the Valley Parade grandstand many hundreds would have died in the inferno, but they remained commonplace at British and European football grounds. Popplewell stated the need for gates in perimeter fencing to be adequate to permit escape onto the pitch, yet at some grounds there were no gates and at others they were very narrow. As we will read in the next chapter, there is little point in having gates if the police fail to open them when an emergency occurs.

On the same day as the Bradford fire a riot took place after the match at St Andrews between Birmingham City and Leeds United. A 15 year old supporter died and 236 people were injured when a wall collapsed.

Popplewell was asked to include the Birmingham riot in the inquiry. His recommendation was that there should be a national membership scheme with only persons holding identity cards allowed to attend matches. Championing the scheme at Luton, Margaret Thatcher pushed strongly for such a system to be introduced across the country.

Just 18 days after the tragic fire at Valley Parade, television audiences across Europe watched another disaster unfold, this time at the UEFA's showpiece European Cup Final, played at the Heysel Stadium in Brussels. Like Bradford, this was a tragedy that should never have happened. Again, although the immediate cause was clear, an undercurrent of neglect, lack of organisation and poor decision making allowed what would have been a relatively minor incident to become a tragedy.

To understand Heysel one has to go back much further than the charge by Liverpool supporters that led to a wall collapsing as Italian fans tried to escape. The previous May Liverpool had beaten Roma at the European Cup Final in Rome. As they left the stadium Liverpool fans were attacked by Roma supporters using iron bars and other weapons. This was not a reaction to defeat, but as the Italian press reported the next day, a premeditated attack with

Roma fans rushing out at the final whistle to collected weapons stashed in their cars. Extraordinarily, Lazio fans, arch rivals of Roma, pushed weapons into the hands of Liverpool supporters, urging them to defend themselves. Hence when Liverpool played Juventus the following year it was against a background of violence from Italian supporters. Whilst in no way excusing the behaviour of some followers of both teams, the events in Rome would have given the match organisers an indication of what may occur as Liverpool played another Italian club.

That Heysel was chosen to stage the match was a shocking comment on the ineptitude of UEFA and dereliction of duty by their team sent to inspect the stadium. It was reported that the day of the inspection was very cold and the officials scarcely bothered to emerge from the warmth to see what should have been obvious to them – that the stadium was simply not suitable to stage a game of this magnitude. The 55 year old stadium had not been well maintained and Liverpool's Chief Executive Peter Robinson urged UEFA to find another venue.

Both ends of the grounds were open terraces, divided into three enclosures, with those at the Liverpool end designated X, Y and Z, the last of these being reserved for neutral Belgian fans. Both Liverpool and Juventus had opposed this, as with tickets on sale in Belgium it would provide an opportunity for fans of both clubs to buy tickets from touts or agencies, with resulting lack of segregation. With a large Italian population in Belgium, many were bought by supporters of Juventus, but mostly families or migrant workers, not hardcore followers of the team.

All that divided supporters of the two teams was a temporary chainlink fence and a central, thinly policed no-mans land. Missiles were thrown between the two sets of fans, with a ready supply of stones simply pulled from the crumbling terraces. As kick off approached a group of Liverpool fans charged across the terraces, through or over the wire fence, and into Section Z. Those experienced in hooligan behaviour observed that there was no murderous intent in the charge by Liverpool supporters. It was the sort of action not uncommonly seen across Europe, and would normally result in opposition fans either fighting back, or backing off. Most of the Juventus fans in Section Z were not the type to stand their ground and moved towards a perimeter wall near the corner flag.

There was a hiatus of about 15 minutes after the charge where a more experienced police force would have moved in to restore order, however when a platoon of Belgian police eventually arrived the first action of their commander was to line them up and inspect them.

Under pressure from the weight of fans, the perimeter wall gave way, the resulting crush leaving 39 dead and 600 injured. Fearing more violence, the game went ahead, with Juventus fans fighting a two hour battle with police at the other end of the ground.

Chief of Merseyside's Serious Crime Squad, Bill Sergeant, led an unprecedented investigation, which resulted in 24 Liverpool supporters being extradited and charged with manslaughter. Fourteen were found guilty, along with Captain Johan Mahieu, the policeman in charge of Section Z and Albert Roosens, Secretary of the Belgian Football Union, who were found guilty of criminal negligence.

Interviewed by the *Liverpool Echo* twenty five years after the disaster, Mr Sergeant cited a catalogue of reasons why a European football match turned to tragedy:

 – *Missiles were thrown from one side to the other. Liverpool fans said they were under attack and they reacted.*
 – *They forced their way through the police line which was ineffectual.*
 – *There were other contributory factors. The police were split into*

civic, district and state police which wasn't right.
– There were lots of problems – radios weren't compatible, there were delays getting reinforcements into the game, and police decided to march onto the pitch rather than deal with what was happening.
– Policing wasn't good enough on every level.
– Pressure from fans trying to escape caused the wall to fall.

Liverpool supporters were rightly blamed for the disaster, but there was little consideration of the underlying causes. The day after the tragedy UEFA's official observer Gunter Schneider said, *'Only English fans were responsible. Of that there is no doubt'*. UEFA, the Belgian police and the owners of Heysel stadium were never investigated for culpability.

Margaret Thatcher put pressure on the FA to withdraw clubs from European competitions and two days later UEFA banned English clubs for *'an indeterminate period of time'*, which was eventually to be five years. There was however no official inquiry into Heysel, but after an 18 month investigation top Belgian judge Mrs Marina Coppieters published a dossier, which contrasted with the one-sided version of events on the British side of the channel. She concluded that perhaps blame should not rest solely with the Liverpool fans, but instead should be shared by the police and football authorities.

To the eternal shame of the British authorities, despite the deaths of 161 supporters at Ibrox, Bradford and Heysel, our football grounds remained unsafe. Lessons were not being learned.

Previous incidents, injuries and even loss of life had not prompted Rangers to deal with the death trap that was Stairway 13. The Safety of Sports Grounds Act brought in after Ibrox did not cover Valley Parade. A warning from the County Council that the wooden grandstand was a fire risk and that accumulated rubbish should be cleared was ignored by Bradford City. Heysel was not a fit stadium to hold a European Cup Final, but requests to change the venue and concerns on ticketing were ignored. Despite these tragedies and their obvious illustration of the need to be able to evacuate areas quickly and safely, little action was taken with regard to the dangers of perimeter fencing.

Four years after Heysel, on a sunny afternoon in Sheffield, 96 Liverpool fans were to die as a result of our failure to learn the deadly combination of poor crowd management and lack of escape routes.

CHAPTER TWO

HILLSBOROUGH

Despite the deaths at Ibrox, Bradford and Heysel, if ever there was another disaster waiting to happen it was at a British football ground.

As we watched tragic pictures of Liverpool fans being carried across the pitch on makeshift stretchers and heard of fans dying crushed against fences, the thoughts of so many football supporters must have been – there but for the grace of God go I. Many supporters, especially those who followed their teams away, had experienced being herded into a packed enclosure, escape blocked by fences, with police watching from outside. Those of us who'd been in the likes of the away ends at White Hart Lane, with its high fenced cages, and Old Trafford, with its spiked overhanging railings, knew how it felt to be packed into in a confined space, barely able to move and surrounded by unclimbable barriers. The authorities were blind to the risks, but so many of us can recount experiences of incidents that could so easily have been a Hillsborough. Mine was at Loftus Road in January 1988.

The fourth round FA Cup fixture was billed as all-ticket and West Ham had sold their 4,000 allocation, but when we arrived QPR were allowing fans to pay at the away turnstiles. It was claimed that 2,000 entered with forged tickets, but no evidence seemed to be provided to confirm this. There was congestion outside the ground, but it was worse inside, with the narrow, low ceilinged corridor that leads to the School End lower tier packed solid. Out of sight, this is where the bodies might have piled up had there been fences at QPR.

By the time we reached the terrace it was pretty much full, although you could still move. I got separated from my friends, but found a position in front of a crush barrier. This was however well before kick off and fans were still pouring in. With turnstiles on only one side of the stand, the left hand side of the enclosure filled more than the right. Not only was the terrace over capacity, but distribution was uneven.

Soon after kick off, as the pressure built to intolerable levels, fans started to climb over the low wall onto the pitch perimeter to escape the crush. At least one supporter was carried away unconscious. There was however no panic, no pitch invasion and no hooligan intent, although BBC *Grandstand* reported it as crowd trouble with West Ham fans invading the pitch. Many supporters simply sat on the side of the pitch to watch the match, but numbers meant that some spilled onto the edge of the playing area. The police response was to bring a dozen horses onto the pitch.

The game was stopped for an hour as the police and stewards tried to find room for the hundreds of West Ham fans who had left the overcrowded terrace. QPR fans were moved in a section of the home end to make space and other visiting supporters found seats in the Ellerslie Road Stand on the side. West Ham had fans in all areas of the ground, segregation was minimal, but there was no violence. The mood remained humorous, with fans singing, *'What's it like to shovel shit'* as a steward cleaned the plastic pitch after the police horses and pretended to throw dung into the crowd.

How different things would have been that afternoon if fences had prevented supporters escaping the crush. As West Ham supporter and football journalist Mark Segal recalled:

'*I remember being incredibly scared that day and have no doubt that if there had been fences in front of the terrace people would have died.*'

If West Ham fans had died behind fences at Loftus Road it would have prompted a thorough review of safety at football grounds. Then it would have been clear to everyone that the combination of failure to control numbers entering a section and fences preventing escape, is a recipe for disaster. There would then surely have been no Hillsborough. What a terrible reflection it is on those responsible for running and policing football matches that it took the loss of 96 lives before they took seriously the safety of those who watch the game.

It was one of my greatest regrets that I didn't write a letter alerting of the events at Loftus Road, asking why QPR allowed far too many supporters onto the terrace, and warning that if such a crush occurred in an area with fencing people would die. I did write to Lord Justice Taylor after Hillsborough, but by then 96 football fans had lost their lives. Of course any letter to the football authorities would have been ignored, as were the many indications across the country that lack of crowd control, a fixation with preventing hooliganism over safety, poorly maintained stadia and above all, perimeter fences, could lead to disaster.

April 15th 1989 was a day that shocked the country, scarred the lives of hundreds of families and led to a long overdue change to the safety culture of football.

For the second successive season Liverpool were playing Nottingham Forest in the FA Cup semi final. Both games were played at Sheffield Wednesday's Hillsborough ground, where there was a history of overcrowding occurring in the Leppings Lane End.

Soon after the start of the 1981 semi final between Tottenham and

Wolves a crush developed resulting in injuries to 38 Spurs fans, including broken arms, legs and ribs. Further injuries and possibly deaths were prevented by the perimeter gates being opened to allow supporters to escape onto the pitch side.

After this Sheffield Wednesday were prompted to make significant changes to the Leppings Lane End and South Yorkshire Police suggested a reduction in capacity with the terrace divided into sections. Fences were erected to form three pens, but there was no cut in capacity and no system to count the number of fans entering each section. Although Section 8 of the 1975 Safety of Sports Ground Act requires the holder to notify the local authority of any proposed alterations or extensions to the ground which are likely to affect spectator safety, the club's safety certificate was not amended to account for these changes.

In 1985, with Sheffield Wednesday back in the First Division, further changes were discussed, and at the request of police two new fences erected to split the terrace into five pens. A police request to remove some crush barriers that they felt could be used as mounting points to scale fences was refused, as this would have meant an unimpeded run from the mouth of the tunnel to the perimeter fence. The middle barrier in Pen 3 was however modified to facilitate access and in 1986 the barrier nearest to the tunnel removed on police advice to assist flow of fans into the pen.

Dr W. Eastwood, consultant engineer to Sheffield Wednesday, had recommended that separate turnstiles, toilet and refreshment facilities should be built for each section, but this was not done for financial reasons. It would have provided computerised counting for each pen, but in the absence of this the club had to rely on visual monitoring. With the areas directly behind the goal always the most popular, the position of the access tunnel and the lack of signposting of the wing pens, it was highly likely that for major matches the central pens would fill to capacity. With fences preventing lateral movement the terrace was probably less safe than had it remained undivided.

For six years the FA selected other venues for semi finals, but in 1987 Hillsborough was chosen for the match between Leeds and Coventry. The central pens were uncomfortably overcrowded, but the venue was used again for the Liverpool v Forest game in 1988. Again crushing was reported, but the same stadium was chosen for the following season.

For both matches Liverpool had challenged the decision to allocate the smaller terrace to their supporters and the large 'Kop' stand to Nottingham Forest, who despite their smaller average support, were given significantly more tickets (29,000 to 24,000). Similarly both Spurs and Leeds had been given the smaller end, although their support was larger than Wolves and Coventry. The choice of ends had been made to ease segregation outside the ground and in 1989 South Yorkshire Police advised that they would only sanction the use of Hillsborough for the semi final if the ends were allocated as for the previous year. As well as segregation issues, they feared confusion if supporters had to enter different turnstiles to the previous season.

In 1988 Liverpool supporters had to pass through a cordon some way from the turnstiles, where tickets were checked. It has been suggested that this may be partly why in 1989 there were so few Liverpool supporters without tickets, as they thought there would be no chance of getting close to the ground entrances. This type of procedure was fairly common for major matches and the need to start controlling the crowd well back from the entrance to the ground had been stressed by the Moelwyn Hughes Report following the disaster at Bolton Wanderers in 1946. In 1989 the police however didn't institute a cordon to check tickets and control rate of access to the turnstiles.

Forest supporters had 60 turnstiles running the full length of the ground in which to enter the stadium. Liverpool however had just 23, which were all situated in one corner and only 7 of which were for the terrace fans. They were labelled alphabetically, but did not actually run in that order, making it hard to follow the directions printed on tickets.

In order for the 10,100 capacity of the Leppings Lane terrace to enter by the 3pm kick off time, it would have been necessary for the turnstiles to be operating at maximum flow from 1pm, and for 5,000 supporters to have passed through by 2pm. At this time it was noted that the two central Leppings Lane End pens were filling, but those at either side of the end were nearly empty. A message was put out over the public address asking fans in Pens 3 and 4 to move forward to make room for others. Supporters entering the ground were however left to find their own way to the terraces, the option of filling the pens successively having been rejected by the a senior police officer, deciding that supporters should be left to '*find their own level*'.

Meanwhile, outside the ground a large number of fans were trying to enter though the turnstiles, but at 2.30, although they could see Leppings Lane on CCTV and had access to turnstile counting figures, the police control room remained confident that they would get everyone in by 3pm. By around 2.45 however there were still about 5,000 fans outside and a dangerous crush had developed around the turnstiles, with those at the front subjected to intolerable conditions. Police outside radioed for reinforcements and as it became clear that the supporters would not get through by 3pm, asked that the kick off be postponed. The police control room acknowledged, but rejected this request.

Fearing fatalities in the crush, senior police officers outside the ground agreed that the exit gate should be opened in order to relieve congestion. This request was radioed to the Control Room by Superintendent Marshall, who was in charge of the area outside the Leppings Lane turnstiles, and required a decision from Match

Commander Chief Superintendent David Duckenfield. He had only been promoted 21 days beforehand, possessed very limited experience of policing football and had never been in charge of a major match. After deliberation he agreed to the request. Gate C was opened at 2.52pm. It was reported that one steward had four times been asked for his keys to open Exit Gate A, but refused, and that others warned the police that to open the gates would lead to a crush inside the ground.

With the dangerous situation outside the police clearly felt that they had little choice but to open the gate, however although it was not opened for five minutes after the initial request, this time was not used to sort out how the influx of fans would be absorbed inside the ground. No action was taken to block access to the central pens, which were already full to a point where supporters were enduring considerable discomfort, or to direct supporters to the pens on each side where there was still plenty of room.

In five minutes around 2,000 supporters entered through Gate C, most of them following the obvious route and a sign saying 'Standing', walked across the concourse and into the tunnel that led directly to the central pens. Old signs from before the radial fences were erected had not been removed and new ones were inadequate, causing confusion which contributed to excessive numbers of supporters arriving at the central pens

The influx of supporters through the tunnel, accelerated by a 1 in 6 downward slope (considerably steeper than recommended by the Green Guide), added to the pressure in the already overcrowded pens. By 2.54 when the teams came onto the pitch supporters were in considerable distress, unable to move their arms and finding it hard to breathe. There were shouts for help and for the perimeter gates to be opened, but still more supporters flowed through the tunnel.

Under the intense pressure one gate burst open, but a police officer quickly closed it. Shortly afterwards it sprang open again and officers tried to shut it, pushing back fans who spilled out. As the match kicked off some fans started climbing the radial fences to escape into adjacent pens, and others tried to get over the perimeter fence, but were turned back by police who feared a pitch invasion. Near the front fans were weakened to the point of collapse or death, but held upright by the pressure. Further back many fans were in great pain from being crushed against barriers and struggled to breathe, but at the rear many, although cramped, watched the game unaware of the distress at the front.

The police control room had failed to notice the overcrowding and didn't realise that anything was amiss in Pens 3 and 4 until fans started spilling out of the gates. Although they had an excellent view of the terrace and their CCTV clearly showed the supporters in distress and not making moves onto the playing area, incredibly the officers in command assumed that this was a pitch invasion. Rather than taking action that could have saved lives, they called up police reserves and made a request for dog handlers.

At 3.04pm Peter Beardsley hit the bar and Liverpool fans surged forward. At this point (or possibly shortly before) a crush barrier broke in Pen 3, projecting supporters towards the fence, many of them falling with the weight of other fans pilling up on them. In Pen 4, although no barriers broke, two were bowed and supporters also crushed against the fence and wall.

As fans struggled to escape, bodies of dead, dying and injured fans piled up in front of the narrow gates. Those with the strength tried to climb over the fence, now assisted by police and other fans. At the back supporters in the upper tier hauled fans up into the West Stand. Police and fans pulled at the wire fencing with their bare hands, succeeding in getting officers in to help those on the terrace.

Neither ambulances nor the fire brigade were called immediately and both had problems getting close to where they were required.

With just six stretchers in the first aid room and three more in the only (St John's) ambulance at the ground, supporters tore down advertising boards to carry the injured and dead to the far end of the stadium. Many fans tried to resuscitate their fellow supporters. Although there was no call over the public address for doctors and nurses until almost 3.30, some had already come onto the pitch of their own accord to do what they could.

The fire brigade had been called for cutting gear, but remarkably on arrival a police Inspector told them, '*I don't think we really need you*'. Ten further appliances were however called as they carry oxygen and resuscitators. By the time fire fighters reached the terrace cutting equipment was no longer required, although they were able to help with rendering first aid.

Meanwhile, fearing that Liverpool supporters might attack Forest fans at the other end, the police formed a line across the centre of the pitch. This image of many officers standing idle while fans did all they could to help the injured and dying, was to add to the huge resentment against the police for their actions on this fateful day.

94 supporters died on the day and another in hospital four days later. 730 reported being injured inside the ground and another 36 outside. One more, Tony Bland, died almost four years later when his life support machine was turned off after his 'persistent vegetative state' had shown no sign of improvement. Thirty eight of the dead were under twenty years of age.

Based on information given to them by Mr Duckenfield in the control room, FA Chief Executive Graham Kelly and Sheffield Wednesday Secretary Graham Mackrell both told the media that a gate had been forced open and fans rushed in. Thus the public perception of the disaster was that it had been caused by the action of Liverpool supporters, a myth that still persists.

At a press conference later that evening Chief Constable Peter Wright stated that, '3,000 *fans turned up in a ten minute period prior to kick off*' and on *Match of the Day* Graham Mackrell inferred that Liverpool supporters had arrived late. Again this immediately put blame on Liverpool supporters, although the investigation was to find that the build up outside the turnstiles occurred between 2.30 and 2.40pm and that as tickets requested '*the holder to take up position 15 minutes before kick off*', it is debatable as to whether this should be considered as late.

It was claimed that many Liverpool fans had arrived without tickets and a 'conspiracy theory' suggested by South Yorkshire Police, that ticketless fans had deliberately planned to arrive late and create trouble so the police would be forced to admit them to the ground. The investigation was to find no evidence of such a conspiracy and of only small numbers of ticketless fans. The congestion outside was simply due to larger numbers than the turnstiles could cope with, and that inside to poor distribution amongst the pens. The total number of fans entering the Leppings Lane End did not exceed its overall capacity, but again misinformation added to the public view that the disaster was caused by the behaviour of Liverpool supporters.

The day after the disaster Prime Minister Margaret Thatcher, her Press Secretary Bernard Ingham and Home Secretary Douglas Hurd were shown around the stadium by police officials. Ingham told the press, '*I know what I learned on that spot: there would have been no Hillsborough if a mob, clearly tanked up, had not tried to force their way in*'. The police sought to find evidence to support this theory by collecting information on the amount of alcohol purchased in pubs and off-licences before the match. Bereaved families were interviewed immediately after they had identified their loved ones' bodies to ascertain how much alcohol each victim may have drunk before the game. The Sheffield Coroner decided to take alcohol levels from the bodies of every victim, including a ten year old boy. The investigation however found that the great majority of

Liverpool supporters were not drunk or even the worse for drink, but another myth perpetuated.

Brian Clough, Nottingham Forest's manager at the time of the semi final, wrote in his 1994 autobiography, '*I will always remain convinced that those Liverpool fans who died were killed by Liverpool people*', adding on a TV chat show '*They were drunk. They killed their own*'. Seven years later Clough decided to express his regret, saying that, '*Investigations have made me realise that I was misinformed*'. However, it is commonly believed that this 'apology' was prompted by a proposed boycott of *Four-Four-Two* magazine for which he wrote a column, and an instruction to do so by the editor if he wanted to keep the work.

Four days after the disaster *The Sun* newspaper published a story which was based on comments made by Irvine Patnick the Conservative MP for Sheffield Hallam, and an unnamed police officer. Other journalists had apparently been briefed off the record by South Yorkshire Police 'sources' who blamed drunken Liverpool fans for the tragedy, and several papers mentioned these unsubstantiated allegations.

Under the heading 'THE TRUTH' *The Sun's* front page sub headlines claimed that:

'*Some fans picked pockets of victims*'
'*Some fans urinated on the brave cops*'
'*Some fans beat up PC giving kiss of life*'

The paper wrote that '*drunken Liverpool fans viciously attacked rescue workers as they tried to revive victims*' and '*police officers, firemen and ambulance crew were punched, kicked and urinated upon*'. One anonymous police officer was quoted as saying that a dead girl had been abused, while fans '*were openly urinating on us and the bodies of the dead.*'

The people of Liverpool, who understood the real causes of Hillsborough, were apoplectic. It was bad enough to have the nation told that Liverpool fans had caused the deaths of their own, but to claim that they had picked the pockets and urinated on the dead, was a call to arms. There were public burnings with thousands of copies of *The Sun* destroyed, deliverymen and shopkeepers refused to handle it, and a boycott cut sales on Merseyside from 200,000 to a mere couple of thousand. Twenty years later it was still selling little more than 10% of its pre-Hillsborough circulation. *The Sun* eventually printed apologies and in 1999 editor Kelvin Mackenzie told a Commons committee that he *'regretted his mistake'*, but later admitted that he had only apologised because he'd been told to do so by Rupert Murdoch, the paper's owner. In 1989 *The Sun* sold almost 4 million copies and was probably read by 12 million. Many of these would believe what it printed to be true.

There is a commonly held belief that drunk and ticketless Liverpool fans entered via Gate C and rushed into the central pens, resulting in those supporters at the front being crushed to death. CCTV images however show that while the gate was open for 5 minutes, fans walked, not rushed into the ground and, without direction, headed unknowingly straight for the dark tunnel, leading to the central pens.

In December 2007 during a discussion on Safe Standing on the BBC Politics Show, presenter Patrick Burns spoke of Liverpool fans being crushed to death after a late influx of ticketless supporters. Later that year in an episode of EastEnders, mechanic Minty told Jase, *'Five years out of Europe because of Heysel, because they pinned you lot in to stop you fighting on the pitch, and then what did we end up with – Hillsborough.'* The BBC had to apologise for both programmes, although even their apology for EastEnders was incorrect. A BBC spokeswoman said that, *'Minty was actually reminding Jase that football hooliganism at Heysel led directly to the fencing-in of fans at matches'*. Fences were commonplace well before Heysel.

Talking to Sky Sports at the World Cup in South Africa in 2010, Jeremy Hunt, Minister for Culture Media and Sport, praised the England supporters, noting that there had been not a single arrest for a football related offence and saying that, *'the terrible problems that we had in Heysel and in Hillsborough in the 1980s seem now to be behind us'*. Mr. Hunt swiftly apologised saying that he knew that fan unrest played no part in the events of April 1989, but as Margaret Aspinall, Chairman of the Hillsborough Family Support Group, said, *'The problem we have is that Hunt has influence and people listen to him.'*

Even a Safety Officer from a Football League club told me that fans had broken the gate down, but that it was fences which caused the loss of life. He was however firmly in favour of the choice to stand, provided that the terrace was not fenced.

It is perhaps understandable that more than 20 years after Hillsborough there is still a common public perception that Liverpool fans were to blame for the tragedy.

CHAPTER THREE

THE TAYLOR REPORTS

Immediately after the Hillsborough Disaster the Government set up an inquiry under Lord Justice Taylor. Its remit was:

'To enquire into the events at Sheffield Wednesday football ground on 15th April 1989 and to make recommendations about the needs of crowd control and safety at sports events.'

It is not commonly understood that there were two Taylor Reports: the Interim Report, which deals with the causes of the disaster and surrounding issues, and the Final Report, which centres on recommendations including those regarding all-seater stadia.

The Interim Taylor Report

The Interim Report amounts to 88 pages and 41,400 words. It is a document that few football supporters have read, but one that recounts the horrors of Hillsborough and its causes. The report ends with 43 recommendations, which have helped to ensure the safety of football supporters.

The report describes the build up of Liverpool fans outside the Leppings Lane turnstiles, then moves on to explain the reason why the order was given to open the exit gate, and how lack of foresight meant that this decision, which was not necessarily wrong in itself, led to such loss of life. Noting that, *'Having lost control and rejected the option of postponing kick-off, the police were faced with a serious danger of deaths or injuries'*, Taylor concludes that the decision to open the gate was correct.

Crucially however Taylor notes that Pens 3 and 4 were full by 2.50pm and that the access tunnel should already have been closed off by a cordon of a few police officers, a simple exercise which had been carried out in 1988. He states that it should have been clear in the control room, from where there was a view of the pens, that the tunnel had to be closed and that the failure to divert fans to the empty areas of the wings could have averted the disaster. The failure to give that order he describes as, *'a blunder of the first magnitude.'*

The report describes in detail the build up of pressure in the centre pens and the desperate attempts of some supporters to escape. Taylor makes specific reference to the time at which the barrier broke in Pen 3 and that this was after Gate C had been opened, presumably in response to the Counsel for South Yorkshire Police, who at the inquiry argued that it had occurred at around 2.47pm. Taylor states that the Counsel's purpose was to show that there was no link between opening of Gate C and the deaths resulting from the barrier collapse.

The report moves on to describe the gruesome scenes with bodies of the living and dead entwined and rescuers working frantically to free them. Taylor tells how *'press photographers dodged about among rescue workers apparently avid to secure photographs at point blank range of those dying through the wire mesh and those laid on the pitch.'*

He notes that in the control room Mr Duckenfield was primarily concerned about public order and that he told representatives of the FA and Sheffield Wednesday that a gate had been forced by Liverpool supporters. The report tells how, *'He pointed to one of the television screens focussed on gate C by the Leppings Lane turnstiles and said "That's the gate that's been forced: there's been an inrush".'*

Taylor reports in his conclusions the following 'Brief Summary of Causes', which I have quoted in full:

265. *The immediate cause of the gross overcrowding and hence the disaster was the failure, when gate C was opened, to cut off access to the central pens which were already overfull.*

266. *They were already overfull because no safe maximum capacities had been laid down, no attempt was made to control entry to individual pens numerically and there was no effective visual monitoring of crowd density.*

267. *When the influx from gate C entered pen 3, the layout of the barriers there afforded less protection than it should and a barrier collapsed. Again, the lack of vigilant monitoring caused a sluggish reaction and response when the crush occurred. The small size and number of gates to the track retarded rescue efforts. So, in the initial stages, did lack of leadership.*

268. *The need to open gate C was due to dangerous congestion at the turnstiles. That occurred because, as both Club and police should have realised, the turnstile area could not easily cope with the large numbers demanded of it unless they arrived steadily over a lengthy period. The Operational Order and police tactics on the day failed to provide for controlling a concentrated arrival of large numbers should that occur in a short period. That it might so occur was foreseeable and it did. The presence of an unruly minority who had drunk too much aggravated the problem. So did the Club's confused and inadequate signs and ticketing.*

Lord Taylor's Interim Report's recommendations amounted to 2,400 words. I shall provide just a brief summary of some of the major recommendations:

That where a terrace is divided into self-contained areas or pens, the Safety Certificate should specify the maximum capacity and arrangements should be made to count the number of supporters entering this area.

Where there are perimeter fences all gates should be kept open while there are supporters on the terrace.

That crush barriers should be inspected for corrosion and their layout checked to ensure that they comply with the 'Green Guide'.

That there should be an immediate review of Safety Certificates.

That turnstiles serving a given area should be capable of allowing the number of persons equal to the capacity of that area to enter within one hour, and if not that the capacity be adjusted proportionally.

A number of recommendations with regard to police organisation, including the importance of preventing overcrowding and that the decision to postpone a kick off should be taken by the officer in command at the ground, with crowd safety paramount in any such decision.

Various recommendations with regard to control rooms, communications, coordination and first aid.

It is a sad reflection on those responsible for safety of football grounds that these simple and common sense recommendations were not in place long before Hillsborough. Had they been so no one would have died on the Leppings Lane terrace.

The Interim Report did not recommend the removal of either fences or standing areas. It did however make the eminently sensible recommendation that after calculation of terrace capacity from the Green Guide recommendations of crowd density, a further reduction of 15% should be made, 'to improve safety margin'. This recommendation considerably improved both safety and comfort for standing supporters.

The Final Taylor Report

Lord Taylor's 109 page Final Report, which was presented to Parliament in January 1990, begins with a damning paragraph headed 'Previous Reports Unheeded':

'It is a depressing and chastening fact that mine is the ninth official report covering crowd safety and control at football grounds. After eight previous reports and three editions of the Green Guide, it seems astounding that 95 people (eventually 96) could die from overcrowding before the very eyes of those controlling the event.'

He continues by quoting from Popplewell's report:

'almost all the matters into which I have been asked to inquire and almost all the solutions I have proposed, have been previously considered in detail by many distinguished Inquiries over a period of 60 years'.

Lord Taylor's 76 recommendations are too long, complex and in some cases technical, to cover in detail, but the list of headings illustrates the extent of his work.

All-Seated Accommodation
Advisory Design Council
National Inspectorate and Review Body
Maximum Capacities for Terraces
Filling and Monitoring Terraces
Gangways
Fences and Gates
Crush Barriers
Safety Certificates
Duties of Each Football Club

Police Planning
Communications
Co-ordination of Emergency Services
First Aid, Medical Facilities and Ambulances
Offences and Penalties
Green Guide

The best known of the report's recommendations and the one which has had a huge effect on most of our football grounds, is all-seating, Taylor starting this section of the report with his much quoted words:

'There is no panacea which will achieve total safety and cure all problems of behaviour and crowd control. But I am satisfied that seating does more to achieve those objectives than any other single measure.'

The first of his report's final recommendations was:

'The Secretary of State should ensure that spectators are admitted only to seated accommodation at matches played at sports grounds designated under the Safety of Sports Grounds Act 1975 in accordance with the timing set out in Recommendations 2 to 4 below.'

Recommendations 2 to 4 set out a programme for the phasing out of terraces by gradual reduction in capacities, and that standing should be abolished by August 1999. Due to the larger crowds in the top two divisions of the English League he recommended that these should be all-seated by the start of the 1994/95 season. His report noted that redevelopment of grounds to meet these recommendations would involve clubs in considerable expense and made various suggestions as to how assistance could be provided.

Taylor makes a number of comments as to the greater comfort of standing which we will consider in Chapter Nineteen, as these are considered by some to be quite contentious and not valid contributions to his justification of all-seater. His description of standing on a terrace with surges and swaying had already become far less relevant after the capacity cuts that followed his Interim Report.

In addition to safety and comfort Taylor concludes that seating has distinct advantages in crowd control, pointing out that with CCTV police can zoom in to pinpoint seats occupied by trouble-makers and that numbered tickets help to identify forgeries.

He notes that the evidence he received was overwhelmingly in favour of more seating accommodation and that most were in favour of reversing the two thirds to one third standing / seating ratio. Notably however, he does not state that this evidence is in favour of all-seating, just more seating. Taylor acknowledges that there were those who wished to retain a proportion of standing accommodation, including the FA and supporters' organisations. He considers their main arguments of a desire to maintain the traditional terrace culture, that all-seating will reduce capacities and increase admission prices, but largely dismisses these. He accepts that clubs may well wish to charge more for seats than standing, and gives the example of Ibrox where seats were 50% more expensive than standing (£6 v £4), which Taylor states is, 'not a prohibitive price or differential'.

Under the heading 'The Trend in the UK', the report then describes how a number of clubs had already converted or announced their intention to convert to totally or predominantly all-seating. He mentions how Coventry City and QPR converted seating areas back to standing under pressure from supporters, but stated that since Hillsborough, 'thinking has changed'. Taylor notes that the trend towards seating is even stronger in Europe and is 'now being driven by decrees of both national and European football authorities'

The report goes on to say that he believes supporters will get used to sitting and that evidence shows they prefer this to standing. Taylor comments that they will rise from their seats at moments of excitement, but then sit down again.

He then considers whether his recommendations about seating should be confined to just football grounds, or include other sports such as rugby and cricket. Taylor notes that whilst misbehavior at these grounds has been minimal, there is still a risk of overcrowding and comments that, *'There would seem little reason for requiring a fourth division League club to convert to seating whilst permitting major rugby clubs to keep their terraces indefinitely.'* His conclusion is that the all-seater recommendation should apply to all grounds designated under the Safety of Sports Grounds Act. The Act defines as 'designated' as any sports ground with minimum capacity of 10,000, however the Secretary of State has reduced this to 5,000 for grounds occupied by Premier League and Football League clubs.

Lord Taylor had set up a Technical Working Party under the chairmanship of Professor Leonard Maunder, to review the technical aspects of the Guide to Safety at Sports Grounds. The Working Party's report is included as an appendix in Taylor's Final Report. It included many recommendations on ground design, capacities etc and in relation to standing recommended:

'Whilst standing accommodation is not intrinsically unsafe, all-seater stadia bring benefits to spectator comfort, safety and crowd control. The implementation of higher proportions of seated accommodation should be governed by common high standards of design and construction.'

The Technical Working Party of experts, which Taylor used to guide him in making many of his recommendations, referred to implementation of '**higher proportions** *of seating accommodation'*. Taylor had noted that the evidence he received was overwhelmingly in favour of **more** seating accommodation, not all-seating. His recommendation was however that *all* standing accommodation should be removed.

In addition to all-seating Taylor made a number of recommendations with regard to stadia.

With regard to terracing capacities he repeated the recommendation from his Interim Report that where a terrace is divided into pens or self-contained areas, each should have a capacity specified in the safety certificate, with the number of spectators entering the area counted.

He considered the emotive subject of fencing, noting that after Hillsborough there was a strong clamour to take down fences (as some clubs did) and that:

'It is true, as is often said, that so far no fatality has resulted from a pitch invasion, whereas 95 people died against a fence installed to prevent such invasion. But if fighting between fans starts on the pitch area, it is difficult to stop and injuries can be caused.'

He concluded that fences should not be banned. His recommendation was that all spikes and inward overhangs should be removed and the maximum height of fencing (including any wall on which it stands) should be 2.2 metres. Additionally there should be gates of minimum width 1.1 metres, which should be manned when the enclosure is occupied and kept open when those in command believe this can safely be done. The gates should not be locked when the enclosure is occupied.

Interestingly Taylor thought that some people would consider his limitations on fencing to be too greater relaxation saying that, *'Some may feel I am being naive or over-optimistic in recommending that fencing be brought down to a lower level.'* He considers other methods of preventing pitch invasions, including lowering of fences but with a prohibition against going on the pitch without reasonable excuse, however presumably did not consider that such a prohibition would be effective without retaining fences.

Taylor examined in great detail the merits of the membership scheme that was included in the Football Spectators Act 1989, which had already passed through parliament, but for which the Statutory Instrument for implementation was to await his report. His statement that, '*I also have grave doubts about the chances of its achieving its purposes and am very anxious about its potential impact on police commitments and control of spectators*' resulted in the Government quietly dropping what had been the lynchpin of their policy to deal with football hooliganism.

As we shall discover in further chapters, whilst Lord Taylor made many excellent recommendations which have improved safety for football supporters, not all of his recommendations have been implemented. Time has shown that whilst undoubtedly well intentioned, he was not always right. Furthermore, that there have been major changes relating to supporter behaviour, demographics and safety, which mean some of his recommendations may no longer be considered necessary. Such have been the changes that perhaps an updated 'Taylor Report' is now required.

CHAPTER FOUR

REACTION TO TAYLOR

The Taylor Reports altered the faces of British football grounds and led to a long overdue change in safety culture for the game. It was however far from the end of the debate about Hillsborough, particularly for the bereaved families who believed that there had been an even greater cover-up and attempt to blame Liverpool fans than was suggested by Lord Taylor.

When disasters occur it is normal for the bereaved and survivors to want to know the truth, see blame apportioned and action taken that will stop such a tragedy ever occurring again. Many families of the Hillsborough victims and survivors of the disaster feel that the truth has been suppressed and seek justice for the 96 fans who died.

As is normal practice, inquests into the deaths at Hillsborough were opened and adjourned, so that the bodies could be released for funerals. Then, in an unprecedented move, 'mini inquests' were held, contrary to the normal practice of determining whether prosecutions should take place prior to holding inquests. At each mini inquest details of the deceased were read out, along with their blood alcohol level. Many of these readings were actually negative. Although they felt that the evidence was slanted and one sided, the families were not permitted to challenge it, but the message picked up by the media was one of drunkenness and violence.

In September 1990 the Director for Public Prosecutions ruled that there would be no criminal prosecutions resulting from Hillsborough, stating that in the case of the police there was, *'insufficient evidence to justify proceedings'*. The full inquest resumed two months later.

The coroner imposed a cut off time of 3.15pm, on the basis that all those who died would have received their injuries by then, which meant that any evidence in relation to the response of the emergency services would be inadmissible. The bereaved families considered going to the High Court to have this decision reviewed, but were advised by their solicitors to wait until the end of the inquest and 'add up all the errors'. Once again the jury were subjected to evidence giving a picture of drunken, ticketless fans. Only local residents and licensees who agreed with such a version of events were called and the police used the inquest to reaffirm their view of the disaster. Comparisons were made to the Trafalgar Square Anti-Poll Tax riot. Senior police officers were reminded that they did not have to answer anything that may be prejudicial and were allowed to keep their statements in the witness box. Fans giving evidence however were given no such reminder and had their statements taken from them. Many were subjected to cross-examination and made to feel that they were in some way responsible.

When the jury returned a majority verdict of 9 to 2 of accidental death the reaction of families and survivors was of anger, disgust and distress, with many breaking down in tears.

After much pressure, some families won the right to a Judicial Review, which was held at the High Court in November 1993. Evidence was put before two judges to indicate that the inquest had not been a thorough investigation and that some supporters had died who could have been saved if they had received appropriate treatment in time. The 3.15 cut off time was challenged, with evidence from a forensic pathologist that the deceased could have lived beyond this time, in particular with regard to 15 year old Kevin

Williams. Eye witness evidence from a WPC and an off-duty police officer demonstrated that Kevin was alive after 3.15. Both made statements, the WPC saying that she had felt a pulse and that he opened his eyes and said 'Mum' before he died around 4pm. However during the investigation by West Midlands Police both retracted their statements, although later said that this was done under pressure and that they stood by their original statements.

The official view is that all the victims died from traumatic asphyxia, which left their bodies bloated and blue. Kevin William's mother Ann said that there were none of these marks on his body and three pathologists had told her that he died of swollen airways caused by broken neck bones. If this were the case a simple tube down his throat would have saved him. The judges concluded that no new inquest was necessary.

Taylor did not criticise the ambulance service, although said that both they and the fire brigade should have been called earlier, and that there was, *'insufficiently close cooperation between the police and emergency services'*. Many people however believe that the delay in paramedics getting to the victims may have cost lives.

The Major Accident Vehicle was not called for until 15.29. Forty two ambulances arrived at the ground, but just one made it onto the pitch. The vehicles and around 80 trained crew were kept outside by the police, an officer saying that they couldn't go onto the pitch because fans were 'still fighting'. Tony Edwards, the only professional paramedic to make it to Leppings Lane, was quoted in *The Independent on Sunday* (November 2000) as saying that the operation was *'chaotic'*. He said that the basic technique of inserting airways into casualties' mouths was barely administered.

Mr Edwards was one of a number of witnesses who were not called to give evidence at the inquest, but have bitterly criticised the emergency response. Casualties were mostly laid on their backs rather than in the recovery position and some had clothing covering their faces even though no qualified person had determined that they were dead. Just fourteen of those who died were taken to hospital. Tony Edwards was only able to reach casualties because his driver ignored the police command and drove through. He is still haunted by his decision to leave the ground, taking three patients to hospital, but with hundreds of others in need of help, which for so many came too late.

When in opposition the Labour Party had promised a new inquiry into Hillsborough. After they came to power in May 1997, Home Secretary Jack Straw set up an independent Judicial Scrutiny under Lord Justice Stuart-Smith. This was commonly believed to be a fresh inquiry, however appeared to have no clear remit and was to look only at fresh evidence. The tone was set early on when meeting with bereaved families Stuart-Smith said to them, *'Have you got a few of your people or are they like Liverpool fans, turn up at the last minute'*, a comment for which he apologised, but suggested that perhaps he had pre-conceived ideas about the disaster.

At the Scrutiny, for the first time the families had access to statements submitted to previous inquiries and found that many of these had been altered. When in 1998 the Home Office made available statements taken by police officers on the day of the disaster, family lawyers estimated that 183 had been subject to editing. Critical comments from PCs relating to lack of leadership, poor communication and how crowd control tactics differed from previous years were altered or edited out completely.

When South Yorkshire Police were ordered to make available documents relating to Hillsborough, ten boxes of unsorted papers were 'dumped' in a House of Commons library. Amongst them a list entitled 'Amended Statements' contained the names of 163 officers and another with 248 names notes the date that statements were vetted. On a front page of the amended statements were handwritten notes setting out the sections to be changed. One read:

'Last two pages require amending. These are his own feelings. He also states that PCs were sat down crying when the fans were carrying the dead and injured. This shows they were organised and we were not. Have (the PC) rewrite the last two pages excluding points mentioned.'

The Scrutiny heard evidence as to how two police officers had tried to save Kevin Williams, that he had opened his eyes and spoken before dying at 4pm, and how both had been pressurised to change their original statements. Stuart-Smith chose not to accept this.

Lord Justice Stuart-Smith ruled that there was no basis on which there should be a further Judicial Inquiry or re-opening of the Taylor Inquiry.

One more question has never been answered. Between 4.30pm on the day of the disaster and 9.00am the next morning, two CCTV video tapes were removed from the locked control room at Hillsborough. Who took them and why has never been answered. No details of any investigation by South Yorkshire Police have been published. No suggestion, other than the obvious one that they contained footage that certain people wished to remain secret, has been put forward.

Some of Lord Taylor's comments about 'Policing on the Day', reflect shamefully on South Yorkshire Police.

'In all some 65 police officers gave oral evidence at the Inquiry. Sadly I must report that for the most part the quality of their evidence was in inverse proportion to their rank. There were many young Constables who as witnesses were alert, intelligent and open. By contrast, with some notable exceptions, the senior officers in command were defensive and evasive witnesses.'

'When Mr Marshall's request came, Mr Duckenfield's capacity to take decisions and give orders seemed to collapse. Most surprisingly, *he gave Mr Kelly and others to think that there had been an inrush due to Liverpool fans forcing open a gate. This was not only untruthful. It set off a widely reported allegation against the supporters which caused grave offence and distress. It revived against football fans, and especially those from Liverpool, accusations of hooliganism which caused reaction not only nationwide but from Europe too.'*

'It is a matter of regret that at the hearing, and in their submissions, the South Yorkshire Police were not prepared to concede they were in any respect at fault in what occurred. Mr Duckenfield, under pressure of cross-examination, apologised for blaming the Liverpool fans for causing the deaths. But, that apart, the police case was to blame the fans for being late and drunk, and to blame the Club for failing to monitor the pens. It was argued that the fatal crush was not caused by the influx through gate C but was due to barrier 124a being defective. Such an unrealistic approach gives cause for anxiety as to whether lessons have been learnt. It would have been more seemly and encouraging for the future if responsibility had been faced.'

In August 1998 the Hillsborough Family Support Group commenced private prosecutions against Chief Superintendent David Duckenfield and Superintendent Bernard Murray, his second-in-command on the day. The case came to court in July 2000 and lasted for six weeks. After four days of deliberation the jury found Murray not guilty of manslaughter, but announced it could not reach a verdict on Duckenfield. Although they indicated that with a little more time they may reach a majority verdict, the judge decided against this and also refused a retrial.

In July 2000 the Police Complaints Authority had instructed South Yorkshire Police to commence disciplinary proceedings against both Duckenfield and Murray. In November Duckenfield however resigned from the force due to ill health, South Yorkshire Police permitting early retirement on full pension as he was suffering from severe depression and post-traumatic stress. Disciplinary action against him therefore could not be concluded and South Yorkshire Police decided that it was unfair to proceed with action against Murray alone.

Some may understandably argue that any pain felt by Duckenfield and Murray was insignificant compared to that of the injured and bereaved, and hence they should be pursued and face the consequences of their errors. However, perhaps it is right that no one or two individuals should be seen to take the blame for Hillsborough. Duckenfield and Murray made horrendous errors that led to the deaths of 96 fans, and their actions after the tragedy were highly questionable, but it would be wrong to concentrate blame entirely on individuals.

Whilst predominately with South Yorkshire Police and some individual senior officers, the blame for Hillsborough extends to all those responsible for safety at football grounds. Responsible to varying degrees, not only for Hillsborough but for the potentially dangerous conditions at other grounds, were football clubs (notably Sheffield Wednesday with regard to Hillsborough), the Football Association, local authorities and successive governments. Also those who failed to heed Popplewell's recommendation with regard to full access to the pitch in an emergency and didn't consider the danger of fences, plus those supporters whose behaviour had led to the belief that fences were necessary and contributed to the blinkered approach of the police. Perhaps the media's hysteria in reporting disorder related to football was also a factor contributing to this approach.

Shortly after the tragedy Margaret Thatcher chaired a cabinet meeting at which the appalling events were discussed with Home Secretary Douglas Hurd. In 2009 a Freedom of Information request from the BBC to see the minutes of this meeting was refused by the Cabinet Office. A ruling by Information Commissioner Christopher Graham, who criticised the Cabinet Office's *'unjustified and excessive delays'*, and ordered the documents to be released, was appealed by the Government in August 2011. Little wonder that supporters still believe that a cover-up took place.

It wasn't until October 2011, when a 140,000 signature online petition triggered a parliamentary debate, that the Government agreed to disclosure of documents. During the debate Maria Eagle, Labour MP for Garston and Halewood, said that the Hillsborough families have had to endure one of the most disgraceful examples of *'official skullduggery and lies.'* David Cameron's office said that all relevant papers had been handed over to The Hillsborough Independent Panel, which had been set up in 2009 to consider ways of creating an archive of Hillsborough material and ensuring that as much information as possible was disclosed to the public.

Lord Taylor's proposals for all-seating of football grounds were accepted by the Government, although in 1992 they decided to allow clubs in the two lowest divisions of the English Football League to retain some standing areas provided they met certain criteria. The Government however chose not to implement Taylor's recommendation that 'designated' stadia used by other sports should also be made all-seated.

In order to implement some of Taylor's key proposals and to oversee the safety and licensing of football grounds, the Government set up the Football Licensing Authority (FLA). This body had originally been conceived to implement the national membership scheme and its new role was to:

'Monitor local authorities' oversight of spectator safety at international, Premiership and Football League grounds and ensuring through a system of licensing that these grounds became all seated.'

There followed the largest programme of building work ever seen at British sports grounds. Clubs such as Sunderland, Derby County,

Reading and Bolton chose to move to new purpose-built all-seated grounds. Others either built new stands, or simply bolted seats onto existing terraces. A few deadline extensions were permitted where clubs could demonstrate that their plans could not be achieved within the set timescale, but by the mid 1990s the top two English and top Scottish leagues were almost completely all-seated.

CHAPTER FIVE

HOOLIGANISM

Whilst Ibrox, Valley Parade, Heysel and Hillsborough could and should have been avoided by adequate safety management, any discussion on football disasters and the move to all-seated grounds must consider the role of hooliganism.

Football hooliganism, a term created by the media in the 1960s, is hardly a new problem. As early as 1846 the Riot Act was read during a match in Derby, with troops called in to deal with the disorderly crowd. From the 1880s trouble was occurring regularly, with fighting at local derbies and attacks on opposition players or referees not uncommon. Some rivalries were intense, few greater than those between West Ham and Millwall. A fixture at the start of the 1906/07 season was reported to have been a violent affair, with one player hurled against a metal advertising board and Millwall finishing the match with only nine men after two were stretchered off following heavy tackles. Fighting took place in the stands and the East Ham Echo reported that, *'From the very first kick it was seen that there was likely to be trouble. All attempts at football were ignored'*.

'Modern' football hooliganism first occurred in the late 1960s, peaking from the mid 70s to mid 80s, and as stated in Chapter One, was already declining by Hillsborough. It is however difficult to gauge the extent of hooliganism by studying media coverage.

As seen with *The Sun's* disgraceful lies after Hillsborough, reporting the truth is not necessarily a priority for the tabloid press, and football supporters seem to be fair game for the kind of sensationalist copy that boosts circulation. Indeed journalists have been accused of actually encouraging hooliganism, with reports of fans being paid to start trouble and the Daily Mirror's publishing of a hooligan league table. Headlines such as '*Let's Blitz Fritz*' (The Sun) and '*Achtung Surrender*' (Daily Mirror), prior to England's Euro 96 semi final with Germany, did little to stem xenophobia

Major outbreaks of trouble, whilst now very rare, attract disproportionate media coverage, particularly if television footage is available and if the clubs involved have a 'reputation'. If a match is disrupted by crowd behaviour, the reaction from media, politicians and football authorities is far greater than where disorder occurs outside the stadium, even if the latter is more serious. Trouble after matches between Birmingham & Aston Villa and Sheffield Wednesday & QPR in 2010 attracted far less attention than that at West Ham v Millwall the previous year. Coverage of the trouble at Upton Park concentrated mainly on pitch invasions, which were largely celebratory rather than violent, the media reaction no doubt fuelled by the involvement of Millwall. Many questioned whether BBC's *Crimewatch* programme's decision to show photos of supporters who ran onto the Upton Park pitch was the best use of its air time, and how many serious criminals whose faces could have been displayed avoided arrest as a result.

These were however very isolated instances. Violence inside football grounds is now extremely rare. By way of illustration, having attended at least thirty matches a season, I cannot recall seeing a punch thrown in the last twenty five years. Where hooliganism now occurs to an extent is outside and around grounds, but also occasionally in a more organised way, some distance from the match. Rival 'firms' arrange to meet up to fight, but innocent bystanders are rarely involved.

Whilst England supporters, and to a lesser extent fans following their clubs away in Europe, regularly caused trouble, this is now virtually unheard of. At Euro 2000 in Belgium and Holland 958 English supporters were arrested, but at the following tournament four years later just one English fan was arrested at a venue city, and this for a drug related offence. No England supporters were arrested at the 2010 World Cup in South Africa. Our supporters are now more likely to be the innocent victims of attacks by foreign fans and police forces, often with greater violence than was perpetrated by the old English hooligans. What was called the 'English Disease' is now a far larger problem in parts of southern and eastern Europe, although it receives much less publicity.

The degree of both drunkenness and violence are far lower than that seen in many town and city centres every Saturday night, but the media, police and politicians seem to consider that football merits highly disproportionate attention. That's not to say that the problem has totally gone away, but that it is far less serious than thirty years ago.

Home Office figures from November 2010 illustrate the rarity of football violence. Of over 37 million people attending 'regulated' domestic and international football matches in England and Wales during the 2009/10 season, just 3,391 were arrested, less than 0.01%. Arrests were down 10% from the previous season. There were no arrests of English or Welsh fans at international away matches. More than 90,000 English and Welsh club fans travelled abroad to Champions League and Europa League matches. These 42 fixtures resulted in just 12 arrests. Over all matches the average number of arrests inside and outside stadia was 1.05 and at 70% of matches there were no arrests.

The figure of 3,391 includes not only specific football offences such as pitch encroachment, but also a wide range of generic criminal offences considered to be committed in connection with a football match and occurring at any place within a period of 24 hours either side of a match. Arrests for possession of drugs, drunkenness and even driving home from the match over the alcohol limit, can be included in the football statistics. There is little doubt that many of those arrested are not what would commonly be viewed as football hooligans.

It should also be noted that police are far more likely to arrest someone at a football match than for similar behaviour elsewhere. Whilst the many 'fly on the wall' documentaries often show police officers using discretion, and for example just telling someone worse for drink to go home, the Crown Prosecution Service guidelines for dealing with football supporters state:

'The Association of Chief Police Officers (ACPO) and the Crown Prosecution Service (CPS) will continue to operate a robust prosecution policy for football related offences during 2009/10 and beyond. This means that there will be a presumption of prosecution whenever there is sufficient evidence to bring offenders before a court on appropriate criminal charges and where a Football Banning Order is considered necessary.'

'Other options, including a Conditional Caution, simple Caution or of a Penalty Notice for Disorder will only be offered in extremely exceptional circumstances.'

If the same standards were used in town centres every Friday and Saturday nights our police stations would be overrun.

Significantly the Home Office publish only arrest figures, not convictions. As with all arrests, a proportion will be found not guilty. It is conviction, not arrest rates that provide a true picture, but the Government choose not to publish these figures.

The 2010 figures for example include medical student Tommy Meyers, a Crystal Palace supporter who was arrested at Reading railway station, and while he was on the ground, restrained and handcuffed, had a police dog set on him. A deep bite to his face required 30 stitches, but although the hospital dispensed painkillers and antibiotics, the police refused to allow Meyers to take these until the next morning. By then they were not effective and after taking himself back to hospital he was told that an immediate operation was vital, otherwise the infection could spread to his lungs and he would die. Almost a year after the incident he still has breathing problems, his voice is affected and he has permanent nerve damage. Tommy Meyers was arrested because an officer said he had been assaulted by him ten minutes earlier and that despite the fast moving situation he had kept his eye on him. Despite the number of police officers, football supporters and members of the general public on the station, no one came forward to say they had witnessed the supposed assault. Meyers was acquitted in court.

In the year to November 2010 1,025 new banning orders were issued, bringing the total to 3,248. Since 2000 92% of individuals whose banning orders expired were assessed by police as no longer posing a risk of football disorder. In the words of the Home Office, 'Banning orders work'.

Contrasting the efforts made to deal with football hooliganism, when besuited racegoers fought with chair legs and champagne bottles at Royal Ascot in June 2011, a racecourse spokesman described the brawl as 'unfortunate'. None of the participants were arrested and there was no Crimewatch photocall. More than 50 people were however arrested during the five day race meeting. Two weeks before Ascot, on a packed train returning from the Epsom Derby, a fight broke out amongst race goers. A woman was badly burned as she forced open the doors and stepped on a live rail. There were no arrests.

Before moving on from matters of policing and arrests, I should say that some progress does appear to be being made. The Football Supporters' Federation meet regularly with police officials, putting forward the concerns of fans. The day after Tommy Meyer's case was publicised in The Guardian, along with half a dozen supporters of different clubs, I attended a meeting with Assistant Chief Constable Garry Forsyth of West Midlands Police, the force viewed by many football fans as the worst at dealing with us. ACC Forsyth acknowledged his force's reputation and was very willing to listen to our comments and suggestions. Such dialogue will hopefully lead to a better understanding between fans and police, and a reduction in conflict.

Lord Taylor considered at length the problem of hooliganism and stated that, '*I must record that there are grounds for cautious optimism about misbehaviour inside football grounds although the same cannot be said for behaviour outside and en route*'.

He describes how away supporters are handled and comments that the further away from the ground spectators spread, the less the police can do to prevent sporadic confrontations, but states that, '*By and large however, the police measures have worked to prevent violent outbursts in and around the ground.*' Taylor considered alcohol sales in grounds and stated that he did not believe it appropriate to relax restrictions, although hoped that in the future a better atmosphere at football grounds may justify bans being relaxed. That alcohol is now sold in grounds for the vast majority of matches, and in both seated and standing areas, is further evidence of improved behaviour.

Taylor also states that pockets of away supporters in home areas form a focus for hostility and that violence often results. Sometimes away supporters can still be seen in home seats, but this is almost always due to difficulty in getting tickets for their own area, and not of aggressive intent. Generally if they keep quiet no problems result. There is almost an unwritten rule that away fans are accepted in home stands provided they don't show allegiance to their club. If however they do so, sometimes a degree of hostility may still result, and the supporters are likely to be moved or ejected by police, but violence is very rare. Much has changed in the last 25 years.

The problem of football hooliganism, whilst still present, is greatly diminished. There is no single reason that explains this, but a number of related factors.

As already discussed, from the mid 1980s hooliganism was starting to decline. This was some years prior to all-seated stadia and the improvements in ground facilities, increased CCTV etc that came in after the Taylor Report. To an extent types of behaviour come in and out of fashion. In the 1970s it was a regular occurrence for large groups of mods, rockers and skinheads to cause mayhem at seaside resorts every summer bank holiday. Whilst this is no longer seen, now the police have to deal with drunken disturbances in towns and cities across the country as pubs and clubs turn out on Saturday nights.

'Taking' of home ends started in the 1970s, but had stopped well before terraces were seated following the Taylor Report. Most trouble makers had no wish to cause injury and simply ran with the crowd in their tribal behaviour. The deaths at Heysel following that charge by Liverpool fans must have had a moderating effect on the behaviour of many who had never considered the possible consequences of their actions.

An important factor is policing and attitude to fans. Prior to Hillsborough and the Taylor Report, policing of football supporters had frequently been ill thought out and confrontational. Fans were herded from station to ground, kept in pens with no officers standing amongst them and often ejected for spurious reasons. There was little respect in either direction between police and supporters. There is still much more to achieve in terms of balanced policing of football, but in understanding, planning and resources, it has come a long way since the early 1980s.

The knowledge that offenders are likely to be caught and that consequences will be severe are major factors in the reduction in hooligan behaviour. For many years supporters who deliberately entered an opposition area of the ground were generally just moved to their club's section, and those who ran onto the pitch often allowed back into the crowd. Any that were convicted mostly received relatively small fines. A huge advance came with the introduction of high resolution CCTV in and around grounds, so that potential troublemakers knew they were very likely to be apprehended. Furthermore, those who were caught faced stiffer court penalties, but most effectively, banning orders. Someone who may have run onto the pitch in 1980 would be far less likely to have done so 20 years later when they knew an almost certain life ban from their club would result.

Improvements in stadium facilities, with fences removed, better catering and customer care, have created an environment where supporters are less likely to cause trouble. There is a lot of truth in the view that if people are treated badly they will behave badly, and if supporters are herded and caged like animals their behaviour will reflect this. A less confrontational attitude (although sadly still with too many exceptions) from stewards and police has helped to achieve an atmosphere where trouble is far less likely.

Interviewed by the European magazine *cafebale.com* prior to the 2006 World Cup in Germany, Stephen Thomas, then Manchester Police Assistant Chief Constable and the Association of Chief Police Officers' representative on football security in England, summed up this reason for the drop in arrests:

'15 years ago the stadiums in England had poor toilets and refreshments, and the fans were caged-in behind fences. This created an atmosphere that was particularly conducive to hooliganism and anti-social behaviour. I subsequently learned that people behave differently if they are in a good stadium with good facilities. The whole atmosphere then changes.'

Paul Wheatley the article's author added:

'This dramatic change meant that instead of treating football fans as trespassers to be tolerated, football authorities began treating fans as valued paying customers with a right to attend football matches.'

Finally, and although it is commonly quoted, I can find no evidence to support the view that all-seater stadia are a reason for reduced hooliganism, other than perhaps the higher ticket prices reducing the number of younger supporters. I would therefore exclude the move to all-seating as a reason for the sharp decline in hooliganism, on the basis that the problem was reducing prior to the removal of terraces, that a similar reduction in trouble has occurred at grounds where standing areas remain, and that many thousands of supporters still stand in front of their seats every week.

Those of us who followed our teams away in the 1970s and 80s could quote many examples where some or all of the ingredients of aggressive policing, unsafe stadia, poor crowd management, lack of safety culture and hooligan behaviour resulted in dangerous situations. I shall briefly recount my experiences of an FA Cup quarter final at Old Trafford in 1985.

Overhead line problems meant the trains were delayed arriving into Manchester. We were met by police with snarling dogs, held on leashes so their teeth were just inches from our genitals. One officer informed us quite openly that he hated *'you Cockney bastards'*. There weren't enough buses to take everyone to the ground, so some of us had to wait for them to do a second trip. Rather than escort us to the away entrance the police simply turned fans out of the buses and left us to walk unprotected through Manchester United supporters. With kick off approaching and an urgency to get into the ground, a mass of fans surrounded the turnstiles. Queuing had broken down. Police horses moved in to alleviate the crush, but we were very nearly squashed between a horse and the stadium wall.

Once inside a mass of bodies moved us slowly into the low standing area behind the goal. As we reached the terrace we were greeted by missiles, including golf balls, thrown by Manchester United supporters. The police and stewards were doing nothing to stop this. Realising that the situation wasn't safe I tried to move back from the terrace, but with the mass of supporters still coming in, escape was impossible. I managed to manoeuvre myself into a spot behind a barrier and fortunately the flow of fans entering soon stopped. As the crowd settled it became more comfortable, but had more people gained entry and crushing increased, there would have been no escape. Old Trafford's notorious iron railings with inward facing spikes were certainly not climbable. Of course not every away game was like this and at most matches supporters had plenty of space on the terraces, but such experiences were far from uncommon. It was only a matter of time before conditions would combine to result in tragedy.

Post Hillsborough however we now have safer stadia, crucially without fences, and far better planning. Each club has a Safety Advisory Group (SAG) made up of officials from the club, local authority, Football Licensing Authority, police, fire and ambulance services. These generally meet monthly and consider risks and planning for upcoming games. Plans are made to deal with crowd control and safety, with the latter being paramount. We no longer have the blinkered approach of stopping hooliganism without consideration of safety.

We should consider the possible role of hooliganism in the stadium disasters that occurred in the latter part of the 20th century.

At Ibrox Park there was no suggestion of poor behaviour by supporters. The disaster was caused by unsafe ground design with a long straight exit stairway. Previous incidents had highlighted the risk, but no significant action had been taken. Hooliganism had no part in Ibrox.

At Valley Parade too there was no suggestion of poor behaviour by supporters. The disaster was caused by a combination of a wooden stand, accumulated rubbish and no ban on smoking. The death toll was increased by exits being shut or locked. A letter warning of the risks of the exact scenario which resulted in the 56 deaths had been ignored by Bradford City. Hooliganism had no part in the Bradford fire.

The immediate cause of Heysel was the charge by Liverpool supporters, which led to Juventus supporters backing away and the collapse of a wall. The state of the stadium, ticketing arrangements and poor policing were also to blame, and had any one of these four causes not occurred, loss of life would have been unlikely. We cannot however escape the fact that whatever their provocation on the day or from previous occasions, without the action of those few Liverpool supporters the Heysel disaster would not have happened.

The causes of Hillsborough were more complex, but can be summarised as inadequate planning and crowd control, resulting in severe overcrowding in a fenced area with no means of escape. Lessons had not been learned from previous incidents, so the situation was entirely foreseeable, but failings in policing allowed it to become a disaster. Despite the lies by the police match commander, and in Lord Taylor's words, the presence of an unruly minority who had drunk too much and aggravated the problems outside, it was not hooliganism that caused the death of the 96 Liverpool fans. However, the fact that there were fences and to an extent the police actions both in planning and on the day, reflect on twenty years of football hooliganism, which hence played an indirect part in the Hillsborough disaster.

CHAPTER SIX

ELLIS PARK

Finally in this section we shall move forward to April 2001 and a match at Ellis Park in South Africa between local rivals Orlando Pirates and Kaizer Chiefs. The modern 60,000 capacity all-seated Johannesburg stadium, which had been used for the 1995 Rugby Union World Cup Final, was full 45 minutes before kick off with many thousands more still trying to get in. The few security staff were powerless as thousands forced their way into the ground, where massive crushing built up.

When the game started more surged in with greater force. When Kaizer Chiefs scored, to quote BBC reporter Milton Nkosi, an Orlanda Pirates fan who was at the match and lucky to escape with his life, *'all hell broke loose'*. As supporters died in the stands the match continued, even as the dead and injured were lain out behind a goal. Eventually the game was halted and pictures of bodies and paramedics trying to revive the injured shown on the stadium screen to demonstrate the situation to other fans.

There are many parallels between Ellis Park, Hillsborough and other football disasters.

As with Hillsborough, loss of life was caused by overcrowding inside the ground, preceded by a loss of control outside.

As with Heysel, whilst crowd behaviour was the primary cause, the disaster would not have happened without the failure of the authorities to anticipate or deal with problems. There had been problems at the same fixture three years earlier when police had fired rubber bullets to quell a riot as fans rushed for tickets minutes before kick off, but lessons had not been learned.

As with Hillsborough, the game should not have been started. South African FA guidelines and FIFA rules stated that a match should not commence until the situation outside and inside the ground is under control.

As with Heysel, policing was woefully inadequate. Many security staff were taken off the streets with little training and some took bribes to allow supporters without tickets to enter the stadium. Tear gas was fired into the crowd, causing a panic reaction which either caused or aggravated a stampede.

The official report by Mr Justice B.M. Ngoepe listed fourteen factors which, *'preceded the event and which led to the tragedy and mismanagement'*. Many of these were common to the earlier European disasters and had been covered in depth in the various reports which followed them. Three were particularly relevant to Hillsborough:

– Failure to learn from the lessons of the past
– Failure by the role players to clearly identify and designate areas of responsibility
– Absence of overall command of the Joint Operation Centre

Both Justice Popplewell and Justice Taylor had commented on the number of previous inquiries into safety at football grounds, but sadly for the victims of Ellis Park, so many of the factors that had led to deaths in Scotland, England and Belgium, also contributed to disaster in South Africa.

Less than a month after the Ellis Park disaster, an even greater sporting tragedy took place in Africa, when Hearts of Oak played

Ashante Kotoko in the Ghanaian Premier League. The match took place at the all-seated Accra Sports Stadium. After the home side scored two late goals to defeat Kotoko, visiting supporters threw bottles and plastic seats onto the pitch. The police response was to fire tear gas into the crowd, which resulted in panic and a stampede as supporters tried to escape. In the crush 126 fans died, the greatest loss of life at any sporting event.

Ellis Park and Accra Stadium showed once again that if preparation, crowd control and policing are inadequate, major safety problems may result – even in an all-seated stadium.

We have seen a succession of disasters, all of which were easily preventable. Warnings that would have prevented dangerous situations and averted loss of life, and ticketing advice that would have stopped incidents of hooliganism, were repeatedly ignored. Inquiries by learned judges have investigated and identified the causes of disasters, but whilst their recommendations have prevented recurrence of the same scenarios, it was not until Hillsborough and Lord Taylor's reports that a proper safety culture was introduced to football. It is that culture rather than any of Taylor's specific recommendations that has done more than anything to make watching football safe once more.

Neither Lord Taylor nor any of the other reports into football safety identified standing as a cause of the disasters. At Valley Parade, Heysel and Hillsborough loss of life came from a dangerous situation that supporters were unable to escape from. It is fences not terraces that caused deaths at Hillsborough. The disasters were not caused by standing, but the (partial) implementation Lord Taylor's all-seater recommendation has deprived most supporters of choice as to how they watch their football.

PART TWO

CURRENT SITUATION – SEATS & TERRACES

CHAPTER SEVEN

CURRENT SITUATION

More than twenty years after the Taylor Report, varying degrees of standing can be seen at every league ground. The Government's decision in 1992 to allow clubs in the then third and fourth divisions to retain terraces meant that many clubs chose not to go all-seated. At the start of the 2011/12 season twenty two grounds in the English Leagues One and Two, plus one in the Championship, had at least one standing area, as did many in the lower leagues in Scotland. Chapters Ten to Twelve describe how terracing is working at these clubs.

However, it is not just those grounds with terraces where supporters stand, but also in our all-seated stadia, either at moments of excitement or for the whole game. Lord Taylor's statement that, '*I am satisfied that in England and Wales as in Scotland and abroad spectators will become accustomed and educated to sitting*', has proved to be far from the case. He anticipated that in the early stages of conversion there may be instances of fans standing on or in front of seats, because this is what they were used to or to register a protest, but not that it would continue indefinitely. Indeed the degree of standing in front of seats has increased over the last ten years, and to many supporters the seat is simply a convenient place to hang a coat or rest their legs at half time. In following West Ham it is many years since I sat for more than few minutes at any match.

There are no figures published for numbers persistently standing in front of seats, so to gauge the extent of this I've had to use my own observations and those from other supporters.

The figures below are the numbers of away supporters (some are approximate) and an estimate of the proportion that stood throughout the game at Upton Park for matches at the start of the 2011/12 season.

Cardiff City	970	95%
Leeds United	3,000	100%
Aldershot	2,500 (approx)	65%
Portsmouth	2,284	98%
Peterborough	2,416	40%
Ipswich Town	2,500 (approx)	99%
Blackpool	1,500	10%
Leicester City	3,000 (approx)	98%
Bristol City	1,792	99%
Derby County	1,600 (approx)	90%

The Cardiff following was much reduced because the Metropolitan Police insisted that supporters would only be permitted to attend if they travelled by coach, collecting tickets at South Mimms Services, which resulted in a partial boycott in protest. The police decided to put Cardiff supporters in both tiers and about 50 of the 200 or so in the upper tier chose to sit. It was noticeable at the Derby match that there were plenty of spare seats where people could sit towards the front, but most supporters chose not to move to these.

In the same season I went to the first seven West Ham away games and from an averaging following of 3,075 the numbers who sat never exceeded single figures. After missing the eighth game at Hull, I went to Coventry where the entire 6,300 following stood, and a week later was one of 1,300 West Ham fans who travelled to Middlesbrough on a freezing Tuesday night. Again everyone stood, but rather than allow us to spread out so that any who wanted to sit could find seats at the front, Middlesbrough kept us in a restricted area, with the lower section empty. At every game there must have been some fans who would have preferred to sit, but with the vast majority wanting to stand and no choice provided, they were forced to stand up.

Members of the Stand Up Sit Down internet forum (www.susd.vitalfootball.co.uk) have for some years been posting information on numbers standing. From their observations and with help from others, I've been able to compile data for some clubs on approximate numbers who typically stand in front of their seats for the whole 90 minutes. As away allocations vary I've shown an average percentage of standers, but for home games actual numbers.

	Home Number	Away %
Arsenal	1,300	90%
Aston Villa	5,000	95%
Brighton	800	75%
Bristol City	900	60%
Chelsea	1,000	80%
Coventry	1,000	50%
Derby	1,000	50%
Leicester	1,200	70%
Leeds	8,000	99%
Liverpool	4,500	99%
Manchester City	4,000	90%
Manchester United	7,500	97%
Newcastle	1,000	99%
Norwich	2,500	95%
Nottingham Forest	1,000	60%
Preston North End	600	35%
Southampton	2,000	99%
Stoke	800	90%
Sunderland	1,000	60%

Swansea	1,250	80%
Tottenham	2,500	90%
West Ham	7,000	95%
West Brom	1,600	10%

It should be noted that these are estimated average figures and that larger numbers often stand for big matches, for example up to 18,000 at Old Trafford. For normal league matches at Liverpool around 2,000 stand for 90 minutes at the back of the Kop, but for games such as Manchester United and Everton the Kop's entire 12,500 capacity stand up. For the biggest European matches about 5,000 also stand in the Anfield Road End, plus sometimes a few hundred in the Paddock and Main Stand.

The authorities however sometimes seem to want to play down the amount of standing. For example, in November 2011 on BBC Radio Leeds, Chris Patzelt General Secretary of the Football Safety Officers Association, said that often across the country standing often occurs only at moments of excitement and that at Anfield the Kop all sit except for European games. This is not what I've seen on my visits to Anfield or have been told by Liverpool supporters. A few days after Mr Patzelt made his comments all 12,500 on the Kop stood for 60 minutes against Manchester City, and around 8,000 stood for the whole game.

At a rough estimate I believe that across the country around 65,000 supporters stand in front of their seats for the whole match each weekend, making a total in the region of 3.4 million for a season. If the numbers who stand on terraces are added, around 85,000 stand up each week, a total of about 4.2 million over a season.

Currently clubs are not officially permitted to openly sell tickets for front rows to those who wish to sit, and towards the back of the stand for supporters who wish to stand. Some clubs will try to provide front seats to those who request them, perhaps because they have children or find it hard to stand for long periods, but they cannot be seen to allocate seats on the basis of preference to stand or sit. This would be viewed by the authorities as condoning standing. A number of clubs do have seated areas where standing is tolerated, if not officially permitted, sometimes in a 'singing section' where like minded fans can congregate. The clubs however do not want attention drawn to the unofficial arrangements, so I will not name examples.

Attempts to enforce all-seating are extremely varied and often not consistent between home and away supporters. At some grounds people are constantly asked by stewards to sit, with threats or actual ejections made, but at others supporters stand every week in what have effectively become unofficial standing areas. Standing, particularly by away supporters, is often tolerated, either because if everyone stands clubs know it is impossible to stop, or because they don't consider smaller numbers standing at the back to be either a safety risk or customer care issue.

Generally when large numbers of fans stand no efforts are made to get them to sit, other than perhaps a token announcement. If supporters decide to stand in large numbers it has proved to be virtually impossible stop and the police and / or clubs take the decision not to attempt it. Sometimes stewards try to persuade fans to sit, row by row, starting from the front, but invariably before they get more than a few rows seated their team will attack or a song starts, and everyone stands again.

When West Ham played at Nottingham Forest in August 2011, all bar a handful of the 3,000 following stood. Soon after kick off, when a steward waved at supporters to sit down, the lady next to me, who was watching the game with her mother and young son, told him to give up, shouting – 'We Stand'. Not one fan sat down and the stewards soon moved on to the Forest fans who were standing in two areas of the ground. Again they were unsuccessful, only once getting most to sit, to which the immediate response was 'Stand up if you love Forest' and everyone on their feet again. It isn't just young males who want to stand and it is simply not possible to force fans to stay seated.

On one occasion we were in the front row of the Clock End at Highbury, when an Arsenal steward, obviously fed up with his unsuccessful attempts to get us to sit, walked along the row saying, *'I'm supposed to be trying to get you to sit. I know you won't, but I have to be seen to be trying'*. Needless to say we all continued to stand. The regulation is unworkable.

Whilst often no action is taken to stop people standing, when stewards do try to eject supporters incidents of conflict happen on a regular basis. Generally these occur when stewards act in a heavy handed manner, often when one individual exceeds his or her authority.

For example in October 2011 when Manchester City played Aston Villa at Eastlands, in an area where everyone was standing, a steward asked a 60 year old man to sit. It appeared to be a tactic of the stewards to pick on an individual and threaten to eject them, presumably hoping that this would persuade others to sit. The man didn't sit down and the steward said she would get the police. By the time the police arrived the man was sitting, but refused to get up and be ejected. A potentially serious incident then took place as police and stewards waded into the crowd, and the man ended up on the floor. The incident was filmed by supporters and the man can clearly be heard telling police that he takes five tablets a day for a heart condition. He had to be helped by medics, who eventually led him away. City supporters around him were not surprisingly incensed, but to their credit their anger did not extend to violence. Home and away supporters were standing in other parts of the stadium without stewards intervening, but the incident took place in an area where some wanted to sit and others to stand. Intervention may have been required, but it seems that the stewards concerned could have acted more reasonably.

The following month, after a number of Motherwell supporters were ejected for standing at Aberdeen, Leeann Dempster, the club's Chief Executive was quoted in the *Daily Record* as saying:

'Clubs have guidelines but each club uses its own interpretation. We are prepared to an extent to tolerate some things and we work to engage with the fans. We're asking people to come and pay money. When they've paid we tell them they can't sing, shout, stand up or dance around. I fear they might start asking themselves. Why are we coming. Why are we paying money for this?'

After the match Aberdeen fans had contacted radio stations defending the Motherwell supporters, and claiming that Old Firm supporters get away with standing at Pittodrie when other clubs don't. The following day the *Daily Record* included another article, which said that Celtic were one club starting a feasibility study into opening a standing area and quoted SPL Chief Executive Neil Doncaster as saying:

'We are very much open to looking at ways to improve the match day experience and one of the most common suggestions from fans is safe standing. The introduction of safe standing would require a change to SPL and SFA rules as both prohibit standing in the top flight. Clubs would have to vote to change our rules but we are open to the idea if anyone wants to explore safe standing.'

The extent to which efforts are made to stop standing in seated areas appears to vary according to the views of the individual safety officer, FLA Inspector or local authority. For example Sunderland and Nottingham Forest have both cut away allocations of some clubs due to persistent standing on the basis that it is unsafe. The reasoning is apparently that supporters are less likely to stand if they know that this will result in fewer tickets for future matches at the same stadium, however it is highly debatable whether the objective is achieved. Those fans who are able to get tickets generally still stand, so all that has been achieved is to reduce the total numbers, whilst risking away supporters buying tickets in home areas. If it was truly considered that there was a safety risk this could be mitigated by accommodating the reduced number of fans in the normal area, reducing the density, for example by selling tickets in every other row. That this is never done suggests that perhaps safety is not the main motivation for reducing allocations. If a few clubs deem it necessary to cut allocations, why don't the rest?

Since standing in seated areas is an issue between clubs and supporters, rather than a matter of law, it is up to individual clubs how they deal with it. As we have seen, some clubs are very strict in attempting to tackle this practice, taking measures such as ejecting people who stand. These practices can create significant public order problems, although there is little evidence of them being effective. Other clubs take a more relaxed approach to this, particularly where it is not causing problems, for example a club safety officer stated in a letter to an FSF member, 'We take a somewhat relaxed view (on standing) provided the individuals are not causing annoyance to other spectators or obstructing other spectators views.'

At matches where the away support is less than the number of seats available, it is normal for those supporters who wish to stand to occupy the back rows, while those who prefer to sit go further forward. This self regulation allows choice for all supporters, but whether it is tolerated by clubs and their stewards varies from ground to ground. For example, in following Torquay I have been threatened with ejection for standing towards the back of a stand at Rushden, Barnet and Southend, but stood without problem at Orient, Northampton and Tottenham.

Torquay's recent visits to Barnet provide further illustration of the desire of supporters to have a choice as to whether they may stand or sit, and the impossibility of getting fans to remain in their seats.

Accommodation for away fans at Underhill has changed a number of times, but for some years was a temporary uncovered seated stand at the south end of the ground. Sometimes away fans would also be given the south section of the East Terrace, as was the case in May 2001 when Torquay brought 4,000 fans for a relegation decider, half of whom were locked out (despite Torquay's advice Barnet had refused to make the game all ticket). When this was allocated those in the seats tended to sit, but if no terrace area was given fans wishing to stand would occupy the back rows of the South Stand. Sometimes this would be tolerated, others not, one match providing a fine example of why unless choice is provided, the ground regulation relating to standing in seated areas is unenforceable.

Around a third of Torquay's 300 or so following stood at the back, but were soon asked by stewards to sit. When this failed a senior steward arrived and tried to persuade fans to take their seats. He was unable to explain why other than, *'it's the regulations'* and wouldn't accept that fans could stand at moments of excitement. After about 15 minutes with fans sitting for a minute or so then getting up as Torquay started to attack, one fan turned and addressed us all; *'Come on lads, he's only doing his job, sit down for the man'*. The moment a hundred Torquay bottoms touched their seats he jumped up again with the shout, *'Stand up if you love Torquay!'* The result – three hundred Torquay fans stand to sing, the steward gives up and more than the original hundred end up standing for the whole match.

Torquay took 702 supporters to Barnet for the first match of the 2006/7 season, a very hot August afternoon. Away fans were now allocated the East Terrace North, but although the South Stand was virtually empty, no seats were provided for visitors. St Johns' Ambulance volunteers had to assist several elderly fans for whom having to stand in the considerable heat was too much, ironically bringing a chair for one gentleman to sit down on. Afterwards I wrote to the FLA Inspector who agreed that it was not desirable for away fans to have no seats allocated.

In 2011 most of Torquay's 493 fans were again in the East Terrace North, but now there was also a new temporary 246 capacity seated stand in the north east corner. Although only an extra pound entrance, this was not full, the majority choosing to stand on the terrace. With a choice of accommodation not one fan stood in the seats.

Examination of this League Two fixture illustrates what can be seen at grounds across the country – that supporters want a choice to stand or sit and that if this is provided there is rarely persistent standing in seated areas.

Whilst this widespread standing is providing a choice for some of those who want to stand, it is causing a customer care issue that needs to be resolved. Supporters who prefer to sit, and particularly children who may be unable to see and those who are unable to stand for long periods, can have their enjoyment ruined by others standing in front of them. This is less of a problem at home games where most people know which areas to avoid if they want to sit, although without guidance from the club selling tickets it can be a problem for occasional attenders. At away games however it is common for an entire following to stand, meaning that unless they have front row seats, those who are unable to do so can't see the match. It is clearly unacceptable that anyone should be unable to see the pitch or feel that they cannot attend a match because others wish to stand. A choice of standing or sitting areas would allow everyone to watch the match as they wish.

Finally, perhaps we should understand why supporters want the choice to stand. This can be split into practical and emotional factors.

Supporters can choose a spot on a terrace, if necessary arriving early to do so, whereas seats, especially for away games, are often allocated with no opportunity for selection. When standing someone can move if they don't like the company of those close to them, or if the person in front is particularly tall, but if an area is full one has to stay in the allocated seat. It is often hard for groups of friends to get seats together and a line of seats is less conducive to conversation than a standing group.

Prior to Upton Park becoming all seated, I stood for many years with a group of friends in the same spot on the North Bank. We knew that there would always be some of us there and it became a meeting point where people we hadn't seen for a while could turn up knowing they'd meet old friends. Now just two of us still go regularly, but in a mainly season ticket area, friends or family can't sit with us for the occasional game. It was on the North Bank that I introduced my wife to my friends, but the inconvenience of all-seating means that football has become less of a social occasion. It is said that all-seating increases diversity, but it has made it less convenient to take my family to an occasional game, so having the opposite effect.

When fans are asked why they want to stand the commonest response is atmosphere. Like minded fans can gather together and support their team vocally with songs and chanting. The atmosphere they develop is enjoyed by others who sit and the television companies who broadcast matches. When cameras pan to supporters singing they are invariably standing and commentators frequently refer to people on their feet when a match is exciting.

Under the heading 'Sit Down if You're Rocking the Boat', Simon Inglis in *Football Grounds of Great Britain* (1996) wrote:

'But football grounds should always be for fun, and while we all deplore the foul language and raucous behaviour, passion must never be pummelled into passivity. Live games call for live responses, and we must all – crowd and crowd managers alike – play our part in the event. We have come to watch football, not a video screen. We are not Americans!'

There is a camaraderie on the terraces that isn't found when everyone sits. It's natural to stand to sing and the atmosphere in all-seated stadia is commonly viewed as inferior to that where fans stand. Those who want to sing are often mixed with supporters who prefer to sit quietly, stifling the less inhibited feeling that comes when like minded people get together. Many fans say that they feel part of the whole event by standing, in a way that they don't if forced to sit. It is perhaps significant that generally people who watch football see themselves as supporters, implying an involvement, but that the FLA, Government and Taylor Report use the word spectator. People want to watch football in different ways, and to provide choice improves the enjoyment for everyone.

CHAPTER EIGHT

THE LEGAL POSITION

It is under the Football Spectators Act (1989) that the Government possesses powers to enforce all-seater stadia. As mentioned previously, the Act passed through parliament prior to the Taylor Report, but was not implemented until after its publication.

The Act covers three main areas:

- A national membership scheme, under which only spectators permitted to attend designated football matches are authorised spectators. The scheme to be overseen by the Football Membership Authority.

- A licensing system whereby stadia require a licence to admit spectators for designated football matches. The scheme to be overseen by The Football Licensing Authority (FLA).

- A system whereby court orders can be made and enforced against persons convicted of certain offences, imposing restrictions preventing them attending matches played abroad.

The national membership scheme has never been enforced (with good reason). The system of court banning orders has been introduced and has proved relatively successful.

The licensing system, overseen by the FLA, has been introduced, and it is this area which relates to standing.

Section 11 of the Act covers the, *'power of the Secretary of State to require conditions in licences relating to seating'*, with the critical clause is as follows:

'The Secretary of State may, by order, direct the licensing authority to include in any licence to admit spectators to any premises a condition imposing requirements as respect the seating of spectators at designated football matches at the premises; and it shall be the duty of the authority to comply with the direction.'

Currently the Government directs the FLA to make it a condition of issuing licences to clubs playing in the Premier League and Championship that their ground is all-seated. This condition is however not imposed for clubs in Leagues One and Two. If a club is promoted to the Championship it is permitted a maximum three years after which the ground must be all-seated. These three years do not have to be consecutive, but are totted up, so that once promotions and relegations mean that a club has spent three years in the Championship, it must be all seated. The date from which years in the Championship are counted is unclear, but is assumed to be around 1993.

If a club that has converted to all-seating is however relegated back to League One, it may not revert to having standing areas. Any club that has had an all-seated stadium, regardless of the division it is playing in, must remain all-seated.

The Football Spectators Act does not therefore, as is commonly believed, state that stadia in the Premier League and Football League Championship should be all-seated. It simply says that the Secretary of State *may* direct the FLA to make conditions regarding seating a condition of granting the licence which is required for each ground. The Act also states that the Secretary of State shall consult with the FLA, which may make recommendations as it thinks fit.

The all-seater requirement could therefore be relaxed if the

Government so wished, without the need for new legislation. The Secretary of State could simply repeal the Regulations.

The situation in Scotland is different as the Football Spectators Act applies only to England and Wales. The Scottish Premier League however requires that all clubs under their jurisdiction have all-seated grounds. I understand that they were 'instructed' to make this a condition of membership of the league, otherwise the FLA, which does not cover Scotland, would be extended to include their grounds. With powers now devolved this is no longer an issue.

The law relating to spectators standing in seated areas is far less clear. Lord Taylor did not expect that supporters would continue to stand once grounds became all-seated and therefore did not make specific recommendations on this issue. The Football Spectators Act does not specifically cover standing in seated areas.

The FLA have been directed by the Secretary of State for Culture, Media and Sport, to include the following two conditions in the licences it issues to clubs under The Football Spectators Act 1989:

a) 'Only seated accommodation shall be provided for spectators at a designated football match'.

b) 'Spectators shall only be admitted to watch a designated match from seated accommodation'.

It is therefore a condition of the licences issued to all Premiership and Championship grounds that standing areas cannot be provided, and that spectators can only be admitted to watch from seated accommodation.

These conditions are however subject to interpretation, and it is debatable as to whether they actually forbid standing in seated areas. Generally 'seated accommodation' is a term used to define an area of a stadium in which seats are provided. If someone chooses not to use the actual seats as they watch from this area, they would seem to be still complying with the regulation. This is a grey area of law, which has not been tested in the courts.

Entry into Premier League and Football League grounds is governed by a club's ground regulations, which are based on model ground regulations recommended by the Premier and Football Leagues. The following condition is contained in those regulations:

'Nobody may stand in any seated area whilst play is in progress. Persistent standing in seated areas whilst play is in progress is strictly forbidden and may result in ejection from the ground'.

The regulations give the clubs power to eject supporters for persistent standing, and to take other sanctions against them such as withdrawal of season tickets. They do not however define 'persistent standing' and if fully enforced would prevent supporters standing to celebrate a goal. Given that standing is generally defined as 'the upright position', it is questionable as to whether supporters are even permitted to walk to the toilet whilst play is in progress! It should however be noted that these are regulations recommended by the Premier and Football Leagues as a condition of entry into private premises, but they are not law. Standing in seated areas is not against the law. This was confirmed by the Department for Culture, Media and Sport who wrote to the FSF in 2008 saying, *'At no point has it been argued that the individual spectator commits a criminal offence by standing in a seated area'.*

Notwithstanding this, most football supporters probably believe that persistent standing is contrary to the law, something that they are often told by ill-informed stewards. They also commonly believe that the practice is not unsafe, and the regulation unnecessary. History has shown that laws which are generally viewed to be unreasonable have proved to be difficult to enforce, and this is clearly proving to be the case with standing at football matches.

In addition to the regulations laid down by the Government, both the Premier League and the Football League have their own regulations covering standing areas.

The Premier League Regulations state that, 'Spectators admitted to a registered ground shall be offered only seated accommodation, the majority of which shall be covered, and there shall be no standing terraces.'

The Football League Regulations state that, 'Each Championship Club shall with effect from the start of season 2012/13 (or with effect from the start of its third season in the Championship if later) only admit spectators to seated accommodation, and there shall be no standing terraces.'

These are however simply the rules of membership and not a legal requirement.

Examination of the legal situation shows quite clearly that the all-seater requirement is a matter of regulation rather than statute. The Government Minister has the power to permit safe standing areas without the need for new legislation.

CHAPTER NINE

PROPOSED SOLUTIONS

It is clear that many supporters want to stand and that if this choice is not provided it's almost impossible to prevent them from doing so, with the resultant customer care issues affecting those who prefer or have to sit. The regulation is unworkable, but those who oppose its relaxation do not propose any realistic solutions. Firmer attempts to enforce the regulation and prevent persistent standing serve only to alienate fans, cause conflict with stewards, additional headaches and costs for clubs, but still without solving the problem. Ten years of threats, 'education' and 'persuasion' have failed to stop widespread standing in seated areas.

Regardless of the issue of the current uncontrolled standing in seated areas, football surely has a duty to listen to its customers. The customer care issue of standers blocking the view of children and those who wish to sit is entirely valid, but there is another customer care issue – giving supporters a choice as to how they watch football.

Solutions are required which will enable supporters who want to stand to do so in safety, and those who wish to sit to be able to watch the game without having their view blocked. A number of proposals have been put forwarded to meet these objectives.

Safe Terraces

Some people don't like the word terrace as they say it brings images of Hillsborough and of the old, often badly maintained and fenced areas that were seen in many British grounds prior to the Taylor Report. However in my opinion it is not a word we should be scared of. There are twenty three league grounds in England with standing areas, and these are still referred to as terraces. The alternative of 'safe standing areas' implies that these terraces are not safe.

Naturally standing must be safe and the many recommendations of the Taylor Report have ensured that those who stand on our terraces can do so without fear of another disaster occurring. It has ensured that terraces are adequately maintained, that crush barriers are correctly positioned and regularly tested, and has set reduced spectator densities which ensure a reasonable margin for additional safety. Critically, supporters are counted into each section so capacity cannot be exceeded, and fences have been removed allowing escape onto the pitch or to other areas of the ground in case of emergency. Above all, there is now a thorough system of inspection and licensing and a proper safety culture, that ensures football grounds and crowd management procedures meet the required standards.

Those terraces which remain in our lower leagues all meet the stringent safety requirements and they are safe. If they were not there is no way that clubs would be allowed to keep them. As the terraces remaining in Leagues One and Two have been proved to be safe, there appears to be no logical reason why they cannot be permitted to remain if a club is promoted to the Championship. Capacities would be the same and even if crowds are larger, they would always be within the safe limit of the terrace that is calculated from Green Guide guidelines.

The suitability of spectator accommodation should surely be related to objective safety criteria and not the standard of football on the pitch. This is even more perverse for those clubs who have converted to all-seating following promotion to the Championship, but under current regulations cannot bring back standing areas should they be relegated. Here it seems that the type of spectator accommodation permitted is based not on the level of football at which the club is playing now, but where it played in previous seasons. It is an absurd regulation that prevents Luton Town in the Conference, or Bradford in League Two, from having standing areas, on the basis that they were once more successful.

The simple solution for those clubs who still have terraces, would therefore be that provided these continue to meet the Green Guide, they are permitted to remain whatever league the club may be playing in. For those clubs whose grounds are currently all-seated it is proposed that there should be no regulations preventing them from replacing some seating areas with modern safe terraces.

The Globe Arena at Morecambe FC is the only new ground to have been built with standing areas at a club then in the Football League since the Taylor Report, and provides an excellent example of how a ground with terraces benefits both club and supporters. Rather than installing far more seats than required and by building to a realistic capacity, Morecambe limited the cost of the new stadium. Building cheaper terraces on three sides meant that the bulk of the available funds could be spent on an impressive main stand, with ample seats to meet demand, but also sponsors' boxes, meeting rooms and bars that bring in revenue throughout the week. As a result Morecambe are moving from an annual loss to being self supporting, and their fans retain the choice to stand or sit. More details of the Globe Arena can be seen in Chapter Ten.

Convertible Standing / Seating Areas

As it is in England, standing in Germany is an integral part of fan culture. In Germany however every ground has standing areas. Clubs recognise that many supporters prefer to stand, and so provide what their customers want. For example, at Borussia Dortmund the 2011 Bundesleaga champions, a huge standing area at one end of the ground holds 27,000 fans, a third of the stadium's capacity. Such is the popularity of this area that it is sold out to season ticket holders.

In 2000 clubs in Germany faced a challenge. UEFA had stipulated that grounds staging Champions League and UEFA Cup matches had to be all-seated. Supporters however wanted the choice to stand. Accepting that they had to provide seats for European and International matches, the clubs looked for a solution that would enable supporters to stand for other games. The answer was convertible standing / seated areas, with seats in position for the few games regulations required this, but the area in standing mode for domestic matches.

Various designs were installed across Germany and later in other European countries. These have proved popular with supporters and by easy conversion, have allowed clubs to use them in seating mode, not only for their own European fixtures, but for matches in UEFA European Finals.

The Ruhrstadion, home to German club VFL Bochum, has large standing areas which look like traditional terraces. On closer inspection however one can see that on every second row there are metal clips onto which seats can be attached. The safety barriers used for standing, are easily removable when the seats are installed. Conversion back to a standing area is simple, with the seats unclipped and the barriers re-inserted.

Hamburg's ultra-modern Imtech Arena includes 10,000 standing spaces and 45,000 seats. As at Bochum, the area looks like a traditional terrace, with barriers that are easily removable when the stadium is in all-seater mode. The main difference is that when the stand is in standing mode, the seats fold away. Every other step is made of metal and the seats are under these steps. In Chapter Thirteen you will read of my observations on a similar design at VFB Stuttgart.

Many clubs, including Werder Bremen and Hannover 96 in Germany, and Wacker Innsbruck in Austria, use an ingenious design known as variositze, 'rail seats'. These consist of a robust 500mm wide metal seat with a high back, which forms a sturdy 1100mm high rail for safe standing and links together to form a continuous, strong rail right along the row. In standing mode the seats fold up flush between the uprights, thus creating wider clearways than along rows of normal seats. For games where the stadium must be in all-seater mode, club staff can quickly unlock the seats with a special key. The seats are approved by UEFA and FIFA for matches under their jurisdiction, and the rail heights meet the requirements of the Green Guide for barriers in standing areas. Numbers standing can be limited to one person per rail seat, or if a rear step is added a second row of fans can be accommodated, increasing capacity by up to 100% under European regulations and 80% with current UK guidelines.

It is in standing mode, with increased capacity, that both clubs and supporters can gain the greatest benefit from rail seats. Supporters have the choice to stand in an area designed for the purpose and clubs no longer have the impossible job of trying to stop persistent standing. Ticket prices can be lowered, yet clubs can increase revenue.

For example, if 4,000 conventional seats were converted to rail seats, based on the Green Guide recommendation of 1.8 standing fans per seat space, the capacity would be raised to 7,200. If seat tickets were £30 and standing £20 the potential extra revenue would be £24,000 per game, amounting to £480,000 over a 20 match season. The cost of convertible seats is slightly higher than conventional fixed seats, and additional expenditure would be required for example to provide extra turnstiles, toilets, refreshment facilities, and stewards. However, clubs can regain expenditure through the greater capacity that it provides in standing mode, and increased sales of food, drink and merchandise. Maintenance costs for rail seats are lower than conventional seats, which tend to get damaged, for example I understand that Manchester United typically have to replace 300 seats after each match.

All three of these convertible designs work well in Germany and meet their safety regulations. With a barrier along each row, the risk of surging is negated, and it is this system which is proposed by the FSF for use in the UK. As I was to find in Stuttgart, their new convertible standing area seems to be both popular and safe, offering another option that would appear could easily meet the requirements of the Green Guide.

Rail seats, or other convertible designs, could be installed by clubs who are currently outside of the top two divisions in England, but are carrying out ground redevelopment and want to ensure that this will meet regulations should they be promoted to the Championship. By selection of suitable tread depth and pitch, it would be perfectly possible to build a terraced stand which could be converted to rail seating at a future date should this be required.

In 2001 the FLA visited the Volksparkstadion in Hamburg to view the system of 'Kombi' convertible seats then in use. These were a foldaway design of aluminium seats. This stadium has since been demolished and replaced with the Imtech Arena (the stadium name has changed several times under sponsorship). The FLA concluded that:

1. The combination of "Kombi" seats and removable barriers is an ingenious and well-engineered system that overcomes most of the disadvantages, in particular inadequate seats and restricted views while seated, of the standing / seating conversions installed at other German football grounds.

2. This system could, with certain modifications, comply with the safety standards required in England and Wales.

The FLA however concluded that the system could not be installed into any current Premiership or Football League ground, primarily due to the 900mm row depth required. They noted the extra cost of installing such an area over conventional seats and ended the report by stating that, *'the development of the "Kombi" seat system in Germany does not affect the key arguments for or against the retention of the Government's long-standing policy on all-seated grounds.'*

The FLA's visit therefore found no reason why the kombi system couldn't be installed into new stadia / stands, but with no relaxation of the all-seating regulation, it attracted little serious interest from clubs.

Rail seats however can be installed in place of conventional seats in existing stands. They have no set row depth and easily fit onto the 760mm depth which is now fairly standard in modern UK stadia. This is deep enough to put in the rear step, raising capacity in standing mode. The standard row depth in most German stadia is 800mm, which is the depth now recommended for new builds by the Green Guide. The Green Guide also specifies the width of the clearway required along any given row. Installing rail seats along rows with a depth of 760mm leaves a clearway around double the depth required, which is much greater than where the rows are fitted with standard seats and allows easier access, for example for paramedics.

Professor Frosdick, founder member of the UK Football Safety Officers' Association and a noted expert in crowd safety, backed the FSF's campaign for rail seating to be allowed as a safe standing alternative to all-seater stadia in the top two divisions. Speaking at the FSF's open meeting on safe standing held in Liverpool in June 2011 he said,

'I think they've got an irrefutable case to allow clubs and fans the choice of having rail seating. I have spent the whole of my professional life working to make football grounds safer places for

football fans to enjoy their sport, and I would never associate myself with anything that would be to the detriment of the safety and welfare of football supporters.'

Managed Standing in Front of Seats

The ideal solution would be to have purpose built safe standing areas for home and away supporters at every ground. However if these are not provided another solution needs to be found if supporters are to have a choice to sit or stand, and to deal with the issue of persistent standing.

Currently at most all-seated grounds some supporters stand for all or part of the game. This may range from a handful to many thousands, sometimes tens of thousands for big matches. As there are no designated standing areas, those standing may block the view of supporters behind who prefer or need to sit. This is a genuine customer care problem and no one should have their enjoyment spoiled by standing supporters. It is however also a customer care issue that many supporters want to stand, but only 23 grounds currently provide this facility (and some of these only for home supporters).

Standing in seated areas is considered by some people to be a safety risk, although the degree of risk (if any) is highly debatable. It is however undeniably true that it is safer to stand in a gently sloping lower tier than it is in a steep upper tier, where there is a greater risk of falls and potentially even of a supporter toppling over the front wall.

In order to overcome the customer care issues and any potential safety issues, it is simply proposed that there should be designated areas in all-seated grounds where supporters may stand in front of their seats. These would be in lower tiers, where it is generally hard to see a safety risk, and it would be made clear to those buying tickets for these areas that supporters will be expected to stand.

Where away supporters are allocated only one area of a ground it is simply proposed that the front would be for those who wish to sit and the back for supporters who want to stand. The proportion would depend on demand, which varies from club to club.

Standing in front of seats is widespread and the authorities have been unable to stop it. This proposal would simply manage what already happens, to the benefit of both clubs and supporters.

Currently regulations prevent clubs from advertising an area for standing so it would be necessary to either alter the regulation, or for more informal local arrangements to be made. The latter is probably more realistic (and already occurs to a degree at some clubs), as it is more likely that any relaxation in the regulation will be to permit areas that are specifically designed for standing. However, managed standing in front of seats may be a sensible interim solution.

At many grounds it is known that fans will stand in certain areas at every match and a proportion of virtually all away supporters can be expected to stand. The entire away support of some clubs stand at every match. This appears to have become accepted practice, with little effort made to stop supporters standing. Clubs and police know that it is virtually impossible to stop and that to attempt to do so may lead to conflict between supporters and stewards. An informal arrangement would allow clubs to officially make those buying tickets aware of the parts of the ground to choose if they wish to either stand or sit. This already happens at some clubs outside of the UK and it would be a commonsense interim solution here.

CHAPTER TEN

AROUND THE
TERRACES – NORTH

In all the talk about 'bringing back standing' it's often forgotten that we still have many grounds where terraces remain. At the start of the 2011/12 season almost half the clubs in Leagues One and Two offered the choice to stand, as of course do most rugby clubs and many football stadia across Europe. To find out how well this works and whether clubs have plans to redevelop, I visited all 23 Football League grounds where terraces remain. I stood to watch matches at Dagenham, Peterborough, Rochdale and Torquay, travelled to Germany to experience VFB Stuttgart's new convertible area, and to Castleford for a rugby league game. Speaking to safety officers, commercial staff and directors gave an insight into how clubs view their terraces.

In order to ensure that no one was misrepresented, I sent a report of the meeting to the club for approval and if necessary modification, before circulating to the FSF Safe Standing Group and taking out information for this book. For the couple who didn't reply I've assumed they were happy with my report.

I've split the clubs into north, south and west, and hope that Peterborough and Burton will be happier classed as northern than southern. Should you wish to skip these chapters and move onto the nitty gritty of the standing arguments, I won't be offended. Come back to them later, but read the summary at the end of Chapter Thirteen.

ACCRINGTON STANLEY – THE CROWN GROUND

Seldom can one mention Accrington without someone saying 'Accrington Stanley'. The club who resigned from the league in 1962, reformed in 1968 and were promoted back to the Football League in 2006, are famous out of all proportion to their size.

The 5,087 capacity Crown Ground nestles in a pleasant residential area, with views to hills behind the away terrace, and easily holds Accrington's average crowd of just under 2,000. Even the 2010/11 play off semi final attracted little more than 4,000 and only 3,712 watched an FA Cup match against Premier League Fulham the season before. Football League regulations have however forced the club to install additional seats that are not needed, then to keep capacity over the League's minimum requirement, Accrington had to extend the away terrace.

I was shown round by Mick Shutz, the club's Safety Officer. He is also the kit man for away matches, runs the lottery and helps out with commercial matters. Along with the groundsman and one of the club's directors, Mick helped with concreting to reproof the steps prior to installing seats on part of the home terrace. We completed our meeting in the club shop as he printed numbers onto the players' shirts to be worn at the first game of the season three days later.

The Main Stand is seated, as is the Whinney Hill stand opposite, although that has lengths of uncovered terrace at each end. The Sophia Khan Stand used to be all terrace, but seats (which came from St Mirren's ground) were installed in the summer of 2010, at a cost of around £50,000. The seats were put in simply to meet the Football League rule and were not wanted by the supporters who would like them to be removed. The remaining 600 standing places are barely enough for home fans. Interestingly the installation of seats has increased the density of supporters on the terrace, theoretically reducing safety.

The uncovered 1,600 capacity Coppice Terrace at the other end is allocated to away supporters, as are some or all seats in the Whinney Hill Stand. It has been extended with a 'golf style' aluminium stand joined to the back of the original concrete terrace, which is intended to be a permanent arrangement. Extension was required as installation of the seats to meet the Football League's 2,000 covered seat requirement would have otherwise reduced the total ground capacity below the Football League's minimum requirement of 5,000.

Around 40% of capacity is standing so there is a choice to stand or sit, although for bigger games the home terrace sells out, with some fans unhappy that they have to sit. Mick said that every time Accrington Stanley have an all ticket match the standing areas sell out first. He estimates that two thirds of the crowd prefer to stand. All ages stand, from families, to older supporters who will lean on a barrier. Entry is the same price for all areas, so supporters are standing through choice not cost.

Standing in seated areas does not occur and there are no problems with disorder at Accrington. The club does have two fans with current banning orders, both for behaviour at away games, one for racist abuse and one alcohol related. Only one game was policed in 2010/11 and Mick didn't expect police to attend any matches in the next season.

No further development is planned at the Crown Ground, but the new chairman would like to relocate in 3 to 4 years. Mick would want any new ground to have terraces, as would the club's fans.

BURTON ALBION – THE PIRELLI STADIUM

Burton Albion, who were promoted to the Football League in 2009, play in one of our most modern grounds. The Pirelli Stadium was opened in 2005, the club moving across the road from Eton Park. It was built on the former site of the Pirelli Tyres Sports and Social Club, with the land donated to Burton Albion in exchange for naming rights. The £7 million construction cost was financed by sale of Eton Park for housing.

The glass fronted entrance to the Main Stand is an impressive introduction to Burton Albion. The stand contains the club's offices, shop, conference rooms, corporate facilities and dressing rooms. Seats in the centre are for season ticket holders and on the left is a 'nominal' family area. Away supporters are allocated around 400 seats, but if required the adjacent block is shared between home and away fans, with a small empty area between them.

The west, north and east sides of the ground are all terraces of standard modern design. The West Stand is where Burton's more vocal supporters tend to congregate.

Capacity was increased from 6,200 to 6,912 after Burton's promotion to the Football League, by agreement with the Safety Advisory Group, after some minor modifications were made. This extra capacity has not yet been required, the record attendance remaining at the 6,192 who attended Burton's final Conference match. The crowd for the FA Cup fixture with Manchester United in 2006 was just one lower, although 11,000 travelled to Old Trafford for the replay. The average league attendance for Burton's first two years in the Football League was 3,070 and the highest 5,801 (Notts County). The 7,000 capacity is therefore adequate for their current support and as a relatively small town club, probably enough for the foreseeable future.

Approximately 70% of The Pirelli Stadium's capacity is standing. The Main Stand is very rarely full, so there's generally a choice to sit or stand, the majority choosing to stand, although this is only £2 cheaper. In the 2011 Football League Supporter Survey 77% of Burton Albion supporters said they brought their families to matches at the stadium, many of whom choose to stand on the terraces. A high proportion of away supporters tend to stand and Ben commented how pleased visiting fans are to find that they can stand on a terrace. With a choice of accommodation, standing in seated areas does not occur.

In their two years in the League Burton have experienced two problems with crowd control, both with away supporters.

In May 2010 Grimsby Town played their final league fixture at Burton and were relegated. At the end of the match their supporters ran onto the pitch and missiles were thrown. Fifty four Grimsby supporters were arrested. The general view is that some of the away fans were looking for trouble, which would have occurred whether they had been in a seated or standing area.

On the other occasion some congestion occurred on the away terrace because Port Vale supporters arrived late and wouldn't move into the gaps available in the terrace, making it impossible to evenly distribute the supporters. There are three entry points to the terrace but most tried to use one end. Some fans spilled out onto the pitch surround. Space was made on the North Terrace by moving home fans and some Port Vale supporters were moved into this area. There was no disorder or injuries.

There have been no arrests of home supporters at The Pirelli Stadium in the last two years and the only significant safety problem is keeping gangways clear on the terraces. Police are only present for certain games where this is identified as necessary.

Ben told me of one incident where an away supporter had an epileptic fit and had to be taken to hospital. He said that supporters on the terrace parted to allow the paramedic through and that he was easily moved. Had this occurred in a seated area Ben said it would have been less easy to move him.

The stadium was built with a long term vision so it can be expanded if required. Footings were made to allow a second tier to be added if needed and seats could be bolted onto the terrace steps. There are however no current plans for redevelopment of the ground and this is unlikely to be required unless the club makes progress through the divisions.

CARLISLE UNITED – BRUNTON PARK

It is not often that a fire is described as, '*the best thing that could have happened*' and that '*it made the club*', but these were the words of Carlisle United legend Paddy Waters about the blaze that destroyed Brunton Park's wooden main stand in 1953. So determined were Carlisle that the fire wouldn't damage the club, that they played a home fixture with Tranmere just two days later, the players changing at the local swimming baths. The new main stand, which was opened a year later, is still in use and a fine example of a traditional English football stand.

In 1992 Carlisle United were bought by Michael Knighton, who despite his ten often turbulent years at the Brunton Park, remains best known for his ball juggling on the pitch at Old Trafford and subsequent failure to raise the funds to buy Manchester United. Knighton had plans to build a new 25,000 capacity all-seated stadium on the Brunton Park site, but much of the finance was to come from bonds to be purchased by supporters. Uptake was poor, with fans reluctant to pay towards a stadium that many didn't want, and the flamboyant owner had to reconsider his grandiose plans. Eventually just the East Stand was built, with funding from the Football Trust.

I was shown round Brunton Park, which is very much a mix of old and new, by Nigel Dickinson, Carlisle's Operations Manager. With standing on three sides, it is a ground of character and easily meets the club's current requirements in terms of capacity and choice of accommodation.

The design of the Main Stand, with a standing paddock below seats was once common and is far more interesting than more modern seated stands. The central seating section has wooden seats and was used in the filming of the BBC drama *United* that told the story of the Busby Babe's. Although only partly covered, the standing paddock is very popular with Carlisle supporters and there was much opposition when it was suggested the area be seated a few years ago.

Opposite, and looking a little out of place in what is otherwise a traditional old style ground, is the 5,700 seat East Stand. This looks newer than its 15 year age, perhaps because it is rarely anywhere near full (it has been described as a white elephant). The stand is off centre, with one end extending well beyond the goal line and the other falling short, because under Knighton's plan it was intended that the pitch would be moved. Away supporters are accommodated at the north end of the stand.

Where the away club brings a large following the 1,728 Peterrill End is also opened. Other than a small block of seats in the corner which were left over from fitting out part of the main stand, this is a basic open terrace. Carlisle's most vocal supporters tend to congregate at the Warwick Road End, a good sized traditional terrace (capacity 3,300) with a distinctive arched roof.

Carlisle's average attendance for 2010/11 was 5,207, and the largest crowd of 7,412 only 40% of capacity. The average for the past five seasons is 7,798, with the highest attendances for the visits of Leeds, with 16,668 in 2007. The 18,202 capacity is therefore adequate for their current support and would probably be sufficient for most fixtures if the club were to gain promotion to the Championship, although not if it were reduced by seating.

Around 60% of Brunton Park's capacity is standing and with the ground averaging only around one third full, there is ample choice. Terrace prices are only £4 less than seats. With a choice of accommodation, standing in seated areas by home fans is not generally a problem. When away supporters are allocated only seats a proportion tend to stand. If numbers are small stewards ask them to sit, but if large numbers stand no attempts are made to seat supporters. It's a shame that fans who wish to stand have to be made to sit when there is an empty terrace, but unless numbers are reasonable the cost of opening the terrace cannot be justified. Carlisle's location means that away followings are often quite small. There are no significant problems of disorder inside Brunton Park.

There are no current plans for redevelopment, but if Carlisle are promoted to the Championship and come under the '3 year rule', to meet the regulations, even if not actual demand for seats, it will be necessary to make major changes to Brunton Park. It is adjacent to the rivers Eden and Petteril, which flooded the ground in 2005, after which flood defences were erected. These are on the club's land and would restrict the design of, but not prevent redevelopment of the Petteril End.

Brunton Park is an example of ground that is perfectly adequate in terms of capacity and choice of supporter accommodation, but where redevelopment will be required if Carlisle are promoted, with this dictated by regulation not customer demand or objective risk assessment.

Just before this book went to the publisher, Carlisle announced that following a feasibility study which had investigated options for both new grounds and redeveloping Brunton Park, they were looking at moving to a new all-seated stadium at Kingmoor Park. The development was thought necessary in order to meet the requirements for the Championship, which the Carlisle aspired to reach. Commendably the club statement ended by saying, *'Keeping our fans fully informed and gaining their approval is most important, and that is what we will seek to do now'.*

Nigel Dickenson told me:

'Our vision is for the Championship and beyond as we look to have a new stadium funded by enablers – as you appreciate we are very much in the embryonic stage but the club's idea would be an all seater 12,000 initial capacity something along the lines of Chesterfield. There is still a long road ahead and the supporters have to be consulted.'

HARTLEPOOL UNITED – VICTORIA PARK

I visited Hartlepool on the eve of the first game of what promised to be an exciting season, the club having taken the bold decision to reduce season ticket prices to just £100 for all areas of the ground. The aim was to combat falling attendances, improve atmosphere and get more supporters into the habit of going to Victoria Park. The excellent response meant that virtually the whole of the home areas sold out to season ticket holders, with very few tickets available on a match by match basis.

Maurice Russell, Hartlepool's Safety Officer, showed me round. A former police officer, he has much experience policing matches in the North East. Victoria Park was modernised in the 1990s and provides a good standard of mixed seating and standing accommodation.

The single tier 1,599 seat Cyril Knowles Stand holds the dressing rooms, family area and executive boxes. To the right the Rink End has 1,033 seats for away supporters. The Town End covered terrace holds 1,775 and is where the club's more vocal supporters stand. The two tiered Niramax Stand is the most interesting stand at Victoria Park, consisting of 1,617 seats in the upper tier above a 1,832 capacity uncovered terrace. Current ground capacity is 7,858.

Hartlepool's average league attendance for 2010/11 was 2,933, with a highest figure of 4,084 (Sheffield Wednesday). The five season average is 3,973, showing a steady drop of about 500 each season from 5,087 in 2006/7. Only two crowds have exceeded 7,000 in the last five years (both for visits of Leeds United).

The first game of the 2011/12 season (Walsall) however attracted 5,170, double the attendance for the same fixture last season, and the average for the first seven league games an 88% increase at 5,512. Whilst the 7,695 capacity was easily adequate at 'normal' prices, the £100 season tickets meant that the ground was much fuller.

Almost half Victoria Park's capacity is standing. Maurice told me that people love to stand, that the terraces are the most popular areas with more choosing to stand than sit, and that a good mix of ages go on the terraces. He said that they are happy to stand in the rain and that supporters were choosing to stand through choice not cost. His view was that terraces work perfectly well at Hartlepool. There is however no choice for away supporters who are allocated only seats.

There are no significant problems of disorder inside Victoria Park and only a handful of matches are policed. Around 100 stewards are employed, all of whom are local and not from agencies. There is occasionally trouble in the town, the most serious when Sheffield Wednesday visited, although of the twelve people charged only two had actually been to the match.

Maurice agreed that the fact that there are people who attach themselves to Hartlepool and occasionally cause trouble, but that there is no disorder in the ground, adds to the evidence that terraces do not lead to crowd trouble. In the last two years there have only been two ejections (both for using laser beams) and one arrest in the ground. In recognition of this Hartlepool received a letter of commendation from the Safety Advisory Group.

There are no problems with keeping gangways clear. Maurice said that 20 years ago fans wouldn't keep them clear, but now they have been educated to do so. Persistent standing in seated areas occurs commonly in the away end, where no choice of accommodation is provided. The FLA are very hot on this (FLA Inspector is Rick Riding who has made a big issue of persistent standing at Sunderland), but if fans refuse to sit Maurice said there is little they can do. Letters are sent to visiting fans, but announcements asking supporters to sit have resulted in more standing up.

Unusually at a ground where there is choice, Hartlepool had a problem with a small group of home fans standing in the block of seats next to the away fans. This is surprising as they could have stood on the terrace below. It was dealt with by allocating these seats to the local college.

Very few injuries occur at the ground, but Maurice told me of two occasions where supporters collapsed and had to be resuscitated. One was a man on the Town End terrace who 'died' for five minutes before being revived by a paramedic. Supporters parted to allow people to reach him and Maurice said that he considers it easer to deal with casualties on a terrace rather than in the seats.

Hartlepool are currently planning a major extension and refurbishment of the away end, but have no plans for home areas or to move from Victoria Park. It's not intended that the two terraces will be replaced, but if the club were promoted and remained in the Championship, seats could be fitted onto the terraces to meet the regulation. The resulting loss of capacity would however mean that the ground was too small for likely demand.

MACCLESFIELD TOWN – MOSS ROSE

Moss Rose is a small but pleasant ground, that has been considerably improved since 1995, when its failure to meet Football League requirements denied Macclesfield promotion from the Conference.

What was just a grass bank at the Star Lane End has been replaced by a covered terrace, four rows of which have light blue seats that came from Maine Road. Dean Holmes who showed me round said that although there's no extra cost to sit, most supporters prefer to stand on the terrace behind. At the opposite end away supporters may stand on the open Silkman End terrace, or sit in 410 seats allocated in the Alfred McAlpine Stand. Whilst Macclesfield's more vocal supporters tend to frequent the Star Lane End, older fans who choose to stand can generally be found on the London Road side of the ground, where there's a 1,220 capacity open terrace in front and either side of the old main stand.

Moss Rose's capacity of 5,988 has proved ample for a club whose average league crowds for the last two seasons were 1,807 and 1,887, both the lowest of the 92 league clubs, although in January 2009 6,008 watched the home FA Cup tie with Everton.

There are no problems of disorder inside Moss Rose, nor is there any standing in seated areas. Macclesfield frequently have no arrests in a season and have been called the 'best behaved fans in the league'. Dean said all ages stand on the terraces.

I showed him the table of injury figures submitted by clubs to the FLA for 2009/10, from which I'd calculated injury rates based on attendances. This showed that Macclesfield's 13 reported injuries at roughly one per 7,350 attendances appeared to be the highest rate of the 92 league clubs. Dean was surprised at this, but said they do get some injuries from supporters being hit by the ball, including a broken hand last season.

Club Safety Officer Dave Towns explained to me that the figures reported to the FLA included incidents from other events, such as minor injuries occurring to players that were looked at by a Red Cross first aider during a community 5 a side competition held at Moss Rose. He said that all incidents, from wasp stings to hand burns from drink spills are recorded, enabling the club to remove or reduce risk, but that if purely football spectator injuries were submitted to the FLA Macclesfield would not have the highest rating. It therefore appears that Macclesfield Town is another example of differences in reporting injury figures meaning that comparisons between clubs are of very little value.

Macclesfield are involved in plans to move to a new ground in South Macclesfield Development Area. This would be a 'Sports Village', with facilities for other sports, as well as women's football. It appears that the move is some way off at the moment and there are no firm plans for the stadium design.

MORECAMBE FC – THE GLOBE ARENA

Since the Taylor Report only one new ground has been built with standing areas at a club then playing in the Football League – Morecambe FC's Globe Arena. This however provides an excellent example of how terraces can be incorporated into modern football grounds, allowing supporters to keep the choice as to how they watch and saving clubs the expense of installing seating, which is neither needed or wanted.

Morecambe were promoted to League Two in 2007 and moved from Christie Park to the 6,334 capacity Globe Arena at the start of the 2010/11 season. I met with Brian Fagan, a club director, to view the new ground and discuss why they chose to include standing areas. Brian oversaw the project to construct the new stadium.

The Globe Arena is an impressive stadium for a League Two club and the approach towards the main stand suggests a larger, higher level ground. It is still in the town, but further from the centre than Christie Park. The ground is named after Globe Construction who built the stadium.

The 2,200 capacity Main Stand includes the club's offices, bar, changing rooms, press area and its very impressive suites and sponsors' boxes. There's even a local police station, which the club provides free of charge and is used by officers policing local estates. It is significantly higher than the other sides of the ground, particularly the North Terrace opposite, giving the stadium a slightly uneven feel. Supporters buying premium seats in the centre section gain entry to a lounge with a bar and food available. The end block of seats is allocated to away supporters, who share facilities with the away terrace. There's an excellent view of the pitch from all seats, and should the football not hold their attention, supporters can enjoy distant views of the Lake District mountains and Pennine hills.

The 2,029 capacity West Terrace has 18 steps with two crush barriers running its full length. These are positioned with only three steps above the upper barrier and three below the lower one, which appears to be a strange arrangement, but was required to meet the Green Guide. There's no concourse below the stand as Morecambe changed their plans for this to reduce cost. Instead supporters use a concourse behind the stand, which has a refreshment kiosk, but is uncovered, not unnaturally causing fans to complain when it's raining. Some large umbrellas have been erected as a temporary measure and the club intends to build a canopy over the concourse as costs permit. There's space to build an upper tier should increased capacity become necessary.

The North Terrace is just 5 steps deep, has a large gap in the centre and holds just 620 supporters. Facing south, the terrace is popular on sunny days, but less so in rain. It is the cheapest area of the ground. Behind the terrace are a number of training pitches which the club rents out, providing a source of income, plus at the east end, a gym and offices that are used for community activities. Whilst there is space to enlarge the terrace, Brian considers it more likely that the club will build additional offices and classrooms for community and educational activities.

The covered East Terrace for away supporters is raised above pitch height and set back a little from the goal line. This is because Morecambe decided to save money by not putting in the lower steps, as it was considered that the 1,485 capacity would be adequate for away support. The capacity could be increased by adding the steps if required. The concourse behind the stand is very narrow and the club accept that this was a mistake. In order to prevent congestion stewards sometimes have to control the rate of access as fans use the facilities behind the stand.

All the terraces have been designed with steps large enough to install seats should this be necessary in the future. Interestingly the 2:1 ratio of standing to sitting capacity is roughly the same as the national average prior to the Taylor Report.

Morecambe's objectives in moving to a new ground were:

To provide sources of income separate from matchday ticket and related sales.
To build a ground that would meet current capacity requirements and those for the foreseeable future.
To provide a ground that looks and sounds right, and that gives fans what they want.

The Globe Arena was financed by the sale of Christie Park to Sainsbury's, plus some money put in by the chairman. The club sought finance from the Football League Trust, but were denied because of a rule which allowed £2.4 million for clubs which were resident in League Two prior to 2005, but only £750,000 for those admitted to the League after that date. Deductions for earlier funding for ground improvement would have reduced any assistance available by the amount of any previous grants. This effectively meant that the Trust could dictate their requirement for an all-seater stadium for circa £600,000 grant aid. The club decided to provide what was financially viable and was what the majority of supporters wanted.

Prior to moving, Morecambe was run at an annual loss. With the additional income streams from the Globe Arena they expected to be self supporting within two years. Lounges have sold extremely well and are regularly used for meetings through the week. The majority of the money was spent on the Main Stand, as it was this that would provide ongoing income. Funds were insufficient to make the whole of the ground seated, but this was not considered as supporters wanted the choice to stand.

Morecambe believed that as a small town club with relatively low attendances, there was no need to build a large ground. A capacity of 6,000 would easily hold their normal support and be adequate for the highest attendances the club had attracted. The average attendance for the three seasons prior to the move was 2,409, with only one match attracting over 5,000 (5,268 for the last ever league match at Christie Park). Hence Morecambe saw no need to build a larger ground, the Globe Arena being easily adequate for the foreseeable future. Average attendance for the first season at the new ground was 2,648, although this was a poor season on the pitch. The club say they are ambitious and have set their sites on promotion to League One, and there is potential to expand the facilities within the guidelines for such a promotion.

Given the choice, Morecambe fans would have liked to have simply moved the Home Stand which they loved from the old ground, rather than build a new stand. The club investigated moving this, which was only ten years old, but found that it was cheaper to build a new stand. Fans said that they wanted standing areas so these were provided, although cost was also a major factor. The club couldn't have afforded to build a 6,000 capacity all-seated stadium, but saw no need to do so as many fans prefer to stand. A seated stand was considered on the north side, but would have cost £350,000 and was not needed, so the small terrace was constructed.

Brian believes that the mix of seats and standing is right for their supporters. The 2,200 seats don't normally sell out so supporters have a choice to stand or sit. With a minimum price differential of only £1 and plenty of seat availability, clearly many Morecambe supporters prefer to stand.

There is no hooligan problem at Morecambe and no standing in seated areas. In May 2011 Football Intelligence Officer PC Will Nelson was quoted as saying that he had followed the club home and away all season and has *'nothing but praise for Shrimp's fans'*.

The Globe Arena is an impressive stadium of which Morecambe FC are rightly proud. It is a part of the community and far more than just a football ground. By investing in facilities that provide additional income on match days but also throughout the week, Morecambe expect to be self sufficient, something that could not have been achieved purely through ticket sales.

By providing ample standing accommodation Morecambe have given supporters what they want – choice. Hence they do not have the problems of standing in seated areas seen at all-seated grounds. By building to a realistic capacity and with three sides of the ground as terraces, they have been able to minimise costs and allocate most of the available finance to areas that provide an ongoing income.

Morecambe FC have shown that it is perfectly possible to build a new ground with standing areas, and that this has considerable benefits for both the club and its supporters.

PETERBOROUGH UNITED – LONDON ROAD

Peterborough United are a club who are close to and listen to their fans, meeting monthly with the three supporters' organisations. They are supportive of standing and if it were in their control would have kept terraces at both ends of the stadium. Perhaps it helps that their Chief Executive Bob Symns grew up on the terraces of White Hart Lane and has experienced rail seats while following Spurs in Europe. Promotion to the Championship in 2011 however meant that unless they are relegated, having already played one season at this level, (their 1992 season was deemed not to qualify) London Road must be all-seated by August 2013.

The club see themselves very much as a part of the community; in Bob's words, 'a community hub', and the planned redevelopment of their London Road ground will enhance this position.

Redevelopment is to be paid for by the city council, who own the ground. It will include premises for other uses, mainly health, leisure and education based. The Probation Service currently use offices in one corner of the ground and included in the rear of the new away stand will be premises for a university level STEM Centre for the teaching of science, technology, engineering and mathematics. The stadium will form part of a large redevelopment on the south bank of the River Nene. A new ground had been discussed, but the recession stopped this happening.

London Road is a traditional stadium, which when I visited had seats on the sides and terraces at both ends. The Family Stand is fairly new, but the rest of the ground has been largely unchanged for many years.

The 3,475 capacity Moy's End Terrace has made Peterborough a popular away trip with visiting supporters for many years, but is to be replaced by a 2,500 seat stand in 2012. Whilst Peterborough and their fans would have liked it to have remained a standing area, with the council footing the bill, they had the final say.

The 2,667 capacity home terrace is expected to be rebuilt in 2013 with improved facilities, and possibly a hotel. The club have told the council that they want this to be a 50:50 split of standing and seating. They would like the 2,500 capacity lower level to be rail seats, which will cater for those supporters who want to stand now. Fans are lobbying the council for this, but cost is however likely to be a challenge as again, the council are paying. Bob told me that if rail seats cannot be installed, Peterborough *'will look for a compromise, such as wider seats so that if supporters did stand at any time there will be sufficient space to overcome the safety concern of supporters spreading into gangways'*.

The current traditional terraces are popular with home and away fans, although they're dated, with limited facilities. Around 40% of London Road's capacity is standing and supporters of all ages choose to stand. The majority however prefer to sit. With a choice of accommodation, standing in seated areas is usually only a problem insofar as from some seats it is necessary to stand when others lean forward for example to follow play in the corners.

Although Peterborough have a small group of 20 to 30 'risk' supporters, there are virtually no problems of disorder inside London Road. The club has good relations with the police, who didn't attend all games in League One, but probably will do so in the Championship.

Total capacity prior to redevelopment is 14,584. This compares to an average crowd of 6,449 for Peterborough's last season in League One and 8,913 for the previous season in the Championship. The ground with its existing terraces would therefore have been of adequate size, but had capacity been lost due to the regulation requiring all-seating, it would probably have been too small for demand for the visits of the likes of Leicester, Leeds and West Ham.

London Road meets Peterborough's current needs and despite limited facilities at both ends, is popular with both home and away fans. Whilst the redevelopments will make some improvements, it is a shame that two terraces that have proved safe and popular for many years have to be lost.

Peterborough v Leeds United

I returned to London Road for a Championship fixture against

Leeds United, where a 12,880 crowd saw an exciting and controversial match. Peterborough's Lee Tomlin was sent off in the first half for a foul that seemed to arise from frustration at the referee refusing to allow a player to return after treatment, but the home side's ten men fought well, equalising for 2.2 in the 88th minute. The point that their spirited display deserved was however taken from Peterborough, when Leeds' substitute Lucciano Becchio scored following a dispute free kick, well after the indicated four minutes added time was up. Despite all the drama, excitement and frustration, there were no problems with behaviour from either set of supporters.

With all home areas sold out the club had asked supporters to arrive early for the 12.00 start, but a delay on the trains meant that I didn't get there until twenty minutes before kick off. There was however no hold up in getting into the ground and I was able to find a spot on the London Road Terrace, noting that both sets of fans were already singing.

Peterborough's vocal support was disappointing in the first half, mostly consisting of a loud and annoying drum with a small group of singers. When the drummer stopped playing more tended to sing and in the second half, as the excitement grew on the pitch and the drummer kept quiet, the home fans became impressively loud.

During the warm up I nearly became an injury statistic as a ball whizzed over my head, hitting the man behind. Four members of Peterborough's staff, including the player responsible for the wayward shot, checked he was OK. Fortunately he was otherwise this would have been another injury allocated to terracing.

The terrace was at capacity but I had plenty of room, with no one on the two steps in front or more than a metre to my right. It was fuller in the middle where the more vocal fans gathered, but there was still plenty of space to move about. The front row was occupied mainly by children with parents and although predominantly male, there were a good number of women of all ages on the terrace.

The 4,236 Leeds supporters were split between the Moys End Terrace and Main Stand. I watched the terrace closely and saw no problems of behaviour. All bar about twenty visiting fans in the seats stood up for the whole game, something which is unusual when choice is provided. No efforts however were made to get them to sit. I can only conclude that the vast majority of Leeds fans prefer to stand.

I had chosen this match because with large numbers of home and away fans on the terraces, and Leeds fans having (perhaps undeservedly) not the best of reputations, it represented a test for an old ground with standing accommodation. The stadium, terraces and supporters passed the test with flying colours.

And one final observation – despite their excellent behaviour, why did the police consider it necessary to film Leeds supporters after the match as soon as they started singing outside the ground? Filming of supporters as they arrive at railway stations and leave grounds is becoming almost routine, but does not help to foster good relations between police and fans.

ROCHDALE – SPOTLANDS

With all four sides having been redeveloped in the last fifteen years, Spotlands is regarded as one of the best grounds in the lower league, a sharp contrast to years gone by. Hence no further development is planned, unless of course this is forced on the club by promotion to the Championship. The 1,898 capacity covered Sandy Lane Terrace provides choice for home supporters, although visitors have only seating in the impressive Willbutts Lane Stand. Current ground capacity is 10,429, which is ample for demand, Rochdale averaging 3,389 for the last three seasons, with a maximum of 6,483 for the local derby against Oldham.

I visited for a Johnstone's Paint Trophy fixture against Walsall.

Cutting the admission price to £5, and just £1 for children, with a 7.15pm kick off, proved successful in attracting a good crowd of 2,089, including plenty of families. Sadly the game failed to provide the entertainment that might entice them back – a dire first half, some improvement after the interval with both sides scoring, then straight to penalties. Even these weren't particularly exciting with Walsall managing to score only one of their four. The highlight for me though was to see 38 year old Jimmy Walker in goal for the Saddlers – a hero at West Ham for his performances in our 2005 promotion season and perhaps even more so for saving a Frank Lampard penalty at Stamford Bridge.

Standing on the Sandy Lane Terrace I noted a wide range of ages and a reasonable number of females. Almost half the group of teenagers who stood behind the goal were girls. I spoke to one couple with two young children (3 and 5), who said that they go on the terrace as the children prefer it as there is more space to move about, but they get bored in the seats. Whilst not perhaps an argument for terraces in the Premier League, this was an example of standing increasing diversity. Although prices were the same for all areas roughly 400 chose to stand on the terrace, about 20% of home fans. Walsall brought about 180, about half of whom stood at the back. There was no persistent standing of home fans until the last few minutes when some youngsters at the back stood, and for penalties when everyone behind the goal stood up.

SCUNTHORPE UNITED – GLANFORD PARK

Glanford Park opened in 1988 when the club moved from the Old Show Ground. It was the first new ground to be built in the modern era (post war).

There's an interesting story as to why it has one of the smallest pitches in the country. The builders asked how large the pitch should be and were told to make it the same size as the Old Show Ground. They took measurements between the two touchlines and the goal lines, and used these for their designs. It was only when the new stadium was completed that it was realised they had left no allowance for the run off outside the lines. Hence the pitch had to be made smaller than the old ground. In a nice mixing of units Scunthorpe show it on their website as 112 metres x 72 yards.

Easily reached by car at the end of the M181 motorway, but a few miles from the town centre, it's a compact single tiered stadium, with a 2,773 capacity covered terrace for home supporters, which is the most popular area of the ground. The away end was built as a terrace, but converted to seating by bolting seats onto the steps. This conversion was made just before the Government relaxed the regulation on the 3rd and 4th divisions, a decision that due to the reduced capacity, General Manager David Beeby told me has cost Scunthorpe a lot of money over the years.

David is very familiar with the standing issue, as had Scunthorpe not been relegated from the Championship at the end of the 2010/11 season, the three year rule would have meant that the remaining terrace would have to be seated. In conjunction with the FSF, supporters launched a campaign to have the three year rule suspended, which was backed by the club and local MPs. Relegation however means that this is on hold, unless Scunthorpe are again promoted to the Championship.

Scunthorpe's average league attendance for their last two years in the Championship was 5,965, with season highs of 8,921 (Newcastle) and 8,122 (Leeds). The average for their last season in League One (2008/9) was 5,020 with a maximum of 8,135 (Leeds). The League Cup fixture against Manchester United in October 2011 attracted 9,077. With relegation to League One their 9,088 capacity was expected to be adequate for most if not all games. Had they avoided relegation and been forced to seat the home terrace, capacity would have been reduced to 7,465, which has been exceeded on nine occasions in the last two seasons.

There is adequate capacity for home supporters to have a choice to sit or stand. Many families and children choose to stand and the biggest uptake for terrace season tickets has been amongst 14 and 15 year olds. Away supporters have no choice and some or all tend to stand in front of their seats. If just a few stand stewards try to get them to sit, but if all 1,600 do they accept it's not possible to stop.

David believes that supporters should have the right to choose whether they watch football from seats or terraces. He said that Scunthorpe is not an affluent area and cheaper terrace tickets help enable the less well off to come to games.

We discussed the new Football League rule that states clubs must be all-seated after two years in the Championship. David thought this is worded incorrectly and should say three years to match the Government regulation. He said that the ruling was originally worded wrongly as it said three consecutive years. His view is that the regulation should be based on terrace size, not the division in which the club is playing.

David said that terrace supporters tend to enter the ground earlier than those in the seats and for big games not to move from their positions (so as to gain a good spot and not lose this). Hence for big games the club takes less money for refreshments in the terraced stand.

Scunthorpe have a few 'risk' fans, but a zero tolerance policy, with supporters banned if necessary. There was a problem with behaviour of a few fans in the seats next to the away supporters and some were banned for a while. When they were allowed to return this was initially for a probationary period, on the condition that they only used the area furthest from the away fans – the North Terrace. This is an interesting illustration of poor behaviour and terraces not being linked – the poor behaviour was in the seats and the supporters told they must use the terrace on completion of their bans. There were no problems on the terrace during Scunthorpe's three years in the championship.

There are no current plans to install seats or redevelop unless the club are promoted, although before the recession there was investigation into moving, with Glandford Park and its surrounds to be sold for housing. Scunthorpe don't want to go all-seated, but if they are forced to will put seats on the terrace, reducing its capacity by more than half. Based on the previous two years, all-seating would mean that it's likely that for an average of at least four games each season the ground could not accommodate all those wishing to attend matches.

CHAPTER ELEVEN

AROUND THE TERRACES – SOUTH

AFC WIMBLEDON – KINGSMEADOW

Just nine years after their formation, and to the pleasure of football supporters across the country, AFC Wimbledon regained the Football League place that had been taken from them by that new club in Buckinghamshire. AFC is owned by its supporters, via a one fan one vote trust. They share Kingsmeadow (The Cherry Red Records Fans' Stadium) with Kingstonians, from whom they took over the lease in 2003.

The ground is painted partly in the red of Kingstonians and partly the yellow and blue of Wimbledon. With terracing on three sides, the 1,265 seats in the Main Stand don't meet the demand from home fans, let alone visitors. Club Secretary David Charles told me that Wimbledon had to turn down 100 season ticket requests and that only 26 seats are available to away supporters, just for those who are old or infirm. Kingsmeadow is therefore a rare ground where it's additional seating not standing, that is required to provide choice.

A rare sight in a football ground were litter bins, a sign perhaps that when supporters own their club they're more inclined to keep it tidy. An even stranger sight was a neat square of bare earth in the centre circle, where the grass had been removed. This I was told was as a result of some people breaking into the ground in the early hours of the previous Saturday night, removing the sprinklers and having a kick about. Unfortunately they replaced one sprinkler head upside down and when it was turned on the downward pressure of water lifted the surrounding turf!

The covered 1,000 capacity Tempest End is the popular home terrace and Wimbledon supporters now also have most of the Kinston Road End, which used to be allocated to away fans. Visitors are given the corner, including some of the John Smith Stand, a partly covered terrace.

The stadium's capacity of 5,100 is only marginally over the league's minimum limit. The average crowd for Wimbledon's first few League Two games was around 4,300 with fans having to be turned away on two occasions, so improvements will be required. It's intended that the Kingston Road End will be seated from August 2012, and the John Smith Stand remodelled to improve the rake and view. Currently the three steps in the open sections and six steps under the low roof are very shallow.

David told me that many people prefer to stand and that visiting supporters often say they are pleased to be able to do so. Under 16s are charged just £2 (£25 for a season ticket) and a lot of children stand on the terraces. There are virtually no problems of disorder inside the Kingsmeadow, nor are there problems of standing in seated areas. David said that a walkway gives easy access to the terraces and they all work well.

The Cherry Red Records Fans' Stadium, whilst adequate for non league and a league club with smaller crowds, needs some work if it is to enable AFC Wimbledon to fulfil their ambitions. This is in hand, and as one would expect from a club owned by its supporters, will retain plenty of choice to either stand or sit.

ALDERSHOT TOWN – EBB RECREATION GROUND

Like Accrington, Aldershot Town are a resurrected club. In March

1992 Aldershot FC went out of business and were expelled from the Football League. Just a month later, at a meeting attended by 600 supporters, Aldershot Town FC was born. Starting in the Diadora Isthmian League Division Three, where their away support regularly swelled average attendances of 90 to over 1,000, the club quickly moved through the leagues. In August 2008 they regained their place in the Football League, continuing to play at the council owned Recreation Ground, which is currently sponsored by EEB.

The ground has spectator accommodation on only three sides, the flat High Street End having been out of use since 2008 as Football League rules state that standing areas must be terraced. With 72% of capacity terracing, it has one of the highest proportion of standing accommodation in the Football League, however a club spokesman told me that there is adequate seating for their normal attendance and that around 60% choose to stand. Aldershot averaged 2,487 in 2010/11, with a three season high of 5,023 (Brentford). In October 2011 a capacity crowd of 7,044 filled the EBB Stadium for a Carling Cup tie against Manchester United.

It is an interesting and atmospheric ground, especially in the torrential rain that fell throughout my visit! The stadium hasn't changed a great deal since the days of Aldershot FC and although in the town centre, is pleasantly situated with tall trees overlooking the pitch. There is terracing on three sides, with seating areas in the centre sections of both the South and North Stands. The East Bank is a traditional terrace with an unusual barrel roof and creates a good atmosphere. An empty section adorned with a selection of supporters' banners separates the home and away areas. In addition to the 751 terraced spaces, away supporters have the adjacent uncovered terrace which holds 390, plus 179 seats on the South Stand.

Aldershot say they have a long term 'desire' to develop the existing ground, but nothing currently in progress.

BARNET – UNDERHILL

Underhill currently offers a good mix of standing and seated accommodation for all fans, with the East Terrace which is split between home and away supporters, helping to generate a good atmosphere. The 2,540 capacity is split into 1,280 home and 1,260 away, although this can be reduced if a sterile area is needed between the two sets of fans. Opposite is the Main Stand and at the ends of the ground are very contrasting structures: the new South Stand, a family stand which replaced uncovered temporary seats, and the 644 capacity North Terrace. A temporary stand in the corner allows the choice that was not always available for away supporters. The North West Terrace, an uncovered standing area holding just 536, is situated next to the Main Stand.

I was shown the 5,200 capacity ground by Darran Wood, Barnet's Commercial Manager. The eight foot slope from end to end is very evident, and adds to Underhill's charm. Darren told me that although the capacity is sufficient for their current support, many people in the area are used to watching Arsenal and Tottenham and the better facilities that they provide. He felt that a new all-seated stadium would generate increased support, although agreed with me that this could be achieved if some terracing was kept, and that they would then not instigate a problem of standing in seated areas.

Standard ticket prices for the East Terrace are just £1 less than the South Stand, but many of all ages choose to stand. Darran told me that there are supporters who have stood on the uncovered North and North East Terraces since they were children, and choose to do so even if it is raining, despite the option of a covered terrace or of seats that are only £3 more expensive.

Whilst adequate for their attendances (average 2,249 in 2010/11), Barnet have been considering moving from Underhill for many years. A new ground may provide opportunities for additional income, but could take the club away from its Barnet roots. Darran wasn't able to give me any information about the current situation with regard to a possible move. It is a subject that raises strong opinions from both supporters and borough's residents. The goings on at Barnet over the years could fill a book themselves and it is probably best that I don't attempt to write about what has become a sensitive issue.

Barnet v Macclesfield Town

A week after meeting Darran, I returned to Underhill for a Friday night match against Macclesfield Town, standing on the East Terrace with the home fans. And what an enjoyable experience it was. The game was interesting, with Barnet scoring two penalties within three minutes to win 2.1 and Macclesfield having six players booked plus one sent off, but it was standing on the terrace with Barnet's friendly fans that made the evening.

The Friday kick off seemed successful, with the 2,200 attendance an improvement on Barnet's recent home crowds, despite Macclesfield bringing only around 100. The change of date was made after some visitors had bought train tickets, so their club provided a free coach as compensation. As they do occasionally when the away following is small, Barnet allocated only the temporary seated stand, and gave the whole East Terrace to home supporters. Around a third of Macclesfield's fans stood at the back and weren't asked to sit.

Ticket prices were reduced to £10 for all areas except the Main Stand, but despite no cost difference it seemed that more fans had chosen the terraces than to sit in the South Stand. The North and North East Terraces were sparsely populated, but a good number stood on the east side, particularly around the half way line where the singers gathered. An excellent atmosphere was generated under the roof, with more singing than one often hears from home Premier League fans. The songs in the lower leagues are often different too, with more variety and less based on whatever the 'tune of the moment' is.

There was a camaraderie and social aspect on the terrace that isn't found in seats. Fans were meeting friends and could move to talk to people. At half time I chatted to a few supporters who told me how much they enjoy the terrace at Underhill. Tom Hammond said that he lives near Watford but comes to Barnet because they have terraces. If Barnet went all-seated he'd follow a non league team where he could stand. When travelling away where Barnet are given a seated area he stands at the back, but says it isn't the same as a terrace.

Strangely six police officers were present, although they stood in the corner for the whole game with nothing to do. Apparently they often choose to attend even though the club don't pay for them. Maybe there aren't any burglars to catch in Barnet! The behaviour of both sets of fans was exemplary, and far better than the drunk and anti social city workers that I encountered on my journey back through London. There were no policemen to look after them though.

A banner held up by supporters in the South Stand urged Barnet to stay at Underhill. It will be a sad day if the club move from this cosy stadium, that is so loved by both home and away fans, and which is plenty adequate for their support.

BRENTFORD – GRIFFIN PARK

Griffin Park is a traditional football stadium with seated stands on both sides, and the 2,200 capacity Ealing Road Terrace for home supporters at one end. This figure is quite conservative, as it does not include the uncovered corners, so that there is no risk of overcrowding under the covered section in wet weather. Away supporters are housed in the two tier Brook Road Stand, which has 650 seats above a 1,200 capacity terrace. The ground's 12,700 capacity has proved adequate in recent years, Brentford's average league gate for the three seasons to 2011 being 5,632, with a maximum of 10,642 (Wycombe Wanderers).

I had a very useful meeting with Brentford's Stadium Manager Tony Ashley, who has realistic views on standing and policing. (Note that the views that he gave me were his own and may not reflect those of Brentford FC). Tony has 27 years experience in safety management at football grounds, most of which was spent with Oxford United, where he was heavily involved in building the Kassam Stadium.

Tony said that he doesn't have a problem with some standing in seated areas, which can be managed if fans are reasonable and compliant. At Brentford some fans stand in the seated paddock area, but generally only at moments of excitement, not persistently. Those who want to stand for the whole game go on the terrace. Most away supporters who want to stand use the terrace, but there are sometimes some who insist on standing in the upper tier seats, perhaps because there is a better view from here. Unless there are just a few standing in the back rows, stewards intervene and occasionally supporters are unreasonable.

Tony said that safety officers have an impossible job in trying to stop persistent standing, as unlike drunkenness, racist or offensive chanting, there is no legislation to back them up. They are being asked to enforce something that is not enforceable by law. He thinks that the legislation is confusing and not helpful, but that if too much pressure is applied the Government may make standing in seated areas a criminal offence. (It is however difficult to see how this could be defined or policed).

He told me of an occasion when Oxford took just 19 supporters to a midweek away match almost 200 miles from London. The supporters all stood at the back of the stand and were ejected by stewards. Hundreds of home supporters were standing with no efforts made to stop this. Tony intervened and was able to get the home club to allow the Oxford fans back into the ground.

Tony's view is that the alcohol rule is an anomaly, as beer is sold in grounds, so a supporter may enter sober and leave under the influence. There is a pub outside each corner of Griffin Park and he would prefer that alcohol was not served in the ground. It has been stopped in the away end, due to difficulties with queuing and the small concourse, rather than behaviour of supporters who had been drinking.

There is often 'banter' between away supporters and Brentford fans in the seats at the away end of the paddock at Griffin Park, but Tony's view is that if this does not cross the line of being offensive he will ask that the police and stewards do not intervene. He said that most of the problems of behaviour, such as abuse and obscene chanting come from the terraces at Griffin Park. It is of course arguable whether this is a product of the terrace itself, or the younger supporters who gather there. Tony feels that the freedom of movement on the terrace and a feeling that supporters can become anonymous (although they can't as they are covered by CCTV), is a major factor in such behaviour. There are however 80 year olds who stand on the terrace and most supporters cause no problems. Most of the problem supporters are aged 15 and 16 and won't accept discipline. Tony's view is that if these people were banned from Griffin Park they would cause trouble elsewhere in the community. The club instigated a security patrol every ten minutes and this largely eradicated the problem on the terrace.

There are no major problems with disorder at Brentford. Only some matches are policed and these by the minimum of one sergeant plus 6 constables. Tony said that it is no harder to eject a supporter from the terrace than the seats, but that different techniques are used. In both instances his preferred tactic is to wait until half time or the end of the game, then talk to the supporter, if necessary telling them that they will get a letter from the club advising of a four match ban.

Very few injures occur at Griffin Park and there is no difference between the seated and standing areas. The most common are slips, trips and falls, plus occasional fans hit by the ball. The majority of injuries treated are brought into the ground, with supporters taking advantage of first aid staff for existing conditions or injuries that occurred en route to the match.

Based on his experience as a supporter and safety officer, Tony's view is that supporters should have a choice to stand. He is aware of rail seats, but has a concern that in a large area of say 5,000 seat / 10,000 standing capacity, supporters could congregate in one area, with an unsafe density. I explained that it's not envisaged that standing areas would be this large and that each section would be separate, but he pointed out that this would add to stewarding costs. Tony's view was that rail seats might work in a new build, but he can't see a club converting an area to them due to the rake of many seated areas, plus the extra costs of additional toilets, turnstiles, stewards etc.

Brentford are owned by a supporters' trust backed by a benefactor whose aim is to gain promotion to the Championship in two years. To meet the regulation for the top two divisions and to increase income (Griffin Park has no executive boxes), the club plan to move in 2 – 3 years to a new all-seated stadium.

CRAWLEY TOWN – BROADWOOD STADIUM

A pleasant mile walk from the station along the tree lined Brighton Road leads to Crawley Town's Broadwood Stadium. On the edge of the town, and just off the A23, trees around the ground give it a more rural look than one would expect for a new town club. Built in 1997, but looking newer, when I visited the Broadwood Stadium comprised a main stand with terraces on the other three sides. The open terrace on the side was however to be replaced by a seated stand during the 2011/12 season.

After chatting with three ladies in reception who were working hard dealing with ticket sales for Crawley's first season in the Football League, I met with Bruce Talbot, the club's Media Manager. Bruce allowed me to wander around the stadium taking photographs as I pleased – a strange experience being the only person in a football ground. I have to confess to whistling Bubbles as I walked along the terraces.

The stadium is dominated by the smart single tier Main Stand, which runs about two thirds the length of the pitch. Virtually identical 1,500 capacity covered terraces at each end wrap around on the west side, so are slightly longer than the pitch width. Both have 8 steps with the only crush barriers at the front. The North Terrace has two barriers about a third of the way along from the west side, allowing it to be split into home and away supporters, although if required away fans are given the whole end.

The uncovered East Terrace was to be replaced by a 2,000 seat stand. This will be a covered temporary stand (like those at Brighton's Withdean Stadium). Away supporters will be given part of this stand rather than the current block in the Main Stand.

Football League regulations required that Crawley install a further 1,000 seats by May 2012, hence the new East Stand. Crawley's average attendance for 2010/11 was 2,535, more than double the previous season. The highest home crowd was 4,145 for their FA Cup 3rd round victory over Derby County. League status has increased interest in the town and around 1,000 season tickets were sold, about 50% of which are for standing. The average attendance for the first seven Football League matches was 3,059, up on the previous year, but well below the 5,005 capacity.

Around 75% of capacity is standing, and this will reduce to

approximately 45% once the new stand is built. Seat tickets are £19 and standing £16, so Bruce agreed that supporters stand through choice not cost. He saw no reason why the terraces at both ends should not remain indefinitely – unless of course the club reach and sustain Championship level.

DAGENHAM & REDBRIDGE – VICTORIA ROAD

Since 1955 Dagenham have played at what most people still call Victoria Road, but is now officially the London Borough of Barking and Dagenham Stadium. Victoria Road has however existed as a football ground since 1917, when it was used by the Sterling Works side, whose factory was situated alongside. Dagenham & Redbridge FC, who were promoted to the Football League in 2007, was formed from a merger between Dagenham and Redbridge Forest in 1992. It is quite an amalgamation of East London clubs, Redbridge Forest having been formed in 1988 by a merger of Walthamstow Avenue and Leytonstone & Ilford, the latter of which resulted from the joining of the two clubs in 1979. The club's current support come from all of these clubs.

I was shown round the 6,000 capacity stadium by Club Secretary Terry Grover. With seats on two sides and standing on the other two, Victoria Road meets the needs of Dagenham & Redbridge FC and its fans.

The fairly modern Main Stand runs for three quarters the length of the pitch, is slightly raised, and has six rows of seats, plus three sponsors' boxes. The block at the east end is used for pay on the day, with 200 to 300 seats usually available. Towards the west end, the 200 seat Family Stand occupies the remainder of the south side of the ground.

The modern all-seated Marcus James Stand was built in 2009 and mainly houses away supporters, although if a large following is not expected home fans may be given part of the stand. At the opposite end is the 1,080 capacity open Bury Road Terrace. Supporters enter by turnstiles on the south east corner to the Bury Road End, but may stand either on this terrace or the North Terrace. Unusually the capacities of the two terraces are combined for monitoring purposes and supporters are free to move between them.

The North Stand is a traditional covered terrace running the full length of the pitch. It's normally used just for home supporters, but occasionally if the away club is bringing a large following (e.g. Charlton), up to 300 away fans are accommodated on the end of the terrace. Two sets of barriers are simply clipped into place to divide the terrace, with a sterile area between the sets of fans. A wooden walkway has been built to allow fans to walk from the Marcus James Stand. Standing tickets are sold at the turnstiles and these have to be shown to stewards to enter the terraced area.

Dagenham & Redbridge's average attendance for 2010/11 was 2,769, with a highest figure of 4,448 (MK Dons). The average for the four seasons which they have been in the Football League is 2,228. The record attendance is 5,949 for an FA Cup match with Ipswich Town in 2002.

Approximately 65% of Victoria Road's capacity is standing. The Main Stand is very rarely full, and if necessary home fans can usually be given space in the Marcus James Stand, so there is a choice to sit or stand. The majority always opt to stand, with many children and families on the terraces.

Away supporters usually only have a seating area allocated. Occasionally some will go on the home terrace (e.g. Orient), but no problems have resulted. It is a shame that the end section of terrace that is occasionally given to away supporters cannot always be available, but presumably this is due to the extra stewarding costs.

With a choice of accommodation, standing in seated areas by home fans doesn't occur, but with no choice for most games, it is normal for some away fans to stand, usually those towards the back. Terry told me that stewards ask them to sit, but they often stand again once the stewards moved away.

There are no problems with disorder. Police choose to attend every game, but are only required to do so for certain fixtures, and it's only these where the club pay for them. For the match versus MK Dons in January 2011 there was no segregation. This fixture was chosen as both clubs have similar family based support, with no history of trouble. It was agreed with the police, Football League and Safety Advisory Group. Terry said that this was a 100% success.

There are currently no plans for redevelopment of the ground and this is unlikely to be required unless the club makes progress through the divisions. If this were occur it's more likely that they would have to move rather than redevelop Victoria Road.

Dagenham & Redbridge v Plymouth

This League One relegation clash took place on a remarkably warm Good Friday afternoon, with temperatures reaching 27°C. Having had ten points deducted for entering administration, victory was virtually essential for Plymouth's chances of avoiding the drop. The visitors bought a noisy 804 following, comprising almost a quarter of the 3,559 attendance, Victoria Road's fourth largest of the season.

The £18 entrance price was £4 lower than for seats, although both reduced by £2 for advance purchase. Plymouth fans of course had no alternative but to pay the seating price. As entry for standing allows access to either the Bury Road or North Stands, fans can move to escape rain, or as was the case today, bright sunshine that by the second half was in the faces of those behind the goal. I chose the shade of the North Stand.

Part of the new Marcus James Stand was given to families of Dagenham's academy players. The stand was shared with Plymouth, although so many visitors turned up that the cordon tape had be moved, reducing the gap between the two sets of fans. Indeed the away area was pretty much full with only odd seats empty, which caused some problems as latecomers sat in the aisles. The only action of the afternoon for the five police officers on duty was to assist stewards to move a few fans into seats. Around 100 stood for the whole game, with no efforts made to get them to sit. Clearly others would have preferred to stand, but rose only at moments of excitement or for occasional songs.

There were a few empty seats in the home areas, but despite the small price difference a far larger number chose to stand. This included supporters of all ages, including a boy of about three on his Dad's shoulders and his slightly older brother who sat on the barrier that protects the wall fronting the terrace. I noted another Dad carrying a stool for his young son, something that used to be common in my early days of watching football, but I hadn't seen for many years.

With West Country connections my allegiance was for Plymouth, although standing in a home area of course I couldn't show it. I'd chosen my spot towards the away end of the terrace, where about twenty five Dagenham lads sang throughout the first half. The empty section of terrace was hardly necessary, there being little interaction. The best Dagenham could come up with for terrace wit was to suggest that Plymouth fans sing only when they're farming and where they may wish to insert their pasties.

Plymouth made far more noise than the home fans, who only sang in numbers once all afternoon. Strangely they had a drummer close to the halfway line but I heard no singing from there, just his rather monotonous beat. 'Green and Yellow Army' however rang out long and loud from the away end.

Dagenham kicked towards the away end in the first half, so a number of supporters moved towards the other end for the second half. I took the opportunity of the break to wander round, take some photos and make use of the good standard toilets. The aroma of frying burgers had been wafting along the terrace since before kick off, but I resisted the temptation, sticking, almost literally, to my rather melted chocolate bar. As I returned to the North Stand a man who appeared to have collapsed was being attended by first aid staff. He was easily wheeled out in a casualty chair, something I noted that would have been more difficult had it of occurred in the steeper seated areas.

And finally to the game, which both sides had plenty of chances to win. Button in Plymouth's goal made some good saves, but overall as an (almost) impartial observer I think I can say that the visitors deserved their one nil win, courtesy of a free kick from Rory Patterson. Eight hundred loud and happy Devonians left through the Tea Bar Exit (how lower league is that!) as instructed by the public address, while Daggers fans muttered as to what might have been.

STEVENAGE – THE LAMEX STADIUM

Formerly known as Broadhall Way, the Lamex Stadium is a tidy, single tiered ground, which has been improved by Stevenage as needs required, and has terracing on two sides. Three sides are of good League One standard, whilst the fourth, a small terrace is more typical of a non league ground.

The Main Stand and South Stand are modern seated stands, with the other two sides terraces. The 700 capacity North Terrace behind one goal is covered for about three quarters of its length. Stevenage intend to replace this with a 2,000 seat stand, but there is no timescale for this. Opposite the Main Stand is the 3,000 capacity East Terrace.

Almost half the Lamex Stadium's capacity is standing. Club Secretary Roger Austin told me that for crowds of 3,000, supporters are typically spread around the ground as follows:

Main Stand – 1,000
East Terrace – 1,500
North Terrace – 300
Away Seats – 200

Around two thirds of home supporters are therefore choosing to stand, but there is no choice for away supporters who are allocated only the 1,392 South Stand seats. Stevenage allow accompanied children under 11 free admission to the terraces, and quite a few families take up this offer.

The current ground capacity is approx 7,100 and Stevenage's average attendance for 2010/11, their first season in the Football League, was 2,898. The highest ever attendance at the ground was 8,040 for their FA Cup match with Newcastle in 1997, when a temporary stand was erected. The proceeds of this match paid for the East Terrace roof.

There are no significant problems of disorder inside the Lamex Stadium. Persistent standing in seated areas occurs commonly in the away end where no choice of accommodation is provided. Some or all of the away fans usually stand and Stevenage don't try to stop them doing so unless they stand on the seats.

Very few injuries occur at the ground. The most common injury is supporters being hit by the ball, which Roger said occurs more in seated areas as it is less easy for seated supporters to move and dodge the ball. His view is that it is easier to remove casualties from a terrace than seated areas.

The Lamex Stadium is a small ground, but adequate for the club's support. There is a good choice to stand or sit for home supporters and this works well. Away supporters are allocated only seats and hence often some or all stand in front of them. Whilst future redevelopment of the North Terrace will lose some standing places, the large East Terrace will still provide plenty of choice for home supporters.

WYCOMBE WANDERERS – ADAMS PARK

Adams Park, a pleasant stadium on the edge of a tree covered hill on the outskirts of High Wycombe, is unusual in being shared on equal terms between Wycombe Wanderers FC and London Wasps rugby club. Unlike most ground shares it is not a tenancy, and the stadium plus both clubs are owned by Wycombe's chairman Steve Hughes. It provides an interesting contrast between the two sports.

The ground's capacity is limited to approximately 10,000 due to concerns about emergency access, as it's served by a single dead end road. This is easily adequate for Wycombe's normal requirements, with an average league gate for the three seasons to 2011 of 5,050 (highest 9,625 – Notts County). It is however insufficient for London Wasps, both because they fill the ground for most games and because the Rugby Union Premiership stipulates a minimum 15,000 capacity. Wasps are regularly fined for the ground being too small and may eventually be forced out of the Premiership if they can't meet the requirement.

With the 1,974 Greene King IPA Terrace at one end, Adams Park, which is dominated by the two tier Frank Adams Stand, provides a choice of accommodation for home fans. Typically around 1,200 stand on the terrace, around a quarter of Wycombe's crowd. For football children are permitted on the terrace and charged just £7, but for rugby no one under 1.2 metres height is allowed to stand.

For Wycombe matches visitors are allocated the 2,000 seat Dreams Stand, and unless a large following sell out the stand, these are unallocated. Hence those who wish to stand do so at the back.

Stewards generally only intervene if supporters stand in the aisles, become rowdy or stand on seats. For rugby the seats are allocated, as supporters fill the stand and prefer to sit.

I met with Jack Tose, a member of the safety team at Wycombe, who told me that there are no significant problems of disorder at Wycombe matches. Neither are there for Wasps, although they do get the occasional rugby fan who has drunk too much. Jack commented that the atmosphere is different for rugby, with no segregation and no banter between opposing supporters. He said that there are no problems with crowd control on the terrace, that supporters keep aisles and hatched areas free, and don't stand in front of the emergency exit gates.

The safety and control facilities at Adams Park are very impressive for a lower league club, perhaps reflecting that this is a dual use stadium. Fifty five CCTV cameras allow police and safety staff to monitor supporters in and around the ground. There are few injuries, mainly occasional trips and supporters hit by the ball. The latter tend to occur behind the goals.

Wycombe and Wasps had plans to move to a new stadium complex 2 miles away, but the council refused planning permission. The move was driven by Wasps' need for a minimum 15,000 capacity, as Wycombe are very happy with what they have now.

There has been some investigation into expanding Adams Park, probably by a two tier stand in place of the terrace, plus a new access road, however this is now unlikely to take place. London Wasps have been put up for sale and it's probable that they will move away from Adams Park. Knowing that Wycombe fans want the choice to stand, the club were considering constructing the lower tier of a new stand with convertible rail seats, but it now appears that the stadium, which meets their current needs, will stay as it is.

CHAPTER TWELVE

AROUND THE TERRACES – WEST

BRISTOL ROVERS – THE MEMORIAL GROUND

Perhaps the most unusual of all our league grounds, the Memorial Stadium, which Rovers purchased from Bristol Rugby Club in 1998, still has very much the look of a rugby ground. The stadium is dominated by tall stands on either side, both of which have seated areas above terraces. With its glass fronted hospitality boxes, the DAS Stand looks more like a cricket pavilion than part of a football ground.

Only a quarter of 12,000 capacity is seats, of which 265 are allocated to visitors in the South Stand. This too is an unusual construction. It was originally erected as a temporary stand, is commonly called 'the tent', and to complete the multi-sport feel of the ground, looks as if it's been borrowed from a horse jumping event! Up to 933 away supporters are also accommodated on the open Uplands Terrace. Home fans can stand on either side of the ground, or on the 3,710 capacity Bass Terrace, where the more vocal supporters tend to congregate behind the goal. Part of the terrace on the west side of the ground is designated as a Family Enclosure, a rare example of a family area being standing.

Although currently in League Two with crowds averaging around 7,000, Rovers have the potential to attract considerably more, however many years without success, including ten years where they played at Bath City's Twerton Park, have diminished the active support. Plans to redevelop the Memorial Ground were put aside in 2011, in favour of a new all-seated stadium to be built on the Frenchay campus of the University of the West of England. It is the club's view that the Memorial Stadium is no longer fit for purpose and doesn't fit with their aspirations, whereas the new ground will allow them to build for a better and sustainable future. The move will be partly financed by the sale of the Memorial Ground to Sainsbury's.

Dave Harper, Rovers' Safety Officer wasn't available when I visited, but gave me his view by email, stressing that this was a personal opinion and not on behalf of the club:

'I can say that the terraces do work well for the vast majority of matches but are tested when we have near capacity attendances in the areas concerned. There is still an element of pushing and it is a difficult job to keep the gangways clear. Although I agree that the use of properly constructed terracing is safe, I still err on the side of all seater stadia.'

The Memorial Ground is one of the few places where I've stood on a terrace to watch West Ham in recent years. Almost 11,000 attended the Carling Cup fixture, which West Ham won 2.1. The game passed off without problems and it was notable that given a choice of terracing, far less West Ham supporters than usual stood in the seats.

I spoke with Mark Willis, who has watched Rovers for more than 30 years, and who told me that the general view of supporters is that they don't want to move to an all-seated stadium. The objection is not to moving, but that the proposed stadium will take away the choice to stand. Mark sees watching football as a social occasion, meeting friends on the terraces, only some of whom have season tickets, but unless everyone buys tickets together this isn't possible in an all-seated ground. He said that the majority of Rovers fans currently stand on the terraces and believe that any new ground should be built with standing areas, but with the potential for conversion should the club reach the Championship.

CHELTENHAM TOWN – ABBEY BUSINESS STADIUM

Formerly known as Whaddon Road, the Abbey Business Stadium has undergone extensive development since the club started moving up the leagues in the late 1990s. I was shown round by James Brown, (Media Officer).

The Stagecoach West Stand has 1,068 seats above two sections of paddock terracing, the Paddock Area with a capacity of 704 and the Tunnel Enclosure 370. James told me that the paddocks are popular areas and that many of the supporters standing here have done so since the club were non league. Opposite this is the In2Print Stand, a 2,000 seat single tiered stand

The curiously named Speedy Skips Stand (sponsored by a local waste management company, not a high speed snack!) is a covered 1,980 capacity terrace. This is the home end where Cheltenham's more vocal supporters stand and is popular with younger supporters. The Hazlewoods Stand at the other end, a covered all-seated stand, has capacity for 1,100 and replaced a terrace. It's allocated in whole or part to away supporters.

42% of capacity (and 50% of home capacity) is standing. The ground is usually not much more than half full, so home supporters have plenty of choice to stand or sit. A wide age range of supporters choose to stand. There is however no choice for away supporters who are allocated only seats, although often some or all stand in front of them. There are no significant problems of disorder at the Abbey Business Stadium.

Cheltenham have no further redevelopment plans for Whaddon Road as they plan to move to a new ground inside the racecourse perimeter. There's no set timescale for this but the chairman would like it to be in 4 to 5 years. This is expected be a 'dome' stadium, but there are no firm plans. It is not yet known if it will include standing areas.

Whilst Whaddon Road is adequate for the club's current needs in terms of spectator accommodation, Cheltenham Town say they need a new ground in order to bring in revenue. It is envisaged that the new ground will be a 'sports hub' and not just used for football. The aim of the move is to make the club self sufficient. The current ground is owned by the council, but the club own the stands. It's envisaged that funding for the new ground will come from the club, council and racecourse. Cheltenham haven't yet consulted with supporters, but say this will take place once the move is confirmed.

With a three season average attendance of 3,340, and maximum of 5,726 (Leeds), the 7,100 capacity Abbey Business Stadium is adequate for the club's support. It seems a shame that in order to make the club self sufficient Cheltenham have to move.

EXTER CITY – ST JAMES' PARK

In the summer of 2003 few Exeter City supporters would have believed that just eight years later the club would be looking at ground developments with a view to possible Championship football. City had just been relegated to the Conference and when, with debts mounting, the police raided the club to take the chairman, his wife and the vice chairman for questioning, its future looked bleak. Having already entered administration in 1994, this was the second time that Exeter had faced closure. The first time the club was saved by selling St James' Park to Beazer homes for £650,000 and the second by the majority share holder who asked the Supporters' Trust to take over running of the club. The Trust owns 63% of shares and Exeter City are therefore a club who understand and listen to supporters' views.

Successive promotions took Exeter from the Conference to League

One and after finishing just one point off the play offs, they are planning for the possibility of promotion to the Championship.

I met with Andy Gillard, Operations Manager, who gave me a tour of the ground and showed me copies of proposed redevelopment plans. These he had to take off the boardroom wall, as the Chairman, who was involved in a long and obviously confidential phone call, politely ushered us out. I did however get to shake hands with Rob Edwards, Exeter's first team coach, who I'd last seen inspire City to a remarkable four goals in twenty minutes comeback to beat Torquay in the Conference play off semi final at Plainmoor.

St James' Park is a traditional football ground, with seats on the sides and terraces at the ends. The ground is owned by the City Council who bought it from Beazer Homes.

The predominately wooden Grandstand was built in the 1920s and is showing its age, becoming increasingly difficult to meet safety regulations. The stand is however popular, especially with older supporters who have sat in it for many years, even if some of them find the steep entry steps difficult. The Fire Brigade visit regularly to inspect the stand and plan for emergencies, and in 2011 a big exercise was undertaken involving all emergency services to deal with a Bradford type fire. Around 150 of the 1,690 seats are allocated to away supporters. The Grandstand runs little more than half the length of the pitch, as the railway line that it backs onto allows no space for a full length stand. The Flybe Stand opposite was built in 2001, replacing a covered terrace.

The Big Bank, with capacity 3,970, is the largest remaining terrace at an English football ground. A modern construction built in 2000, it replaced a large open terrace. The small uncovered St James' Terrace at the other end holds 1,053 and receives mixed comments from visiting supporters. Some are pleased to be able to stand, but others complain about the poor view and standard of accommodation.

With an average attendance of 5,393 for 2010/11 and a three year high of 8,549 (Leeds United), the total capacity of 8,829 is adequate for all but the very occasional game, however should they gain promotion to the Championship a larger ground would be beneficial.

57% of St James' Park capacity is standing and supporters of all ages choose to stand. Typically around half the crowd use the terraces and with a choice of accommodation, standing in seated areas is not a problem. There are virtually no problems of disorder inside St James' Park and many matches are not policed.

A problem of overcrowding occurred in the away end at the match against Leeds in January 2010. The club had asked that arrival of coaches was staggered, but the police held them all at the motorway services, so they didn't arrive until just before kick off. The two turnstiles were inadequate for such a large number of fans to enter the ground in a few minutes. Congestion occurred in the corner of the away terrace, which was not helped because the match had started while around 200 fans were still outside. Some supporters had to be moved for their safety, but no injures occurred. The away area was all-ticket and capacity was not exceeded. The problem was caused by the late arrival of visiting fans' coaches and an example of police tactics failing to follow the lessons of Hillsborough. Fortunately there were no fences at St James' Park.

The pitch has now been moved forward and an area in front of the terrace tarmaced. A new walkway allows stewards to move fans to the left hand side of the terrace and the away seats, which are entered by the same two turnstiles as the terrace. These are at one end of the terrace – the old ones at the other end have been closed for many years as they are unsafe.

In 2007 Exeter engaged a firm of consultants to look at possible options for moving the ground. Three sites were considered, but it was concluded that the best option was to stay at St James' Park, which is just outside the city centre, with reasonable transport links.

Problems with the Grandstand (the Safety Advisory Group are pushing for it to be redeveloped), plus the greater security of League One status and potential for promotion, have prompted the club to put together a redevelopment plan, which will increase capacity to 10,500. This is currently at the consultation stage, with supporters and local residents invited to comment.

The plans involve a new away stand, a new grandstand and developments behind the Big Bank, although much to the relief of City supporters, the terrace would remain unaltered. Andy said that feedback from fans has been very positive. The new stands would be financed by a developer and would include accommodation units for the nearby university. The grandstand would be tapered so could extend further than the current stand, although lack of space means that it can't run the full length of the pitch.

It is intended that the new away end will be a covered terrace with 2,700 capacity. Exeter want to provide standing, both because this is what supporters want, and because it will maximise capacity on the small footprint of the ground. Seats would only be installed if the club are promoted and remain in the Championship, when unless it is changed by then, the regulation will require this. If it has to be seated capacity would be 1,650. I showed Andy information on rail seats and suggested that the stand be designed so that these can be installed on the terrace at a later date if necessary. Subject to regulations, this would allow the stand to be used in standing mode with increased capacity.

HEREFORD UNITED – EDGAR STREET

Edgar Street is a ground with character! It has four old stands (one currently closed), but (just) meets the club's current requirements in terms of capacity and choice of accommodation, although its age causes some problems. Various modifications have been required to meet safety requirements and it's an ongoing job to keep it up to standard.

The city centre ground is owned by the council and leased to the club. There are plans to build a new stand at one end and maybe at some stage at the other end. I met with Steve Thomas, Hereford United's Safety Officer, who was formerly Football Officer for the local police force.

One cannot write about Edgar Street without mentioning perhaps the most famous FA Cup goal of all time, when Ronnie Radford's 30 yard strike from the mud prompted an invasion of parka-clad youngsters and led to the then non-league Hereford knocking out mighty Newcastle. Officially there were 14,313 fans in Edgar Street that day, although quite probably more. Now the ground holds just 5,710.

The single tier Main Stand is designated as a family stand, although entry is not strictly restricted to families. Capacity is 1,801, but this is reduced by 5 – 10% as seating is unallocated.

Opposite is the highly unusual Cargill Community Stand, one of the first cantilevered stands to be built in England, which backs directly onto a main road. The stand is divided between home and away supporters. The upper tier is seated with the northern end allocated for home supporters and the southern end (472 seats) for away fans. The stand is very steep and Steve agreed with my observation that this makes it the greatest safety risk in the ground. The front wall obscures the nearside touchline, but supporters don't tend to stand to gain a better view. Steve's opinion was that those visiting supporters who wish to stand use the terrace below. The lower tier terrace is also split around the halfway line, with the home section having capacity of 391 and the away section 233. The capacities are very low in relation to the terraces' area, partly due to the many pillars which obstruct views.

The curved, part covered, 1,689 capacity Meadow End Terrace is where Hereford's more vocal supporters tend to stand. It has a flat semi circular tarmac area to the front on which supporters are no longer permitted to stand. Additional new crush barriers have recently been installed on the terrace. The only significant safety related problem experienced is the constant need to remind supporters not to stand in gangways.

The terrace at the Blackfriars Street End is similar in design to the home end, but with a central wall to split into home and away areas. It has however been closed since 2009 for safety reasons. Whilst the crush barriers were deemed adequate, the concrete failed a strength test resulting in a failed inspection. For the 2010/11 and 2011/12 seasons two temporary seated stands were placed in front of the terrace and these used to accommodate away supporters where the visiting team brought a larger following. When the visiting support was small the end remained empty.

Hereford intend to redevelop the Blackfriars Street end of the ground shortly and plans have been approved for an all-seated stand. The land south of the stadium is to be used for a new shopping centre and it is envisaged that the new stand will link with this. The large footprint of the old curved terrace means that there is room for a new stand, with land behind to be part of the new commercial development. The club chairman is keen for the new stand to be a true family stand, with entry restricted to only those with children. Part of it may however need to be used for away supporters where they bring a following too large for the away sections of the Cargill Community Stand.

There are no current plans to develop the rest of the ground, although the Meadow End Terrace may be replaced at some stage. With the desire of many supporters to stand Steve believes that it is most likely that it would be replaced with a new terrace. It would be difficult to redevelop the Cargill Community Stand due to the small footprint with it backing onto a main road, so Steve expects that it will remain indefinitely.

Hereford's average attendance for 2010/11 was 2,516, with a maximum of 3,942 (Shrewsbury Town). Average for the past five seasons is 2,929. The 5,700 capacity is therefore ample for their support currently and in the foreseeable future. The standing capacity is adequate for demand, although away clubs bringing a large support would ideally have more than 230 standing places. Loss of the Blackfriars Terrace and cuts in capacity to meet safety requirements, means that Hereford are not far above the Football League's minimum requirement, and it is a concern that possible further reductions could result in loss of League status.

Around 40% of Edgar Street's capacity is standing and Steve showed me figures indicating that about a third of the crowd typically choose to stand. For normal games seats don't sell out. Price differentials are only £2 to £3 and Steve said that these fans stand through choice, not cost. With a choice of accommodation, standing in seated areas is not generally a problem.

There are virtually no supporter behaviour problems inside Edgar Street, although they occasionally occur outside the stadium. Hereford don't use police in the ground, just stewards who they hire themselves. The cost of stewarding equates to roughly £1 per spectator. The minimum cost to provide police (they will not attend with less than one sergeant and six constables) is £1,300 per game.

Based on his recent observations and 30 year's experience of policing football prior to taking up the safety officer's position, Steve said that it is far easier to eject supporters from standing areas than from seats. He also said that it is easier to remove anyone who may be injured or ill from a terrace than from seats.

Steve is firmly of the view that standing areas should be retained at Edgar Street.

Edgar Street is a ground with much character, a choice of standing and seating accommodation and a capacity adequate for the foreseeable future. It would be a shame if its unique character is lost by redevelopment.

TORQUAY UNITED – PLAINMOOR

Plainmoor is a ground I know well, having watched more matches here than anywhere other than Upton Park. I was there for perhaps the most famous match of all, against Crewe in 1987, the first year of automatic relegation from the Football League. An equaliser scored in injury time added after Bryn the police dog ran onto the pitch and bit a Torquay player, not only kept the club in the league, but quite possibly saved them from extinction.

Plainmoor wasn't at its best when I visited to watch a match against AFC Wimbledon and meet with the club's General Manager Andrew Candy. The old grandstand was in a state of partial demolition, with a new 1,750 seat stand to be constructed in its place.

As usual I stood on the Popular Side terrace, which runs the length of one side of the ground. Around me I noticed more older people than I'd probably seen anywhere on a terrace, with quite a few obviously over retirement age and a couple in front of me looking to be well into their seventies. Andrew told me that some of these would normally have sat or stood in the old grandstand, but although there were empty seats in the Family Stand behind the goal, they'd chosen to stand. The majority of Torquay fans went on the terrace and no one stood in the seats.

The majority of the 2,353 crowd enjoyed an excellent display from Torquay, with poor Wimbledon defending contributing to a 4.0 home win. Wimbledon's creditable midweek following of 385 stood in the covered 1,050 capacity Sparkworld Away Stand, both sets of fans contributing to a good atmosphere.

The new stand is to be known as Bristow's Bench in recognition of the contribution made to the prosperity of the club by the late Paul Bristow. Unlike the old wooden stand which was shortened after a fire in 1985, it will run the full length of the pitch. It will contain dressing rooms and offices, plus classrooms for the adjacent Westlands School. Funding is coming partly from the school, partly from the Football Foundation and partly from the club. The old stand had a small standing paddock at the front but the new one will be entirely seated.

Currently home supporters have adequate choice, however during construction of the new grandstand Torquay are unable to allocate any seats to away supporters, but once completed they will be given a section of the new stand. Andrew said that few injuries occur to spectators and the only ones he was aware of were from people falling down the steps in the Family Stand. He told me that there are no problems of disorder inside the Plainmoor, nor are there problems of standing in seated areas. Andrew himself chooses to stand on the Popular Side, where Torquay's more vocal fans gather.

In the mid 1980s Torquay's capacity was set at 4,999, the lowest in the league, in order that the ground was not designated so avoided the Safety of Sports Ground Act. In recent years Plainmoor's capacity has been marginally above the 5,000 Football League minimum. Without the grandstand it holds a mere 3,900, which will cause loss of income for some games, notably Plymouth, Bristol Rovers and Swindon. Capacity will however rise to 6,500 on completion of the stand, which should be adequate, the club's average crowd in 2010/11 being 2,630.

Bristow's Bench will complete the redevelopment of Plainmoor. The other three sides of the ground have been rebuilt in the last 20 years and are of a good standard. No further significant work is therefore anticipated in the foreseeable future. Andrew told me that the club have no intention of replacing the two terraces.

And finally, like West Ham, Torquay are a club who rarely have a season without excitement, albeit it often a relegation battle. Since West Ham's last visit to Wembley in 1981, I've watched Torquay in five Wembley finals, plus one at Old Trafford. For the last two of these the club allocated some blocks of seats for 'singers'. Inevitably these became standing areas, but meant that there was virtually no standing in other sections, something that was particularly important with the large number of families attending the matches.

YEOVIL TOWN – HUISH PARK

Yeovil moved from their town centre Huish ground with its famous sloping pitch, to out of town Huish Park in 1990. Access by road is easy, with plenty of parking, but like many new grounds, not so easy by train, with both stations the other side of the town. Having paid £13 for a taxi from the station, I took two buses back. Not surprisingly, away fans tend to arrive by coach rather than train.

I met with James Hillier, General Manager (Stadium), who is responsible for safety at Huish Park. The stadium has terraces at both ends and seats either side.

Both stands are single tier, with up to 540 seats in the Cowlin Stand allocated to away supporters. The terraces are of modern design and with contemporary construction sturdy steel crush barriers, look newer than their 21 years. Both were originally open, but the home terrace was covered about ten years ago. Supports for a roof extend behind the away terrace and look a little odd, but to date no roof has been built for cost reasons.

The theoretical capacity of the away terrace is 1,700, but James has put a limit of 1,500 to provide extra safety margin. The Blackthorn Stand home terrace is a good size, holding 2,500. Yeovil's average attendance for the three seasons to 2010/11 was 4,463 with a maximum of 7,484 (Southampton). The ground capacity of 9,600 is therefore easily adequate for their current needs.

Around 40% of capacity is standing so there is plenty of choice to stand or sit. The only exception is when visiting clubs bring a very small following when Yeovil don't open the away terrace to save costs. This happens in about a third of games and all away supporters are then accommodated in the Cowlin Stand seats. Those who wish to stand tend to go to the back and the club don't stop them standing up. Yeovil make it very clear to visiting supporters that the terrace is uncovered, but even when it is raining some choose to stand and get wet rather than go in covered seats. James told me of an away fan who had gone home soaked to the skin and wearing just his boxers, but wrote to the club to say how much he enjoyed his day at Yeovil!

The price differential is small (£1 to £3) and James said that supporters stand through preference not cost. Supporters of all ages stand, and he finds that home terrace tends to attract younger fans. When supporters have a choice, there is no standing in seated areas, which James views as a big plus of having terraces. He sees them as a good thing and says they take problems away. He also understands the desire of fans to stand and to show their emotions at matches.

There are virtually no problems of disorder inside Huish Park and no more issues in home terraces than there are home seated areas. Most matches are not policed. In the coming season Yeovil expected to have police attending only four fixtures – Exeter, Bournemouth, Sheffield United & Sheffield Wednesday.

Yeovil have about 45 stewards on their books and supplement these with agency stewards when required. They share stewards with Bournemouth and Exeter when fixtures allow. No one specific person is tasked only with checking for overcrowding (as the Taylor Report recommended), but it is a duty of all stewards who are all trained to NVQ2 in Spectator Safety.

Yeovil have no real 'risk' supporters and is very much a family club. Typically there are only one or two arrests per season, although last year eight or nine Exeter fans were arrested for alcohol offences.

There are few spectator injuries at Huish Park. The most common is from being hit by the ball, which occurs more often on the terraces simply because these are behind the goal. When a practice goal was placed in front of the main stand someone got hurt by a ball there. Other than this there are no more injures on the terraces than in seats. Slips, trips and falls, are the next most common injury and these are spread evenly around the four sides of the ground. Some injures are pre-existing, such as a supporter bitten by a dog on the way to the ground and one who hurt himself climbing over a fence taking a short cut en route to the match. In such instances supporters tend to go into the ground knowing there are first aiders there, but they then are logged as football injuries. James believes that it is easier to get to a casualty in seated areas than a full terrace (but not one that is less full), however it is easier to evacuate someone from a terrace than seats.

Away supporters on the open terrace are carefully managed. The terrace is in three sections, with supporters free to move between them, but the one behind the goal tends to fill first. When this is full stewards close it off with movable barriers and direct supporters to the wings. The terrace has wide aisles with wide openings in the wall at the front. These have been manned by up to six stewards to hold back fans who may run forward celebrating goals, but to allow stewards to be spread more evenly along the terrace, gates are now to be fitted.

Yeovil appreciate that Huish Park was built at a time when facilities were less than people expect now. For example their disabled facilities are poor and there are only four female toilets for the 2,600 capacity main stand. The club want to improve the ground all the way round, starting with the away terrace. A decision on whether to redevelop was due to be made in about 6 months. Then if it is to go ahead the club will look at designs, and seats versus standing.

CHAPTER THIRTEEN

AROUND THE TERRACES – CASTLEFORD, STUTTGART & SUMMARY

CASTLEFORD TIGERS – WHELDON ROAD

I'd never been to a rugby match. The last time I watched rugby league on television Eddie Waring was commentating and I was more interested in waiting for football scores to scroll across the bottom of the screen. Other than those shared with football clubs, few rugby grounds are all-seated, so there was a good choice of Super League clubs where I could stand on a terrace. Castleford, a ground with plenty of terracing, seemed a good place to observe how standing works at rugby and compare this to football.

The first difference was price – just £15 for a Challenge Cup quarter final against Huddersfield. The next was a lack of booking fee, yet the ticket arrived the next day by first class recorded delivery. We football supporters are used to a £1.50 surcharge with the ticket turning up after a week or so by normal post. And the third difference – STANDING – printed on a ticket for a top league club. With just 1,500 seats in the wooden grandstand that runs for only half the length of one side of the ground, most of Wheldon Road's 12,000 capacity is standing.

Slightly confused as to where to enter the ground with no stand name shown on my ticket, I asked a steward, who on hearing that this was my first match explained the various areas of the ground. The covered terrace at one end is used by Castleford's more rowdy fans and it was here that there would be singing. He suggested standing at the corner if I wanted shade, but not too close to the fans who'd be turning out of the pub just before kick off. If I wanted to sit I could pay an extra £3 once inside, or I could stand on the open Railway Terrace at the far end. Alternatively I could go on the covered side terrace, which was where most of the visiting fans would congregate, although there was no segregation. There was no need to decide now though, as one can move between terraces once inside.

The steep steps to the terrace starting as soon as one passes through the turnstile were my first observation that this ground wouldn't get a football safety certificate. The main problem would however have been the freedom to move between terraces and the lack of any way of counting numbers in each area – something that Taylor recommended for all stadia, not just football grounds.

On a very hot day, I took the steward's advice and stood in the corner at the back of the covered terrace, enjoying an excellent burger before the match. Kick off was preceded by an overexcited man on the public address, cheerleaders and ridiculously loud music, that just like at football, drowned out the genuine atmosphere of fans singing.

The terraces were all reasonably full, but there were plenty of empty seats in the grandstand, by far the majority of supporters preferring to stand. As at football, the most vocal fans gathered towards the back of the covered stand behind the goal, but there was a wide mix of people in all areas. Close to me were some young children, two couples with babies in prams and a blind man with his guide dog. Men were drinking pints on the terrace, which is permitted, and a few smoking cigarettes, which I suspect isn't.

The whole atmosphere was much as one would find at a lower

London Road Terrace – Peterborough United

Leeds United fans on the Moy's End Terrace – Peterborough United

Morecambe players train in front of East Terrace – Morecambe FC

Memorial Ground – Bristol Rovers

East Terrace – Burton Albion

The Big Bank – Exeter City

St James' Park – Exeter City

North Terrace – Crawley Town

East Terrace & North Terrace – Crawley Town

Speedy Skips Stand – Cheltenham Town

Niramax Stand – Hartlepool United

Greene King Stand – Wycombe Wanderers

Bury Road Terrace – Dagenham & Redbridge

Diversity on the North Terrace – Dagenham & Redbridge

Cargill Community Stand – Hereford United

Meadow End Terrace – Hereford United

Star Lane End – Macclesfield Town

Silkman Terrace – Macclesfield Town

Sandy Lane Terrace - Rochdale

North Terrace – Scunthorpe United

East Terrace – Stevenage

Blackthorn Stand – Yeovil Town

Convertible Standing Area – VfB Stuttart

Stuttgart fans display flags before kick off

Cannstatter Kurve – VfB Stuttgart v Hannover 96

league football match, but the noticeable difference was that there was no interaction between the two sets of supporters. No songs were sung to each other and when a try was scored there was no mocking of opponents or singing the score. The referee however received customary abuse, although immediately home fans sang suggesting of his participation in certain solo sexual activities, an announcement was made saying that bad language would not be tolerated. Lads being lads, rugby or not, the immediate response was to sing it again!

As for the game; a big man in a shirt far too small for him and unhealthily tight shorts, gets the ball and runs two yards into another big man in similar ill fitting attire. The first man gives the ball to another on his side who repeats the process. Gradually the ball moves up the pitch, until someone drops it, when the other team have a turn and bring it slowly back. After a while someone gets bored and kicks the ball in the air (I think this is what dear old Eddie Waring referred to as the 'up and under'). Someone catches the ball, the crowd cheer and the process starts all over again. Eventually one or other side get the ball to the end of the pitch and ground it behind the line. The crowd cheer, the PA plays loud music and dancing girls run along the touchline. Then someone attempts to kick the ball over the goal and the crowd cheer again, but not so loudly, if he succeeds. Only once did someone dare to do anything different, when a Huddersfield player caught the ball at one end and ran 100 yards to score at the other.

Surprising as it may sound – and much to my surprise after the first ten minutes or so, it was actually very exciting. Castleford opened up a lead, Huddersfield clawed it back, Castleford moved well clear, but with late pressure the visitors almost caught up. Castleford won 22.18, simply because they were better at kicking, after both sides had scored four tries. Oh how the Huddersfield supporters moaned about their kickers on the train home.

So what did I learn on my visit to Castleford? That a rugby ground th 90% standing which doesn't meet the Taylor Report recommendation is considered safe. That like football, the standing areas attract a wide range of supporters. That the crowd create an atmosphere, aren't always polite to the ref, but that opposing supporters appear to ignore each other. Finally I learned that rugby league is actually quite exciting.

VfB STUTTGART – Mercedes-Benz Arena

My only experience of watching football in Germany had been the 1988 European Championship, with dismal England defeats to Ireland and Russia. To see for myself the modern German standing areas and experience the atmosphere that many talk about, I returned to Stuttgart, this time for a Bundesliga game against Hannover 96. The Neckarstadion where I'd stood on an open terrace as Ray Houghton's goal defeated England, has been renamed and rebuilt. Now known as the Mercedes-Benz Arena, it's a highly impressive 60,441 capacity stadium (54,906 in all-seated mode).

The first contrast with England was that my ticket for the Cannstatter Kurve, the brand new standing area for home fans which had only been opened the previous month, cost just 13 Euros (approx £12), and included tram travel from the city centre. A standing season ticket is just 190 Euros. Seat prices ranged from 25 to 42 Euros. The terrace was sold out well before the match, although the 53,000 attendance showed there were some empty seats, especially in the away section.

The terrace is fairly shallow, with steps only about six inches high. Every other step is aluminium, under which are the seats that are installed for international games in order to meet regulations. Capacity is then halved from the roughly 5,000 standing spaces. I understand that the design has been patented by Stuttgart and that any other grounds wanting to use it would have to pay a royalty. Removable barriers are positioned in a staggered pattern, with a maximum of eight rows between them. The low step height and positioning of barriers means that a significant surge could not occur. Unlike in most UK grounds, the gangways are not straight, so the risk of a fall or surge is far less than in many of our seated areas. There were no fences and supporters could have escaped onto the pitch in an emergency.

The terrace is divided into six sections with tickets sold separately for each. All supporters entered the huge concourse by the same turnstiles, but stewards carefully checked tickets on entering and re-entering the terrace, ensuring that people were in the correct block. Hence the numbers in each section are controlled. The barriers between the sections were relatively low, but I saw no one climb them to move to another block. There appears to be a considerable degree of self regulation by supporters. Unlike in England, both beer and smoking were permitted on the terrace.

The majority of supporters on the terrace were males aged 15 to 35, but there were also a good number of older people, women and children. I stood next to a couple in their thirties and close by was a boy of about 12 with his father, and a man on crutches with his wife. There was diversity on the terrace although not so much as in the rest of the ground, however it was clear that the presence of a standing area did not deter many families from attending the match.

Although full, the terrace was not uncomfortable and there was no difficulty in moving to get a drink during the game (the problem with that though was that they don't take cash, only payment on special card, which costs 20 Euros). I estimated that supporter density was similar to that on full English terraces after the 15% post Hillsborough capacity reductions.

Singing started half an hour before kick off, something that rarely occurs in England now and it wasn't drowned out by the tannoy as so often happens pre match here. As in Britain, the more vocal supporters stood behind the goal, with it quieter towards the edges, however the support was markedly different to that we are used to. Huge flags and banners were waved, by agreement of the club. Supporters are searched to ensure they don't bring bottles into the ground, but twenty foot flag poles are OK!

Five supporters stood with their backs to the pitch on a raised platform at the front of the terrace and orchestrated the singing. One had drums, another a megaphone and a third a microphone, and they led supporters in a limited selection of songs, plus clapping and jumping up and down in unison. These choreographed displays contrasted to the traditional style of English support, which is based more on reacting to events on the pitch and banter with opposition supporters. The amount and volume of singing probably matched the best that one might experience from British away supporters at a local derby, but was far better than we hear at typical league games. I could see that the Hannover supporters in the opposite corner were singing and clapping, but with the constant noise from the home terrace, didn't hear them once. Stuttgart was certainly an advert for the argument that standing improves atmosphere.

I chatted to a few fans around me. Rainer and Iris said that they stand for the atmosphere, as it is the natural way to watch football, Rainer adding, 'it's not the opera'. I was told that the old standing area had many barriers (I believe it was rail seats), but that the new one is much better. He said the barriers made it cramped and hard to move, but now it's much easier to move around.

Andreas told me that he has watched football all over Europe and finds the best atmosphere in Germany. He said that Stuttgart were one of the last German clubs to redevelop their ground and that they talked to fans to find out what they liked and didn't like elsewhere – hence the running track was removed and the standing area was enlarged from 1,500 to 5,000 (plus some for away fans). 5,000 however still did not meet demand, as this area sold out first and some supporters stood in the seats behind. The vast majority in the seats however sat for the whole game. When I explained that we can't have terraces in most English grounds because the Government say they are unsafe, he answered in one word – Bollocks!

In summary, I believe that the Cannstatter Kurve is safe as those larger terraces still remaining in England such as Peterborough and Exeter, and safer than standing in seated upper tiers. I suspect that the only reason it may not meet the Green Guide is barrier positioning, which could easily be altered. Although the style of support was different, the atmosphere was far better than most games in England. I saw no reason why such a convertible area should not be permitted in the UK.

TERRACES – SUMMARY

From talking to clubs and watching matches one thing was immediately clear – terraces work.

Supporters want the choice to stand, saying that it is the natural way to watch football and creates the best atmosphere. Often terraces are the most popular area of grounds, with supporters choosing to stand even if the price is the same as seats. All ages choose to stand, with plenty of women and children to be seen on the terraces.

Clubs are happy to offer the choice to stand, as it is what fans want and prevents the problem of standing in seated areas. The terraces do not cause problems with hooliganism, which is not seen in the grounds I visited, although the more boisterous supporters tend to gather on parts of them. On the whole this is probably an advantage, separating supporters who want to sit quietly from those who want to sing.

I learned of only two specific instances of problems with crowd control, one of which was caused by police tactics. On neither occasion were any supporters injured, isolated overcrowding being easily dealt with when there are no fences. Both clubs have learnt from the incidents with action taken to prevent recurrence. A few other clubs commented that there can be issues with managing standing supporters, but control these by good stewarding. I was impressed with the concern and planning that goes into the safety and control of supporters, and it was clear from my meetings and observations that clubs are managing supporters well in both seated and standing areas.

My visits demonstrated how well terracing works and that now we have a proper safety culture, with the dangerous combination of uncontrolled entry and no means of escape both dealt with, they are a safe and popular way to watch football.

I asked one club safety officer why despite almost a third of its clubs having terraces and others believing that there should be choice, the Football League had recently introduced a rule saying that clubs had to be all seated after a maximum of two years in the Championship. The answer I was told was that although the majority of smaller clubs favour permitting terraces, League One and Two clubs have little say, the Football League Board and distribution of votes being heavily weighted to Championship clubs, almost all of which are already all seated. I have since been told by two other sources that the Football League's all seater rule was forced on them by the Premier League as a condition of the revised parachute payment deal, as the Premier League don't want small clubs promoted with grounds they consider unsuitable.

The vast majority of clubs were extremely helpful in allowing me to photograph their terraces and providing information. I am grateful for this help and the time that they gave to show me round the grounds. Only at one club did I have difficulty in getting permission to take photographs, but having initially said no because he didn't want to be associated with a book that might back standing, the chairman later agreed to me taking pictures.

Not all clubs were willing to allow me to publish comments that favoured the choice to stand, even seemingly innocuous statements such as that they had no injuries attributed to terracing, or that it is harder to remove casualties from seated areas. In the most extreme example a club director sent me an email which was very positive about standing and saying that they never have a problem with standing in seated areas as this is prevented by giving choice, which he thought was a strong argument for keeping terracing. However, when I proposed publishing his comments, within an hour of my email he replied saying that he had contacted the club's solicitors and should I use them the club would take legal action against me and my publisher. One wonders why he was unwilling to have his views on standing made public and why rather than simply declining my request, he felt it necessary to threaten legal action.

PART THREE

ARGUMENTS FOR & AGAINST CHOICE TO STAND

CHAPTER FOURTEEN

THE CASE AGAINST STANDING

The best way to outline the arguments against standing seemed to be to ask the various bodies that oppose it. To give them the opportunity to provide a detailed response rather than a standard letter, I outlined some reasons why standing could be reintroduced into the top two divisions and three proposed solutions. My letter, which is shown below, was sent in June 2011 to:

The Premier League
The Football Association
The Football League
Association of Chief Police Officers (ACPO)
Football Safety Officers Association (FSOA)
The Minister for Sport (Hugh Robertson)
The Shadow Minister for Sport (Ian Austin)(Labour Party)
The Liberal Democrat Sports Spokesman (Don Foster)

The Labour Party, Premier League and FSOA failed to reply.

I also sent letters to the Hillsborough Justice Campaign and Hillsborough Family Support Group explaining that I was writing a book on the standing issue and inviting them to let me have their views. Neither replied.

Finally I wrote to Ruth Shaw, the new Chief Executive of the FLA, asking if she would be willing to meet me in order that I could be clear on the current FLA position on various aspects of the issue.

The tone of her reply was far more convivial than many of my previous dealings with the FLA, and whilst her current workload meant she was unable to find the time to meet with me, she was happy to answer questions put to her in writing.

Dear Sirs

I am writing to ask the view of the XYZ with regard to proposals to reintroduce standing areas in the top two divisions of the English football leagues.

Given that standing is permitted in the Leagues One and Two of the Football League, at other sports such as rugby, in football grounds for music concerts and for domestic football matches in a number of European countries, it surely cannot be unsafe. Indeed in his report Lord Taylor stated that 'standing is not inherently unsafe'.

None of the reports into the disasters to occur at football grounds in the 1970s and 80s concluded that they were caused by standing. The main causes of loss of life can be summarised as failure to heed previous warnings, failure to manage crowds, failure to ensure adequate emergency escape routes, and above all, lack of adequate safety culture.

There have been many changes in crowd management, supporter behaviour and safety over the last twenty years. Entry to grounds is properly monitored and controlled so that the capacity of an area cannot be exceeded. Fences have been removed allowing easy emergency escape routes and barrier configuration, design and strength is carefully specified. Spectator density in standing areas has been reduced. Above all there is now a proper safety culture. Properly designed and managed standing areas are not unsafe.

It is said by some that supporter disorder is more likely to occur in standing areas, but there is no evidence that providing the choice to stand increases 'hooliganism'. Indeed hooliganism is rarely seen in our grounds now, whether they are all-seated or with standing areas. The huge reduction in hooligan behaviour is due to factors such as banning orders, CCTV, supporter demographics and fashions of behaviour. If it were simply due to abolishing standing there would still be hooliganism at those grounds with terraces, and the many grounds where large number of home and / or away supporters stand in front of their seats.

There is clearly a demand for standing, as shown both by the numbers choosing to use terrace areas where these remain and the numbers standing in seated areas across the country every week – a problem which causes annoyance for those who prefer to sit and can preclude some supporters from attending games. This problem however very rarely occurs where standing areas are provided.

A simple interim solution would be to designate sections of all-seater grounds where standing in front of seats would be permitted. This would effectively manage the problem of persistent standing which the authorities have been unable to prevent, and improve safety and customer care for supporters, plus remove the ongoing conflict with stewards.

In Germany and some other European countries standing is permitted for domestic fixtures and stadia have a variety of convertible seating / standing areas. These work well, allowing supporters the choice they desire.

Currently twenty three Football League grounds retain standing areas. These meet the laid down safety requirements and provide a choice for supporters. They work well without the problems of safety and hooliganism that many have wrongly attributed to terracing.

The present regulation is clearly unworkable as shown by the persistent standing which occurs at all seated grounds around the country – but not in seating areas in grounds where supporters of each team also have standing areas available.

A number of proposals have been put forward to allow standing areas in all British football grounds.

i) Traditional small 'terrace' areas as currently remaining at 23 Football League Grounds.
ii) Convertible or 'rail' seats as seen in Germany.
iii) Managed standing in front of seats in designated areas of grounds.

It seems to me that all three proposals have considerable merit and could be introduced to the benefit of all concerned, without compromising the safety of supporters.

As an initial step I would suggest that the regulation whereby clubs must make their ground all-seated after having been in the Championship or Premiership for three years should be repealed. It is plainly absurd that the type of spectator accommodation should be determined by the level of football on the pitch, rather than factors such as capacity and safety assessments.

I would be grateful if you could advise whether XYZ would support these proposals and if not, what your objections would be.

Just one response was positive, Luke Norman, Parliamentary Assistant to Don Foster MP, saying that:

'*Modern Safe Standing in the top two professional football divisions in England has in fact been a Liberal Democrat policy for several years. It in a policy that Don himself has promoted and pushed for and in December 2010 he introduced a private member's bill on Safe Standing to the House of Commons.'*

Rather than try to paraphrase, I considered it fairest to use the words of those who oppose standing and although this means that this chapter is mainly made up of correspondence, I think it best that I quote directly from their letters.

Police

Assistant Chief Constable Andrew Holt, the ACPO Lead on football policing, sent me a personal letter and based most of his objections to the reintroduction of standing on the Taylor Report.

'It is interesting that you choose to quote Lord Justice Taylor at the start of your letter. I am of the view that the report to which you refer is a seminal piece of work that has shaped the way in which spectators watch football and perhaps more importantly has shaped the way that Clubs, the Football Authorities and the Police Service ensure that spectators are safe whilst they do so. However I note that you have not included the whole sentence in your quote from Lord Justice Taylor's report, which reads "whilst standing accommodation is not intrinsically unsafe, all-seater stadia bring benefits to spectator comfort, safety and crowd control".

In his report Lord Justice Taylor devotes a large part of chapter two in discussing the merits of all seater stadia versus the provision of standing terraces and covers the arguments that are once more being rehearsed in favour of a reintroduction of standing. In paragraph 61 of chapter two he states "There is no panacea which will achieve total safety and cure all problems of behaviour and crowd control. But I am satisfied that seating does more to achieve those objectives than any other single measure."

At a recent meeting chaired by Don Foster MP all present were asked for their view on the reintroduction of standing. The Football

Association, the Premiership, the Football League, the Football Licensing Authority and the Football Safety Officers Association all spoke against the reintroduction of standing. With the Football Supporters Federation being the only body that spoke in favour of its reintroduction.

I accept that you have presented a passionate and eloquent case, but it seems to me that there is very little support from the Football Authorities for the reintroduction of standing. Taylor is also clear in his view that seating contributes to safety, good crowd control and behaviour. As yet I have not seen any evidence that gives me any reason to disagree with his conclusions.'

Department of Culture Media & Sport (DCMS)

In response to my letter to Hugh Robertson, Dempster Marples from the Ministerial Support Team wrote:

'The current Government position is that it supports the recommendations made in the Taylor Report after the Hillsborough disaster, including that stadia in the top two divisions should be all-seater. It is critical that any debate about this issue is done against the backdrop of the Hillsborough disaster and does not add to the burden of those affected by the tragedy.

It is important to note that the case for maintaining the all-seated requirement is not just about safety but also public order and customer care. As well as all grounds in the Premier League now being all-seater many of the clubs in Leagues 1 and 2 (3rd and 4th tiers of English football) are also all-seater. This indicates that a number of clubs are content to provide all-seater accommodation even when not legally required, as it not only provides a safe, comfortable environment but enables the clubs to control the crowd and deal with issues of public disorder, including coin throwing and abusive behaviour, swiftly and effectively.

I understand those that have to manage or license/certify stadia generally hold the view that the introduction of all-seated stadia has helped to improve crowd management and crowd behaviour, and that it also gives supporters better facilities to enjoy football matches. However, we realise that some supporters miss the tradition, character and history of some of our former grounds.

I also recognise that no-one is suggesting we return to the arrangements that were in place fifteen or twenty years ago and we welcome constructive debate about the issues. Before any change in the legislation, there would have to be a very clear demand, as well as very clear evidence that any such change meets stringent safety standards. It could not happen unless the football authorities, those charged with stadium safety, and the police all indicated their support. At this time, however, there is not an appetite from the police or safety authorities for any change and as such continue to support the existing policy.'

I received no reply to my email to Mr Marples, asking that in light of his statement that the Government supports the recommendations made in the Taylor Report, please could he advise when it will be implementing its recommendation and extending the all-seating regulation that applies to football grounds to rugby grounds.

Notably the DCMS reply did not mention injuries. This was a new development as for some years the standard Government letter on standing referred to injury rates. A letter from High Robertson to Tony Lloyd MP in April 2011 stated:

'The Football Licensing Authority has collected injury statistics for a number of seasons, which suggest that a spectator is less likely to be injured at an all-seated ground than at one that retains standing accommodation. Differences in the way in which statistics are collected by different clubs, and the fact they often rely on self reporting, means there are limitations to the conclusions that can be drawn.'

The second sentence was a fairly recent addition to Government letters and was added after the FSF repeatedly challenged the FLA's figures and the validity of conclusions drawn from them.

The Football Association

Tracey Bates, Customer Relations Assistant, wrote:

'The FA believes that the introduction of all seater stadia, following the Taylor report, has helped to change football, from decreasing levels of football related violence, to increasing numbers of female and young fans attending matches. Any potential change to safe standing as well as having a potentially detrimental impact on crowd management and control, could dissuade female fans, younger supporters and families from attending matches.

A return to standing at football matches would be a retrograde step and would reverse a number of the advances that have made the game as accessible and successful as it is today.

One of our principal concerns about safe standing is crowd management and control. A view widely held by safety professionals is that crowd management is easier to achieve in a seated stadium than in a terrace. For example, it is far easier to deal with a potential disturbance in a seated area, as it allows through the use of CCTV to pin point those causing the trouble alongside the use of numbered seats and ticketing to identify those causing the trouble.

We firmly believe that the use of all seater stadia has resulted in improved public order and safety for football fans in England and continues to provide a better option for in terms of crowd safety and management.'

The Football League

Andrew Pomfret, Customer Services Officer, wrote advising that

The Football League had recently made the following statement:

'The Football League supports the current legislation relating to all-seater stadia in the top two divisions. In our view, it has led to clubs working hand in hand with the safety authorities to deliver a strong record of improvement in crowd management and behaviour. It is not overly onerous on clubs and sensibly balances the need for additional seating with divisional status.

The match day environment of football has changed dramatically in recent years and has played a major role in The League attracting record modern-day crowds, with the highest aggregate attendance for 50 years being recorded last season'.

The Football Licensing Authority

I raised the following questions with the FLA.

1. Many of the objections to standing seem to be based on somewhat generalised statements, or for example stating that other bodies oppose a change in the regulation. The Taylor Report is of course often quoted, although it should be noted that his recommendations on all-seating for 'designated stadia' were against a background of many large, ill maintained, fenced terraces, plus a level of hooliganism far greater than that seen today. Taylor's own recommendations ensured that the terraces which remain are infinitely safer and more comfortable than those prior to Hillsborough.

What are the FLA's specific objections to standing areas which meet the requirements of the Green Guide, such as those currently remaining at 23 English League football grounds, and in other sports such as rugby, being permitted in the top two English football leagues (Premiership & Championship)?

2. Currently if a club is promoted and spends three seasons in the

Championship, its ground must then be all-seated. It is hard to understand why a terrace that meets the Green Guide, has been in use for many years and retains the same capacity, should have to be removed simply because the club is playing at a higher level of football. One would expect that safety would be determined by objective factors related to the area's design, control and the numbers who stand on it, not the standard of football on the pitch.

What is the FLA's objection to the '3 year rule' being scrapped and perhaps replaced with a rule that requires an objective assessment of individual stadia after promotion to the Championship?

3. In 2005 the FLA told Amanda and myself that it would like to see all 92 league grounds all seated.

Does this remain an aspiration of the FLA, or are you content that provided they continue to meet safety regulations, standing areas may remain in the lower two divisions?

4. Standing areas are permitted for domestic matches in Germany and a number of other European countries. Many of these grounds use convertible seating / standing areas, which are only used in seating mode for UEFA & FIFA matches. Some years ago the FLA visited Hamburg to view a design of convertible seats and noted that it appeared to work well, but for engineering reasons could not be installed into *existing* stands in the UK, and did not change their view on standing. The most favoured design proposed for possible use in the UK is now 'rail seats', where there is a waist-high rail in front of every row, preventing any possibility of a cascade effect. These work well in Germany, at clubs such as Hannover, Werder Bremen and Stuttgart and in Austria at Wacker Innsbruck.

What, if any, would be the FLA's objection to 'rail seats' being installed in the UK?

5. I am familiar with the FLA's document *'Standing in Seated Areas*

at Football Grounds, August 2002' and the reasons that the FLA recommended the Minister rejected the proposals of 'managed standing in seated areas' put forward by *Stand Up Sit Down* in 2005. Lord Taylor's prediction that supporters would soon get used to sitting has been proved incorrect. In 2005 the FLA told us that they were confident that this could be stopped by education and possibly other measures, however the extent of standing in seated areas has increased over the last ten years. The FLA also told us that in their opinion standing in seated areas is more dangerous than standing on a designated terrace.

If the FLA does not wish to see standing areas in the top two divisions, which experience widely shows prevents the standing in seated areas that has proved extremely difficult to control, do you accept that any safety risk from persistent standing would be considerably reduced if this standing was managed by permitting it in designated areas of lower tiers, and that this would also overcome the customer care problem?

6. Over the last few years there has been much debate between the FSF and the FLA with regard to injury figures. After a number of errors in the figures were pointed out and the FLA's conclusions disputed, the standard DCMS letter of reply on standing in which they referred to injury statistics collected by the FLA, had a rider added to the sentence on injury statistics. This stated that *'Differences in the way in which statistics are collected by different clubs, and the fact that they often rely on self reporting, means there are limitations to the conclusions that can be drawn.'* The letter which I received from DCMS, dated 6th June, which I assume to be their latest standard letter, did not mention injury figures at all.

Does the FLA now believe that the data available on injuries shows no clear evidence that a spectator is more likely to be injured in a standing area than in an all seated stadium?

7. It is often said that disorder is more likely to occur if standing areas are permitted, although I have seen no specific evidence to support this. I am not aware of a higher incidence of disorder at those League One & Two clubs who retain standing areas, than those who don't. Whilst some safety officers agree with the current regulation on standing, I have spoken to others who favour allowing a choice for supporters to sit or stand as this would reduce / reduces conflict over standing in seated areas.

Does the FLA have any specific evidence which supports the view that if standing is permitted greater disorder may result?

8. It is sometimes said (and was mentioned in an email to me from the FA) that to permit standing areas could dissuade female fans, younger supporters and families from attending matches. I have seen no evidence that fewer female, younger & family supporters attend matches at the 23 grounds which retain standing areas, or those where large numbers routinely stand in seated areas. It is proposed that only relatively small proportions of stadia are converted to seating, so there will remain plenty of seats for those who prefer not to stand.

Does the FLA share the view that that to permit standing areas could dissuade female fans, younger supporters and families from attending matches, and if so do you have any specific evidence to support this?

9. The above questions cover what I have found appear to be the main objections to permitting the introduction of standing areas in the top two divisions. Do the FLA have any other significant objections which you think I should include in the book?

Finding a number of overlapping themes Ruth Shaw chose to address these rather than answer the specific questions as I had put them, but asked me to come back if I required further detail. Rather than reproduce all of her long letter I have quoted the most relevant sections, and sought her agreement that this was a fair reflection prior to publication of this book.

Government Policy

The decision on whether to permit standing areas in the Premiership and Championship is ultimately a matter of Government Policy. It is the current Government view that all-seater stadia are the best means to ensure the safety and security of fans and that they have been a contributing factor to the increased diversity of those attending matches in recent years.

The Government appreciates that some supporters would like to see the return of standing areas at football stadia, but they do not believe that a compelling case has been made to change the policy. In reaching that view, the Government have listened to the views of a range of organisations and individuals not just the FLA.

Extent of Conversion

I am not aware of a current formalised FLA position on whether the organisation would like to see all 92 league grounds becoming all-seater. In some ways it is perhaps more helpful to consider what the FLA aims to achieve in terms of its overall mission to ensure that all spectators regardless of age, gender, ethnic origin, disability, or the team they support are able to attend sports grounds in safety, comfort and security. We work hard at all levels to achieve that, within the existing legislative and policy framework, and will continue to do so.

The FLA's overall position in terms of all seater stadia, can perhaps be best summarised as follows:

While we recognise that there are some fans who would prefer to stand, it is our view that seating is generally safer, more comfortable and enables better crowd management. Seating can make it easier to steward spectators, and identify them if needed. Seating may provide a more defensible space for those who need or want it, including children, elderly people, and people with disabilities. This can help to create a more inclusive and diverse environment.

Persistent Standing

It has been suggested that the existence of persistent standing in seated areas may be a reason to change the current arrangements. However, it has also been suggested that only relatively small proportions of stadia are converted to standing. It would be helpful to understand how it is envisaged this would work in practice, and whether there is any evidence available from other countries on what the impact on persistent standing might be in areas of grounds which remained seated.

The FLA believes that standing in seated areas presents a range of potential safety, crowd management and customer care issues. We agree that not everyone who stands in a seated area does so because they want to, and some are forced to stand because others are, and it is the only way to see. We remain committed to a collaborative way to addressing this situation, which recognises that ground management is responsible for the safety of spectators, but that fans, football clubs, local authorities, and police can all play a role in tackling the issue.

Measures to address persistent standing include educating and persuading supporters, active control of crowds by ground management, and where necessary firm action against supporters who do not comply. We would tend to see the issue of persistent standing as primarily a matter for enforcement, rather than a reason to change the regulations.

Injury Statistics

The FLA has collected injury statistics for a number of seasons which show that a spectator is less likely to be injured at an all-seater ground than at one which retains standing accommodation. Differences in the way statistics are collected by different clubs, and the fact that they often reply on self reporting, means there are limitations to the conclusions that can be drawn. However, the statistics clearly show that the rate of injuries at grounds with standing accommodation is higher than at all seated grounds'.

Public Disorder

'The FLA does not collate statistics on the incidence of public order issues in football grounds, which is primarily a matter for the police.'

Diversity

'The FLA welcomes the many improvements which have made football clubs more welcoming and inclusive environments. As I've set out above, the FLA view is that seating can provide a more defensible space for those who need or want it, including children, elderly people, and people with disabilities, and that this can in turn help to create a more inclusive and diverse environment. However, we recognise that a number of factors may contribute to diversity amongst spectators'.

Time for Conversion

As you know, clubs promoted to the Championship for the first time have up to three years to convert their ground to all-seated accommodation. This was originally intended to ensure that a club which may have three sides of the ground to convert would have the opportunity of three closed seasons to complete the work.

This may be less likely to be the position for clubs gaining promotion to the Championship in recent years, and there could therefore be an argument for the period of time for conversion being reduced. *We believe it is important to strike the right balance between giving clubs sufficient time to make the necessary arrangements, and being fair and consistent with the approach that has been taken in the past at other grounds.*

Other Observations

'*I appreciate your view that some of the arguments made against standing are based on somewhat generalised statements. I am sure that the same could be said about some of the arguments made for standing, and therefore share your view on the value of robust evidence to inform the debate.*'

Ruth Shaw's letter did not give an opinion either for or against rail seats, but stated that there were a number of questions that remain to be answered including practical, technical and financial issues.

Prior to the book being sent to the publisher in December 2011, she confirmed that the statements in her letter reflected the views of the organisation as at the end of October 2011. She also added:

'*The other point I would make in relation to the selected extract on public disorder is that while we do not collate statistics on public disorder as it is primarily a matter for the police, we do work closely with the UK Football Policing Unit to ensure we are aware of significant developments and issues, and we recognise the important relationship between safety and security and the need for an integrated approach to safety management.*'

The next eight chapters consider the various issues raised by those opposing the choice to stand, and discuss the merits of their objections.

CHAPTER FIFTEEN

DEMAND FOR CHOICE

It has often been claimed that there is no demand for standing, hence no need to bring it back. Lord Taylor said that supporters would soon get used to sitting and for some years the FLA seemed to deny that fans wanted to stand up. Those backing calls for standing were portrayed as dinosaurs wanting to return to the bad old days, when we should all be rejoicing in shiny new stadia around the country.

The standard Government reply to those writing with regard to standing says that, *'Before any change in the legislation, there would have to be a very clear demand'*. It is however not hard to make a case that many supporters want to stand and that the majority of all fans want choice to be available.

Let's start with the 23 clubs who still have terraces. At most of these the cost differential is just a few pounds, there are plenty of spare seats, but many (often the majority) choose to stand. Even if prices are the same, many opt for the terraces. It is rarely the case that there are insufficient seats forcing supporters to stand, but that when choice is provided a large proportion prefer to stand up.

Again Torquay provides a good example, this time a home League Cup fixture against Reading in August 2010. A crowd of 2,832 paid the same admission price of £15 for all areas of the ground, but the only seated section that was full was the small area allocated to visitors. There were many empty seats in the Ellacombe Road Stand behind the goal, but more Torquay supporters chose to stand on the Popular Side terrace. There can be no doubt that supporters want the choice to stand.

Where grounds are all-seated supporters still want to stand. Far from getting used to sitting, tens of thousands stand in front of their seats every week. It is true that these will include some who would prefer to sit but are forced to stand because others in front are doing so, but also that many fans remain seated, but would rather stand up.

Would there be a campaign for choice if fans didn't want this? It's an issue that many supporters feel strongly about and one that's raised over and over again when fans meet with clubs. Over the last few years a number of surveys have been carried out asking supporters' views on standing. Whilst these cannot claim to be based on scientifically selected representative samples, as the following tables show, they consistently demonstrate a majority supporting the choice to stand.

Football Supporters' Federation – National Survey – 2009

	Respondents	Stand	Sit	Don't Know	Depends
Do you prefer to stand or sit at football matches?	5,503	50.2%	20.5%	0.9%	28.4%

	Respondents	Yes	No	Don't Know
Do you think supporters should have the choice of sitting or standing, including having areas specifically designed for safe standing?	5,470	89.8%	7.1%	3.1%

Football Fans Census – January 2009

The Football Fans Census is, *'a research organisation founded in 2002 to help make sure that fans were put in the heart of the game's decision-making processes by providing a communication channel between fans and decision makers through ongoing research, consultation and reports'* (www.footballfanscensus.com).

	Respondents	Yes	No	Don't Know
Should fans be given the freedom to choose whether they stand (in "safe-standing" areas) or sit inside football grounds?	2,046	92%	7%	1%

The survey's respondents included supporters of 159 clubs, 46% of whom were season ticket holders.

Football Fans Census – November 2004

The survey considered designated 'Stand Up' areas where supporters could stand in front of seats. The respondents included supporters of 115 clubs.

	Respondents	Yes	No	Don't Know
Should separate 'Stand Up' and 'Sit Down' areas be created in grounds?	1,502	88%	11%	1%

	Respondents	Safe Standing (Modern Terrace)	Stand Up Sit Down (in front of seats)	Neither (I am happy with current situation)	Don't Know
Overall, which of the two solutions to the issue of standing in all-seater stadia do you feel is the best?	1,502	65%	22%	8%	5%

Whilst a large majority of supporters backed the proposal for 'Stand Up' and 'Sit Down' areas in all-seated grounds, the clear preference by a ratio of three to one was for safe standing 'modern terrace' areas.

The Guardian Online Poll – March 2011

	Yes	No
The Guardian has revealed that the government will listen to the case for reintroducing terracing almost 22 years after the Hillsborough disaster. Would you like to be able to stand at top-level games again?	76.4%	23.6%

Bristol City Supporters' Trust – New Stadium Survey – March/April 2008

	Respondents	Yes	No	Don't Know
Would you like provision to be made in the design of one of stands to accommodate a designated area for safe standing should this be allowed in years to come?	2,878	53.5%	37.4%	9.4%

Significantly, a majority of those currently sitting in all four stands at Ashton Gate favoured a designated safe standing area.

Annual Survey of Arsenal Supporters by the Gooner Fanzine – June 2011

	Respondents	Yes	No	Don't Know
Do you support the current Government requirement that Ashburton Grove is all-seated along with all other grounds in the top two divisions?	~2,500	25.9%	49.7%	24.3%

	Respondents	Stand	Sit	No Preference
If you had a choice, would you personally prefer to sit or stand to watch Arsenal at home games?	~2,500	47.1%	35.1%	17.9%
If you had a choice, would you personally prefer to sit or stand to watch Arsenal at away games?	~2,500	57.8%	23.3%	18.9%

Reading Supporters' Trust (STAR) Membership Survey – November 2008

	Respondents	Agree (slightly or completely)	Disagree (slightly or completely)	Neither/ Don't Know
Supporters should have the choice whether to sit or stand at matches	405	59%	29%	12%

Daily Star – October 2011

The Daily Star interviewed 1,000 fans from more than 90 clubs.

	Yes	No	Undecided/ Don't Know
Would you support the introduction of modern, purpose-built standing-only areas within Premier League and Championship grounds?	66%	17%	17%
If modern, purpose-built, standing areas were available, would you personally use them?	48%	26%	26%

Various polls on supporters' internet forums showed a similar picture, with for example Manchester United, Wolves and Reading supporters all strongly favouring safe standing areas. I have been unable to find any polls that do not support the choice to stand.

The Premier League's annual end of season supporter survey has only once included a question about standing. The 2007/8 survey asked not whether fans wanted to stand, but instead about persistent standing, with the aim to determine the scale of this problem, or whether it was a problem at all.

Reponses of 31,005 match attenders to the question, *'Are you aware of people persistently standing around you when you attend matches?'* were:

No, never	19%
No, not as a general rule	36%
Yes, but it doesn't bother me	22%
Yes, and it lessens my enjoyment of the game	10%
Yes, and it increases my enjoyment of the game	14%

15% of all male supporters (7% of female) and 32% of 16 – 24 year olds said that standing increased their enjoyment.

The Premier League's comments on these responses are interesting.

'Over half of the supporters (55%) said that they are not aware of people persistently standing around them – either 'never' or 'as a general rule'. Even those who are aware of it can tend to be not bothered about it (22%) – with just 10% of supporters being both aware and bothered by the persistent standing of those around them. To complicate matters further, 14% of those responding said that it actually increased their enjoyment of the game; deemed, presumably, part of the wider experience of a Matchday atmosphere and ritual'.

The Premier League seemingly found it 'complicating' that people were saying things they didn't want to hear and have never asked this or any similar question since.

It is abundantly clear from all these polls that the majority of supporters believe that there should be a choice to sit or stand at football matches. All of the eleven polls I found showed a majority favouring standing being permitted, with an average of 82% in favour. It is not just younger fans or those who might be expected to want to stand, but a majority of all supporters, regardless of their preference to sit or stand, who favour choice.

There is no doubt that as exhibited by the numbers standing on our remaining terraces and in front of seats at all-seated grounds, and by the consistent results of polls, football supporters want the choice to sit or stand at matches.

CHAPTER SIXTEEN

THE TAYLOR REPORT

I would agree with Assistant Chief Constable Andrew Holt that the Taylor Report is a seminal piece of work that has shaped the way in which spectators watch football and the way that clubs, the football authorities and the police ensure their safety. However it should be considered that this was written over twenty years ago and that since then there have been many changes in football, society and safety management.

Lord Taylor's report was written at a time when hooliganism was a far greater problem than it is today, and when many of our football grounds were old, ill-maintained and lacking more than basic facilities. His report at last led to many changes which have ensured the safety of football supporters, and partly as a result of some of his recommendations there have been huge improvements in supporter behaviour. However, history has shown that Lord Taylor wasn't always right. Were he still alive I'm sure that he would accept that recommendations that are more than twenty years old may not all be appropriate today.

The DCMS wrote that the current Government position is that it *'supports the recommendations made in the Taylor Report'*, but as we will see, it doesn't seem concerned that not all of his recommendations have been implemented.

Lord Taylor starts Chapter Two of his Final Report under the heading *'A Better Future for Football'* with the commendable statement that, *'It is not enough to aim only at the minimum measures necessary for safety'*. This is of course true, but it has also been said that the only completely safe stadium is one that is empty. It is not realistic to aim for total safety, but is the role of clubs to provide 'reasonable safety' for their customers.

His first paragraph says that there should be *'more consultation with the supporters'*. There is generally more dialogue now, but consultation and actually doing what supporters want are another matter. It's not just standing, but issues such as ticket prices and match scheduling, that are regularly brought up by the FSF, but little seems to change.

There are few bigger issues for supporters than their club moving ground, especially if it's to an athletics stadium, but despite pledging to listen to supporters when they bought West Ham, David Gold and David Sullivan refused repeated calls for a ballot to find out the views of supporters as they bid for the Olympic Stadium.

In 2010 the Government commissioned a Select Committee to investigate governance of football. Its report stated that:

'Every club should have a dedicated and mandatory supporter liaison officer', and *'every club should officially recognise the relevant supporters groups or trusts and keep an open dialogue with them. They should hold official and regular annual general meetings at which these groups are invited to take part and at which appropriate financial and other information can be shared and consulted upon'*.

More than twenty years after Lord Taylor's report football clubs were still being told that they should listen to their supporters.

Taylor makes a number of comments with regard to all-seating, that were contentious then and have been shown to be incorrect or even less relevant over time.

The relevance and perhaps the accuracy of his comment that, 'It is obvious that sitting for the duration of a match is more comfortable than standing', are questionable. Comfort is a matter of opinion and includes what one feels happy with, not just physical comfort. Some people are for example more comfortable walking than they are riding in a car, or in a packed pub rather than a quiet restaurant. Many supporters, particularly those of above average height, consider that the very cramped seats that were installed on some terraces are less comfortable then the standing areas they replaced.

Taylor writes that seated spectators will not be in close physical contact with those around them, and will not be jostled or moved about by swaying or surging, or painfully bent double over a crush barrier. It is true that some supporters on the terraces of old were subject to swaying and surging, and that they were not always comfortable, although those who attended regularly knew which areas to stand if they wished to avoid this. Unlike in seats, on a terrace someone can move if they are not happy with their position or people around them. Taylor's comment about being bent double over a crush barrier, whilst relevant to the exceptional circumstances at Hillsborough, is a considerable exaggeration over what occurred elsewhere on even the most packed terraces.

Taylor's own recommendations on terrace capacities however largely stopped the very problems that he uses towards his justification for all-seating. With reduced capacities supporters were no longer so closely packed and the type of discomfort he describes ceased to occur. Prior to Hillsborough, when a terrace was full one could expect to be in physical contact with other supporters, but with today's reduced capacities this no longer occurs. On none of the terraces from which I watched matches when travelling around grounds for this book was I in physical contact with other supporters.

Taylor refers to small or infirm spectators and young children being buffeted and unsighted by more robust people on the terraces, but no one is saying that anyone should be forced to stand. That some people may find something uncomfortable seems a strange argument to add to the case for banning it. A choice of accommodation is what is wanted and those who prefer to sit would presumably do so. It was right to increase the proportion of seating at many grounds, allowing opportunity for all those who want to sit to have a seat, but is the fact that some do not wish to stand a justification for removing this choice?

Lord Taylor wrote that, *'It is true that at moments of excitement seated spectators do, and may be expected to, rise from their seats. But the moment passes and they sit down again'*. On the next page of his report he said, *'It is possible that in the early stages of conversion there may be instances of fans standing on the seats or in front of them because they are used to standing or in order to register a protest, but I am satisfied that in England and Wales as in Scotland and abroad spectators will become accustomed and educated to sitting'*. On this Lord Taylor was wrong. As shown in Chapter Seven, supporters have not got used to sitting and the numbers who stand in front of their seats every week are rising.

Given that standing in seated areas is considered by the FLA to be less safe than standing on terraces, one must question whether had he known that supporters would continue to stand in large numbers, Lord Taylor would have made his all-seater recommendation.

As mentioned in Chapter Three, Taylor stated that, *'The evidence I have received has been overwhelmingly in favour of **more** seating accommodation'*. The Technical Working Party which he set up referred to implementation of **higher proportions** of seating accommodation.

Taylor refers to a survey of Football Supporters' Association members undertaken in November 2009 by the Sir Norman Chester Centre for Football Research. Lord Taylor states that the survey was commissioned to, '*discover the views of committed football fans on a number of the issues after Hillsborough which are covered in my Report. The extension of seating was one such issue.*' He writes that the report states, '*that substantial majorities in the sample were in favour of maintaining the status quo on the seats / terraces balance at their own club.*' Rather than quote these figures Taylor adds, '*However, the Report continues:*

'*53.6% claimed they would actually support the drive for more seating if they were reasonably priced and covered*'. Note the word more is used not all-seating and that Taylor referred to the '**extension of** *seating*' as one issue covered by the survey. He notes that when all-seating was put to the sample there was a majority against it. Taylor then quotes from the report, '*Finally, and perhaps more significantly, opposition to the introduction of all-seated facilities diminishes considerably when one introduces provisos on price and protection from the elements. When this is done, more people support all-seaters than oppose them*'. So in one sentence the report says a (small) majority favour **more** seating if reasonably priced and covered, but in another it makes the same conclusion but says **all-seaters**. Taylor appears to have picked up on the discrepancy, inserting (sic) in the first statement, but makes no other comment. Lord Taylor's selective quoting from the Sir Norman Chester Centre report gives the impression of someone looking for data that supports an existing view, rather than using it to help form a conclusion.

Lord Taylor talks about reversing the two to one standing / seating ratio, but nowhere in his report does he state that he has received evidence that grounds should be totally seated, however this is the conclusion he came to.

Taylor considers the main reasons why some (including at the time the Football Association) wished to retain a proportion of standing room.

The first, *'an emotional one based on the desire to retain the traditional culture derived from the close contact of the terraces'*, he counters by saying that he was not convinced *'that the cherished culture of the terraces is wholly lost when fans are seated'* and that, *'To such an extent as the seating limits togetherness or prevents movement, that price is surely worth paying for the benefits in safety and control'*. The former statement is an argument of subjective opinions, but I would suggest that the view of those who have watched football from seats and terraces and conclude that they still wish to stand, are those with greater relevance. The validity of his latter statement depends on what the benefits actually are, which of course is a matter of considerable debate. Taylor also comments that the lower maximum crowd densities now acceptable take the force out of the argument. On this however he has been proved wrong – supporters still want to stand.

Taylor noted that sitting in the rain is worse than standing on an uncovered terrace, so said that increased seating requires cover to be provided. It was however not until 2007 that the away end at Fratton Park, the last permanent uncovered seating area at a Premier League ground, was covered. Supporters sitting for example in the temporary stand at Wolves, the uncovered stands at the Don Valley Stadium and towards the front of countless grounds around the country, still however get wet when it rains. The Premier League regulation says merely that the majority of accommodation shall be covered.

There are a number of holes in Taylor's response to the second argument that conversion to all-seating will reduce capacities, so many would-be spectators will be disappointed. He comments that this assumes a significantly greater density being permitted for standing places than seating, but the assumption is correct. Current Green Guide recommendations permit 1.8 times higher density for standing than is typically the case for seats. Taylor says that it also assumes that the size of present (i.e. 1989) crowds regularly exceed projected all-seated capacities.

He quotes figures for the 1988/89 season, which showed that at only one club (Liverpool) did the average attendance exceed the projected all-seated capacity. For each club the number of attendances exceeding projected all-seated capacity ranged from 0 to 16, and for 21 out of 44 clubs in the top two divisions attendance never exceeded projected capacity. The Taylor Report words this in such a way as to suggest that the capacity reductions will not be a problem. If the figures are turned round however one could say that the all-seated capacities would mean that at more than half the clubs some supporters will be disappointed at least once per season, at three clubs this will occur at least 10 times, and at Liverpool it will be for most games.

The figures in his report therefore show that in 1989, when Lord Taylor made his all-seater recommendation, reduced capacities would result in stadia being unable to accommodate all the fans wishing to attend a significant number of matches. However things have moved on. Now we have all-seated stadia, some higher capacity, but most lower than when they had standing areas, matches at many top clubs are sold out or almost sold out. In 2010/11 eleven Premier League clubs had average attendances in excess of 90% of capacity. Average gates at Chelsea, Arsenal, Manchester United and Tottenham all exceeded 98% of capacity. Many games are sold out, it is hard to obtain tickets and knowing demand exceeds supply, clubs can charge high prices. If standing areas were permitted, capacities would rise, helping to alleviate the problem.

So we come to the third argument Taylor considered, that of cost. His view was that clubs may wish to charge more for seating than for standing, but that it should be possible to plan a price structure which suits the cheapest seats to the pockets of those presently paying to stand. It could be said that Taylor was right, as clubs who still have terraces tend to charge only a few pounds extra for seats. This however probably reflects the fact that the majority of their supporters don't see the value of paying much more to sit and that clubs need to maximise income from all areas.

Although some argue that standing should be brought back to enable reduced ticket prices, many supporters have said that they would be willing to pay the same to stand as they currently do to sit. Ticket prices have however risen hugely since the Taylor Report. Clubs need the money to fund exorbitant player wages and know that supporters will pay to watch their teams. The recession brought some reductions as crowds fell, but prices have still risen by far more than inflation. A report in *The Guardian* by David Cobb showed that in the twenty years from 1989 ticket prices at the Premier League's top six clubs increased by 719%, ten times the rate of inflation. Whilst not directly down to all-seating, lack of spare capacity must be a factor, hence as illustrated in Chapter Nine, conversion of some seated areas to standing could potentially allow cheaper tickets with no loss of income for clubs.

Taylor notes that, '*The trend towards seating is even stronger in Europe and is being driven by decrees of both national and European football authorities*'. He was correct that both UEFA and FIFA stipulate that all games played under their jurisdiction should be in all-seated stadia, but for domestic games many grounds across Europe have standing accommodation. If the trend in Europe was an argument for moving all-seated in 1989, it is now an argument for bringing back standing areas.

After considering whether all-seating should apply to other sports, as discussed in Chapter Three, Lord Taylor decided that it should not be restricted to football, stating, '*I therefore conclude and recommend that designated grounds under the 1975 Act should be required in due course to be converted to all-seating*'. The Safety of Sports Grounds Act to which he refers defines a 'designated ground' as a sports ground that with accommodation for more than 10,000 spectators or a football ground that holds more than 5,000. This is a recommendation that successive governments have chosen not to implement. The Government also chose not to enforce his recommendation for the third and fourth tiers of the English leagues.

Because the Football Spectators Act 1989 applies only to football, Taylor recommended that the inspecting and reviewing role of the FLA should be extended to cover all grounds designated under the 1975 Act. It was however not until 2011 that the Sports Grounds Safety Authority Bill was passed, allowing the authority to provide advice about safety for any sports ground. In November 2011 the FLA was renamed the Sports Ground Safety Authority. Contrary to Taylor's recommendation, the changes did not extend the FLA's licensing functions or its local authority oversight duties under the 1989 Act to sports grounds other than football grounds.

Taylor talks about hooliganism and notes that, *'incitement from the pitch or bad behaviour by players has a malign influence on the crowd'*. He says that it is up to the players themselves, then referees, managers and club directors to stop incitement by players, adding, *'If and when they fail to use it, the FA must take a firm disciplinary line'*. Clubs and the FA do sometimes take action, although as the maximum fine of two weeks wages is hardly missed by those earning millions, one could argue as to whether this is 'firm'. Bans are more effective, but as in the case of Wayne Rooney's swearing outburst to a TV camera at Upton Park, club's sometimes complain when star players are prevented from playing.

Every week we see players cup their ear, or provocatively celebrate goals in front of opposition supporters. This is the sort of incitement to which Taylor was referring but nothing is done to stop it. The fact that crowds almost always react only verbally or with gestures, is a measure of how much behaviour has improved since Lord Taylor wrote his report.

In Chapter Five we learned of Taylor's cautious optimism with regard to misbehaviour inside grounds and his comment that police measures were by and large preventing violence. His report states that, *'there has to be a police presence at a match to maintain law and order'*, yet many matches (very often in grounds with terracing) are now played with no police present. That police are often no longer required to maintain the peace is a further illustration of how things have changed since Lord Taylor wrote his report.

Taylor notes that much progress had recently been made at a number of clubs in bringing women and children back to football, by creating separate family and membership areas. He suggests that de-segregation in these areas is a good step towards a move away from segregation, which tends to worsen hostility. Few would argue with this, although in general supporters probably prefer the identity and atmosphere that comes from having areas for fans of each club. Taylor's comment is however not an argument for all-seating, just for family areas to be seated.

Lord Taylor considered at length the issues of overcrowding and preventing pitch invasions and concluded that fences should remain, albeit with maximum heights and specified access gates. That for many years there have been no fences at British grounds is a reflection on both the improved behaviour (in seated and standing areas) and the imposition of almost automatic bans for running onto the pitch.

Taylor recommended that for each pen or terraced area of capacity over 2,000 which for any match is expected to be at least one third full, there should be a steward or police officer whose sole duty is to check crowd conditions in that area for possible overcrowding or distress. Enquires have shown that whilst all clubs carefully monitor terraces for signs of overcrowding, contrary to Taylor's recommendation, this is not the *sole* duty of any one person.

Discussing the need to encourage supporters to enter the ground in good time, Lord Taylor noted the absence of pre-match entertainment and recommended that each club should consult with supporters clubs as to the provision of such entertainment. Whether this occurred varied from club to club, but few arrange anything that entices supporters to arrive early. The reason for this is almost certainly that fans simply aren't interested – they go to watch football not dancing girls.

Experience has however shown that crowds now generally arrive much later than they did when all grounds had large areas of standing. Supporters would arrive early in order to secure a favourite position and often would start singing an hour or so before kick off. With places assured in all-seated grounds, less tendency to sing when seated and often very loud public address systems drowning any attempts to do so, the majority now enter in the 15 minutes prior to kick off.

Contrasting with Lord Taylor's comments with regard to encouraging supporters to arrive in good time, it has become a common police tactic to hold back away supporters, escorting fans on foot or in coaches to the ground at the very last minute. Often this results in congestion at the turnstiles, and with some supporters missing the start of the match, ill feeling and raised tempers – just the sort of situation that Taylor sought to avoid.

As we have read, the police tactic of holding Leeds United supporters at the motorway services and bringing them all at once to Exeter City just before kick off, led to a potentially dangerous situation. It is fortunate that the removal of fences, plus many of the measures recommended by Lord Taylor, have improved safety, so that these situations caused by police tactics do not lead to more serious problems.

Various recommendations are made in relation to medical facilities. Taylor describes a *major incident equipment vehicle* used by the Scottish Ambulance Service, which is packed with 50 stretchers, blankets and medical supplies, and deployed at matches with crowds over 25,000. He recommends that this is adopted elsewhere and the Green Guide now sets out recommended medical provision, including for matches where a crowd of over 25,000 is expected, that one Major Incident Vehicle is provided. Actual practice however varies. West Midlands Ambulance Service told me that ambulances are provided according to the Green Guide recommendations, that ten Major Incident Response Vehicles are strategically located across the region to respond to any event that may occur, and that:

As on occasions the expected attendance at some matches may be close to, or even just above 25,000, a number of additional stretchers / further equipment is spread around the ground to overcome the need for a major incident vehicle to be present.'

The North East Ambulance Service however told me that they, *'have a Hazardous Area Response Team who would be deployed in the event of a major incident, and they do mass casualty capabilities. They are not sent to large events as a matter of course, only if needed.'*

Whilst not questioning that adequate medical resources are provided for football matches, I quote this as another example of Lord Taylor's recommendations that has not been followed.

Taylor considers the police policy of admitting fans without tickets, where they judge it best to let them into the ground rather than having them roaming the town. This he says, *'must not be allowed to continue'*. He accepts that in a situation such as that outside Hillsborough when it was a matter of life and death it was correct to open Gate C, but says that, *'when the police have an option to let fans without tickets in or keep them out, their policy must clearly be to exclude them'*. There was no Hillsborough type life and death situation outside Upton Park in August 2010 when the Metropolitan Police allowed a large group of ticketless Millwall fans into the ground. Perhaps the police were aware that it was their insistence on reducing Millwall's allocation, against advice of the clubs, that probably contributed to the fans arriving without tickets?

Lord Taylor is very clear on ticket touting, saying that, '*in my view touting should be made unlawful*'. It is now an offence, but one that the police often fail to deal with. At big matches touts can often been openly seen selling tickets, in the case of West Ham, many being the same faces who have been on Green Street for at least twenty years.

In order to reduce the risk of fans arriving without tickets, Taylor recommended that, '*all-ticket matches should be confined to those at which a capacity or near capacity crowd is expected*'. This recommendation is often ignored, with matches made all-ticket on 'police advice'.

Taylor recommends that, '*clubs should recruit and retain sufficient competent stewards*' and refers to the age, fitness and training. There has been a move away from 'older supporters' acting as stewards, but many fans question the competence of some stewards, and even their command of English. To keep costs down clubs often use agencies rather than employing staff themselves, and I was told by one safety officer that he accepts their standard is not ideal.

The Taylor Report refers to postponing kick offs and recommends that this should be at the discretion of the officer in charge, with crowd safety paramount. Kick offs are occasionally delayed, either due to congestion outside or transport problems, but many supporters believe that the power of television is such that matches due to be shown live are less likely to be put back.

In September 2011 major crushing occurred outside Craven Cottage in chaotic scenes prior to a friendly between Brazil and Ghana. Women and children were in tears and grown men genuinely feared for their safety in the crush as supporters tried to collect pre-booked tickets. Police and stewards failed to alleviate the dangerous situation, or to delay the kick off. As with Hillsborough, the easily avoidable situation was caused by poor organisation, and an unjustified attempt made to blame the problem on ticketless fans.

As was shown at Ellis Park, such a situation can lead to disaster at an all-seated stadium, yet Taylor's recommendation was ignored.

Taylor also considered kick off times, suggesting early starts to reduce the risk of trouble. This does now occur, but it seems that the influence of TV in scheduling can exceed that of the police. For example, the 1999 title decider between Celtic and Rangers was given a Sunday evening kick off for Sky TV coverage, allowing fans a whole day to drink before the match. With a frenzied atmosphere there were several flashpoints and a number of Celtic supporters ran onto the pitch to confront the referee.

Taylor recommends that important public address announcements should be preceded by a loud signal to catch the attention of the crowd, and that this arrangement should be prominently advertised in the programme for every match. It is included in some club programmes, but at many clubs it is not.

In a report of such length it is understandable that there will be occasional errors. For example Taylor says that it was Manchester City not Leeds supporters who tore up seats at Coventry and that the Moelwyn Hughes Report was written in 1924 not 1946: (1924 was the date of the Short Report into the 1923 FA Cup final). More significantly he refers to surging, fighting and coin throwing on the terraces being provoked by scuffles between Wimbledon and West Ham players in a match at Upton Park in November 1989. Having been at the match in question I would not dispute that fans surged downwards and that coins may have been thrown, there was however no fighting amongst supporters. It is easy for an inexperienced observer or second hand report to mistakenly conclude that disorder is more serious than actually occurred.

Lord Taylor made the following much quoted statement with regard to seating:

'There is no panacea which will achieve total safety and cure all

STAND UP SIT DOWN

problems of behaviour and crowd control. But I am satisfied that seating does more to achieve those objectives than any other single measure.'

On first reading it appears that he is simply saying that all-seating is the safest and best option for crowd control. However it should be noted that he says *single measure*. A combination of a number of other measures could potentially have the same effect and it is argued that in the various controls he recommended for standing areas, this has been achieved. Surely it is the overall effect that is important, not the number of separate measures that are taken to meet the objective. Reducing the speed limit by 50% would achieve more than any other single measure to improve road safety, but it is preferred to use a package of measures instead. Contrary to common perception, Taylor's statement does not say that all-seating is the best or only solution to achieving the objectives of both safety and crowd control. It simply says that it is the best single measure. The same objectives could be, and it appears are, met by a package of other measures. If Taylor thought that all-seating was the only solution, would he not have said so?

It is surprising that in a report of such length, Lord Taylor included very little to explain his conclusion that it is safer to sit than to stand. ACC Holt wrote that in his report Lord Taylor devotes a large part of chapter two discussing the merits of all-seater stadia versus standing terraces. Close examination of the chapter shows however that only four of the eighty paragraphs contain his specific merits of all-seating, and that most of it deals with his reasons to counter some of the arguments of those wishing to retain terraces and the financing and implementation of all-seating. Taylor wrote more about comfort than safety, although there is an argument that his comments on supporters being jostled or moved about by swaying or surging could also relate to safety. Having read his entire report several times I can find only two other justifications for Taylor's comment that sitting is safer.

His comment that, *'Those monitoring numbers will know exactly how many there are without having to count them in or assess density by visual impression'*, is of questionable relevance as all areas, whether standing or seated, have set capacities with the numbers entered controlled by turnstiles.

Taylor's statement that whilst there will still be scope for crowd pressure on stairways, *'involuntary and uncontrolled movements occasioned by incidents in the game are effectively eliminated'*, and his comments that numbered seat tickets help identify forgeries that could lead to inflated numbers on terraces, are considered in the next chapter.

Lord Taylor made a very valid statement that *'safety and crowd control are inter-dependant'* and this along with his comments that with CCTV and numbered tickets seating has *'distinct advantages in crowd control'*, will also be considered later.

Having studied the report in detail I wrote back to the Minister for Sport, asking why the Government said it supported the recommendations of the Taylor Report, when at least fifteen of these had not been implemented. The reply from Colin Burton of the Ministerial Support Team was one of the more feeble attempts I've seen to defend the indefensible.

Mr Burton confirmed that the Government continues *'its general support for the Taylor Report'*, although the insertion of 'general' was a change from the original DCMS letter. He pointed out that some of Taylor's 76 recommendations were for the Government, including numbers 1 – 4 about all-seater accommodation, but that many were the responsibility of others, such as the police, football authorities etc, and therefore the responsibility lies with the other parties.

Mr Burton however failed to mention that contained in recommendations 1 – 4, which he accepted were for the

Government, was the recommendation that all designated stadia, not only football grounds, should be all-seated. He was therefore admitting that implementing all-seating at rugby grounds was an action which Taylor recommended for the Government to carry out, but did not explain why although they supported the recommendations, they had not implemented this.

Even more strangely, Mr Burton noted that I had stated that a number of recommendations do not always occur. He commented, *'that does, of course, mean that they have, in general, been implemented but there are occasions where they may not be carried out'*. I somehow suspect that Lord Taylor expected his recommendations to be carried out all the time, not just when it was convenient. The large number of Taylor's recommendations that have not been implemented undermines the argument that all-seating must remain because it was recommended by the Taylor Report.

Only a fool would not thank Lord Justice Taylor for his contribution to making it safe to watch football, but it should be considered that his report was written when hooliganism was a major (albeit already reducing) problem, many grounds suffered from lack of investment and there was inadequate safety culture within the game. As we have seen, not all of Taylor's recommendations were implemented and with all the changes that have occurred in the last twenty years, it seems that there is now a strong case for reviewing his all-seater recommendation.

CHAPTER SEVENTEEN

SAFETY & INJURIES

Safety

One would imagine that with safety commonly perceived as the main justification for all-seater stadia, those who oppose standing areas would present a strong safety argument to support their views. It is however the opposite that is true.

None of the various bodies who replied to my letters gave any specific reasons as to why they considered standing to be less safe than sitting. Neither the FA or Football League mentioned safety, and the police, DCMS and FLA either referred to the Taylor Report or made only general statements.

Lord Taylor's crucial statement refers to seating doing more to achieve the objectives of safety, behaviour and crowd control than any other *single* measure, but doesn't mean that a package of other measures could not work as well or better. He writes surprisingly little to support his statement that seating is safer. The reasons he gives in support of his conclusion are that numbers can be monitored without counting, that uncontrolled movements (surging) are eliminated and that numbered seats help prevent forgeries.

Taylor's comment that in seated areas exact numbers can be known without counting, seems odd given that the strength of his recommendations in both reports that capacities are set and numbers entering controlled. Yes one can see if a seated area is roughly full and therefore from the number of seats know how many people are in it, but one can also know the same information on a terrace from a turnstile count. If too many people aren't allowed onto a terrace it cannot become overcrowded. As seen at Ellis Park, seated areas can also become overcrowded, and it is just as necessary to control numbers entering these. What is crucial for both is that there is a quick means of escape should any emergency or unforeseen circumstance occur. As I have been told countless times – people died at Hillsborough because of fences not terraces. Given that supporters are always counted in to both seats and terraces, Taylor's comment that it is not necessary to count those in a seated area to know how many are present seems to be of little relevance.

Surging and swaying used to be a regular occurrences on some terraces. On Liverpool's Kop the crowd would sway, scarves aloft, to sing You'll Never Walk Alone, and anyone watching film of 1970's matches at Anfield will see fans surge forward every time Liverpool scored at the Kop end. Surging resulted from either a largely involuntary reaction to an event on the pitch, such as a goal being scored, or was generated by a group of fans deliberately pushing forward. It was seen as a part of terrace culture by those who wanted to be in an area where it took place. Such crowd movement did not occur on all terraces and on those where it was seen, tended to be mainly in the central sections behind the goal.

However such swaying and surging does not occur on terraces today. Longer crush barriers allow far shorter unhindered runs, so it would be physically impossible for old style surges to take place. Crowd density is lower and surging is simply not part of modern-day terrace culture. In rail seats, with a barrier between every row of one or two people, surging to any degree is impossible.

In the days before all-seater stadia those supporters in seats generally sat passively, only standing to applaud a goal. For many however watching football is not a passive activity. There is an emotional involvement with the game, their club and fellow supporters, which does not fit well with sitting. Hence in all-seated grounds not only do we see persistent standing, but also communal expressions such as Manchester City's 'Poznan' celebration and West Brom's 'Boing Boing Baggies'. Perhaps these have replaced the surges and swaying, but would it not be better if such dynamics took place on a properly designed terrace?

Taylor is correct that numbered seats can help to highlight forgeries, as if two people attempt to occupy the same seat stewards will soon be called. Technology has however moved on from the time of the Taylor Report. Top clubs now have electronic entry systems where swipe cards or electronic strips on tickets are used to pass through the turnstile. These are far harder to forge and I have been unable to find any evidence that this occurs. Whilst the potential financial rewards from cloning or forging credit cards are high enough for some criminals to take the risk, they are unlikely to do so for the cost of a football ticket. If terraces were to be permitted at top grounds again it could easily be made a condition that such electronic tickets are mandatory.

Entry to all football grounds is now strictly controlled, with turnstiles closed once capacity is reached. If tickets were forged it is possible that those arriving late with genuine tickets may find the terrace closed, a situation that whilst undesirable, is unlikely to affect safety. Forged tickets cannot cause a terrace to be overcrowded and even if it did, a dangerous situation cannot occur if there are adequate means of escape – no fences.

It should be remembered that Lord Taylor was writing at a time when many grounds had huge terraces of up to 20,000 capacity, with far fewer safety measures than the modern standing areas that are now proposed. His conclusion that sitting is safer was made over twenty years ago and based on old style terracing, when crowd behaviour and safety culture was very different from today. At the time of Hillsborough few clubs had safety officers, but now every club has one. Safety Advisory Groups and the licensing system ensure that guidelines are followed so that supporters can watch football safely, whether in seats or on terraces. Safety Certificates are now reviewed annually, or after any incident in which the safety of the public may have been put at risk.

Any debate on safety should not be based on the situation in 1989, but on the current position. It is not relevant to consider the old, large, ill-managed and fenced terraces, or to presume that in modern all-seated stadia everyone will sit down. The relevant comparison is between all-seated grounds where often many supporters will stand in front of their seats for all or part of the match, and modern terrace or convertible areas which meet the stringent guidelines.

In all my enquiries no one has put forward a case as to why smaller modern terraces and rail seats are not safe. It has been argued that crowds are larger in the top divisions, but safety in one part of a ground is not materially affected by the stadium's overall capacity. Logically any regulation should be based on terrace design and capacity, rather than the total number of people at a match.

Perhaps the strongest argument that standing areas are not unsafe is that we still have twenty three football league grounds, countless non league grounds, and many rugby stadia, which have terraces. Further afield, many European football grounds have standing areas, including those at the highest level in Germany. As my travels round the country showed, our terraces work well and the safety officers in charge of them seem happy for them to remain. If terraces were not safe, there is no way that those responsible for safety on either a local or national level would allow them to stay.

Injuries

For some years the FLA have claimed that a higher rate of injuries occurs at grounds that retain terracing, which indicates that all-seated grounds are safer. After figures were repeatedly challenged by the Football Supporters Federation and Stand Up Sit Down, the FLA and the DCMS accepted that differences in the way statistics are collected by clubs, and the fact that they often reply on self reporting, means there are limitations to the conclusions that can be drawn.

In September 2011 Ruth Shaw wrote to me:

'*On a separate point, which you raised in an earlier e-mail about injury statistics, you quite rightly identify limitations to what can be inferred from the information available. It is not always possible to tell from the information provided by clubs whether injuries have occurred in seating or standing areas and it is not always possible to tell whether injuries have been sustained as a result of people standing in seated areas. It is my understanding that under current arrangements first aid personnel are not required to record the circumstances in which injuries were sustained, and a spectator may choose not to disclose this when receiving treatment.*'

In December 2008 Chris Nash carried out an in-depth analysis of the injury statistics which the FLA and DCMS were quoting to support their claim that standing is less safe than sitting. His report cast major doubt over both the accuracy and relevance of the data.

In order to calculate injury rates the FLA needed to know aggregate attendance figures for the season, but Chris found many errors in their data. For example, the 2005/6 FLA report showed a total for League Two attendances that was 180,000 more than is obtained from adding up the figures they showed for individual clubs. Darlington's club website gave a total attendance of 96,571 for their 23 home matches, but the FLA showed a figure of 198,179, more than twice the true number. For Barnet's LDV Trophy match with MK Dons the FLA quoted an attendance of 2,563, but the actual figure was just 991.

The FLA's attendance data (but not injuries) included many matches played abroad, such as the Germany v England game in Munich in 2001, as well as away fixtures for English clubs in European competitions. These figures were included in the Premier League attendances, inflating this total and hence skewing the comparison against grounds with standing areas. It was clear that the injury rates quoted by the FLA contained inaccuracies due to the use of incorrect match attendance figures.

Each year clubs are required to send a return to the FLA detailing the number of injuries sustained within the season. The FLA's policy is to retain this data for six years, however when Chris requested copies of club returns he was told that those for 2005/6 and 2006/7 had been destroyed. For the years where copies of returns could be provided, he found that injury numbers supplied by clubs didn't always agree with the totals quoted by the FLA. Some clubs split injuries into those occurring inside and outside the ground, but it wasn't clear which the FLA used. Premier League club returns for 2001/2 showed a total of 835 injuries (794 occurring inside the ground), but the FLA list stated 850. Again it was clear that there were errors in the FLA's figures.

Putting aside inaccuracies in the data, a number of factors cast major doubt on the validity of the injury statistics to make conclusions about the relative safety of grounds with and without terracing. No grounds are all-standing, yet the injuries aren't split into the type of accommodation where injuries occurred. Neither though are most grounds in effect all-seated, as where terraces are not provided many have 'standing areas' where supporters stand in front of their seats.

The FLA had accepted that a range of factors affect injury levels, including the age of a stadium. Most grounds with standing areas are older, hence a higher injury rate would be expected for reasons unrelated to standing. This observation is supported by Chris's calculation that based on 2005/6 figures, the injury rate in grounds with new terraces was roughly half that at clubs where the terraces were old. Finally Chris noted that the total number of injuries in grounds with standing areas was exceeded by the overall number caused by scalds, suggesting that the removal of hot drinks and not standing areas is the way to improve safety!

Chris compared the injury rates at all-seated stadia and those with terracing in the then Leagues Two and Three. This showed a rate of one injury per 20,528 in grounds with terracing and one per 21,625 at all-seated clubs. Given the many variables this difference of 5% is certainly not statistically significant.

The 2007/8 figures showed a 61% increase in injuries. Chris noted that commenting on this the FLA said that injuries from two clubs were overstated as they had included pre-existing injuries and seemed to pass off a quadrupling of limb injuries as '*a change in reporting practice at one ground*'. There was no comparison between all-seated grounds and those with standing areas, but still much anti standing rhetoric. An '*increase in persistent standing at particular grounds*' was suggested as a possible reason for the sharp rise in injury rates, but no figures were shown to support this and the FLA admitted that '*they do not have firm enough evidence to be confident about this*'.

Chris's report concluded that:

'*Factors such as inclusion of games played abroad, the endemic errors in the attendances and failure to copy down figures from club returns are all basic failings in the data collection process. Without proper data, the arguments are like a house built on sand.*'

After examining the 2007/8 figures Chris added in his report's appendix:

'*The role of governmental organisations is to collect meaningful and reliable data and then conduct proper analysis on it. What the*

FLA *actually do is provide us with a largely worthless jumble of figures and then proceed to make vague, unsubstantiated claims on the back of them'.*

The tone of the FLA's replies, both to the UK Statistics Authority (who had been copied with the report) and to the FSF, was extremely dismissive. The FSF was descried as *'a small vocal pressure group'* and that it *'contends that the policy is solely about spectator safety and is underpinned by the statistics published by the FLA',* none of which are correct. The FLA accepted some but not all of the inaccuracies in their data. They highlighted the difficulty in obtaining *'coherent statistics of any kind out of the clubs',* a statement which probably did as much as Chris's report to question the validity of any conclusions drawn from injury figures.

The 2009/10 injury statistics that were published on the FLA's website in March 2011 showed the number of injuries and frequency of injury per spectator in each of the four league divisions, plus a breakdown of causes of injuries and part of body affected. Their annual figures normally include 92 clubs, plus English and Welsh international stadia, but this year six clubs and the Millennium Stadium didn't report. The total number of injuries from the 87 reporting clubs was 1,386, a rate of one injury per 24,938 spectators.

The rate of injuries increased down the divisions, with figures appearing to show that spectators were roughly twice as likely to be injured at a match in League Two than in the Premier League. The injury rate in all-seated grounds in Leagues One and Two was higher than for the Premiership and Championship clubs, showing that there is a relationship between divisional status and injuries. This could be due to factors such as age of ground, resources devoted to safety, or differences in reporting. This trend means that any comparison of grounds with standing in the lower two divisions, with all-seated stadia in all four divisions, is not valid. It also suggests that a range of factors affect the number of reported injuries, raising questions about the validity of any comparisons.

As we will see, the validity of any conclusions from these figures is highly questionable. Ruth Shaw kindly provided me with the reported injury figures for each club on which the FLA's summary was based. My initial analysis appeared to support the view that the injury rate is lower at all-seated grounds. A comparison of all-seated and grounds with terracing in Leagues One and Two showing roughly 25,400 spectators per injury at clubs with terracing and 35,800 at all-seated clubs; (figures are based on adding 10% to total published league match attendances as an estimate of additional spectators for cup games).

The many variables however mean that comparison is not straightforward. For example, including the attendances at nine home cup matches, Manchester United's 96 injuries equate to a rate of one per 21,367 spectators. This is higher than the average for the 18 clubs with standing areas. If one wishes to use injury figures to compare grounds with and without standing areas, one could therefore quite reasonably conclude that on average it is safer to watch a match at a lower league ground with terracing than it is to do so at the modern all-seated Old Trafford.

When I started to look at Premier League and Championship clubs (for which I added a nominal 20% to league crowds to cover cup matches) the huge range in injury rates cast major doubts over the validity of the data. With just 3 injuries Birmingham City have an injury rate of approximately one per 192,000 spectators and Bolton with 4, one per 125,000. In contrast Aston Villa's 44 injuries equate to 1 in 20,000 and Sunderland's 39 to one in 24,000. Why should there be such discrepancies? In the Championship, Derby with a new ground had 40 injuries at 1 in 40,000, but Ipswich in a largely old ground that might be expected to be less safe, just 7 at 1 in 164,000.

It seems extremely unlikely that Birmingham City's St Andrews ground is ten times safer than Villa Park a few miles up the road.

Similarly, it seems strange that Macclesfield reported 13 injuries, whilst Hereford, Torquay and Accrington, who all have larger crowds, had nil, one and two respectively. Why should there be such variance in the rate of injuries? The most obvious answer must be that it is due to reporting. Clubs have no set guidelines as to how injuries are recorded and reported, and it would appear that as a result the figures submitted to the FLA show huge inconsistencies.

West Ham's 8 injuries at 1 in 96,000 is one of the lowest rates, yet at Upton Park 8,000 to 12,000 supporters stand in front of their seats every game. The statistics therefore imply that this is safer than for example Reading where the vast majority sit but 22 were injured, a rate of 1 in 44,000. If the figures are to be believed we can presumably conclude that standing in front of seats is safer than sitting.

All figures (bar Manchester United which were exact) assume a nominal additional attendance for cup games over the published league figures, however any approximation for attendances is of little statistical significance in relation to the huge variation in injury figures between clubs.

My visit to Macclesfield helped to confirm the inaccuracies resulting from varied reporting of injuries. Not only do the club 'run a tight ship' in recording all incidents from wasp stings to scalds from drink spills, enabling them to reduce or eliminate risk where possible, but the figures they submit to the FLA include injuries from all events held at Moss Rose. Small music concerts, charity matches and five a side competitions are all supported with stewarding and first aid cover, with any incidents recorded in the club's overall injury figures. 42% of the injuries reported to the FLA for the 2009/10 season were minor injuries occurring to players in a community 5 a side competition at Moss Rose. These would have been included by the FLA in their figures that supposedly show that supporters are more likely to get injured at a ground with terracing. It is plain that the FLA are working with flawed data.

The following table shows a breakdown of the cause of injuries.

Cause	Injuries	% of Total
Trips, slips & falls	419	30.2
No details	216	15.6
Cuts	202	14.6
Hit by football	108	7.8
Scalds	77	5.6
Trapped limbs	74	5.3
Public order	73	5.3
Hit by object	53	3.8
Celebration	50	3.6
Wasp	43	3.1
Other	36	2.6
Fell off object / seat	31	2.2
Crush	4	0.3

Trips, slips and falls could of course occur in any area, but it is generally agreed that they are more likely to happen in older grounds where surfaces may be less even. There is no obvious cause of cuts in football grounds, but it seems unlikely that these would occur more on terraces than in seats. I was told at several clubs that being hit by the ball was their most common injury. It is more likely that supporters will be hit by footballs behind the goal (usually when players are warming up), which is where the majority of terraces are, so these injuries could have skewed the comparison to an extent. Were the terraces to be seated it is likely that as was suggested in my visit to Stevenage, more supporters would be injured in this way as it is harder to move to dodge the ball.

That only 30 more supporters were reported injured by public order incidents than being stung by wasps, illustrates the improvement in behaviour that we now see. Trapped limbs are most likely to be related to seats (crushed fingers in seats is a common problem, but rarely reported). The 50 celebration injuries are a fraction of those that occur, but are not reported, when supporters graze legs on seats as they celebrate goals. Just 4 crush injuries, which could have occurred in any area, show that overcrowding is not a problem on our terraces.

Following concerns by the FLA that injury rates were increasing, a study was carried out into consultations with first aid personnel at Villa Park in 2007/8. The results published in *Emergency Medical Journal* showed 78 contacts, none of which were critical. A third were unrelated to new injuries or illness, mostly pre-existing illnesses or *'opportunist presentation of exiting stable problems'*. Persistent standing takes place at every game at Villa Park.

Analysis by Chris Nash in 2008 and my own examination of the more recent figures, show that there are far too many variables, most notably in the collection of data, for any meaningful conclusions to be drawn on the relative injury rates for standing and sitting.

Whilst it is a commendable aim to seek to reduce the number of injuries, at any large gathering of people the occasional injury will occur and a balance has to be found between reasonable safety and enjoyment. If the balance is pushed too far towards preventing risk, we end up with examples of the sort of excessive health and safety zeal that the press love to pick up on. We could see hot drinks banned at football, nets at all sports grounds to protect the crowd from balls and supporters being told to remain in their seats to celebrate goals. What is clear though from the figures is that the rate of injuries at football matches is extremely low. It is safe to watch football whether the stadium is all-seated or has terraces.

CHAPTER EIGHTEEN

LESSONS FROM HILLSBOROUGH

Hillsborough was not caused by terracing, but by the failure to ensure that the stadium was safe, to plan, to manage the crowd, to learn from previous incidents and crucially by the fences that prevented escape. Lessons were learned from Hillsborough and as a result our football grounds are now as safe as can reasonably be expected (no mass gathering of people, whether for sport, music or travel can be guaranteed as totally safe). The Taylor Report said that *'standing is not intrinsically unsafe'* and did not put the blame for the loss of life on the fact that there were terraces at Hillsborough.

Lord Taylor's comments about the evidence of senior South Yorkshire Police Officers to his inquiry, and more recently the incidents at Exeter and Fulham, however suggest that perhaps the police have not learned all they should from the tragedy.

The key lesson learned from Hillsborough was that no longer could the safety of football supporters be largely ignored and hence systems have been set up to regulate and monitor safety. As is seen at many grounds in the UK and across Europe, safety can still be achieved when supporters have the choice to stand.

It is natural that survivors and bereaved families of those who lose their lives in disasters want action taken that will stop others dying in a similar manner. It's right that we should listen to the views of those most affected by tragedies, but should they have the final say on policy?

Safety improvements were made after the Bradford fire, but perhaps the greatest legacy of the Valley Parade tragedy was the Plastic Surgery and Burns Research Unit, that was set up at Bradford University. The pioneering unit, which has been partly funded by generous support of the people of Bradford, was founded by Professor David Sharpe, who treated many of the Valley Parade injured. Twenty five years to the day after the devastating fire, the UK's largest academic research centre in skin sciences was launched at the University of Bradford, a living memorial to those who died at Valley Parade.

Following the Ufton Nervet rail crash, where a train ploughed into a car parked on a level crossing by a suicidal driver, causing the death of five passengers, there were calls for seat belts to be fitted on trains. Peter Webster, whose daughter Emily died in the crash, took a petition to Downing Street and planned legal action to force seat belts to be fitted. It is highly understandable that a bereaved parent would focus their energies into seeking changes that they believed would prevent similar loss of life in future, however seat belts on trains would not give the safety benefits that one might initially think. Research by the Railway Safety & Standards Board showed that they would actually increase injures, mainly due to the strengthening of seats that would be required, which would reduce their ability to deform and absorb energy. For every one live saved they calculated that there would be an additional eight fatalities. The bereaved father was well intentioned, but not sufficiently well informed to be allowed to dictate policy.

Perhaps an even better example is the Automatic Train Protection (ATP) system, which the Hidden Inquiry after the 1988 Clapham rail crash recommended be introduced. It was however fitted on only a few trains. ATP would have prevented the 1999 crash at Ladbroke Grove near Paddington, in which 31 died after a train passed a red signal. The Cullen report into this accident also recommended that ATP, which would automatically stop a train passing a red signal, should be introduced. Instead of ATP, the

Government however installed the cheaper Train Protection & Warning System (TPWS), which considerably reduces risks, but is not a fully automatic computerised stopping system for all trains.

The general view in the rail industry was that ATP was not good value for money in terms of cost per life saved. It was accepted that it would prevent some accidents, but analysing historical accident data showed the cost to be £14 million per fatality saved. In short, money could be more effectively spent on other safety improvements. The Paddington Survivors Group, formed of survivors and bereaved families from the Ladbroke Grove crash, lobbied strongly for ATP to be installed. Their emotional pleas received much publicity, but the Government heeded advice from the rail industry, keeping ATP only as a long term aspiration.

It is right that the views of those who lost loved ones and those who were injured or tramaumatised from their experiences at Hillsborough, should be considered. It should however be recognised that perhaps their understandable emotional involvement means that those closest to the disaster are not best placed to make objective assesment of the situation.

The DCMS statement that, *'It is critical that any debate about this issue is done against the backdrop of the Hillsborough disaster and does not add to the burden of those affected by the tragedy'* is correct in that Hillsborough must be considered. It is however strange that the Government appeared to suggest that in the case of Hillsborough those affected should have more influence than that afforded to survivors groups from other tragedies.

I wrote back to the Minister for Sport, asking why the Government appears to give greater importance to the views of survivors and families of Hillsborough victims, than it does to those from other disasters. Quoting the earlier DCMS response, I suggested that perhaps the burden of those affected by Hillsborough could be lessened if the Government ensured that the *full* story of what happened that day is made public.

Peter Littlefair of the Ministerial Support Team replied as follows:.

'The point my colleague was making in the previous reply was that any debate is against the backdrop of Hillsborough and we must take on board lessons that are learned, the current approach to the issue of standing and safety generally at football followed the Lord Justice Taylor enquiry and report into the Hillsborough tragedy so it's absolutely right that it is one of the things we take into account.'

Whilst this failed to answer my question, it did not support the earlier letter's statement that the debate does not add to the burden of those affected by Hillsborough.

No one is saying that we should not learn lessons from Hillsborough, what I questioned was the level of influence given to some of the bereaved and survivors. It is understandable that those who lost loved ones don't want to see a change of policy on a key recommendation of the Taylor Report, however it is also understandable that they may not be looking at the wider picture.

It is disappointing that neither the Hillsborough Justice Campaign nor the Hillsborough Family Support Group replied to my letters. I understand that the view of both organisations is that standing should not be brought back, but that this opinion is not held by all individuals and that some may not be aware of the extent of official or unofficial standing that currently takes place in English football grounds (including Anfield). However many Liverpool supporters, including some who were at Hillsborough or lost family in the disaster, recognise that as the Taylor Report said, standing is not inherently unsafe, and favour a return to properly managed safe standing. The Daily Star survey in October 2011 found that just 5% of Liverpool supporters blamed the terraces for Hillsborough, 64%

backed standing areas being reintroduced and that 51% said they would stand if given the choice.

Finally, the most obvious lesson from Hillsborough is that caging supporters behind fences, in seated or standing areas, causes a major safety risk. If people can't escape from an emergency, whether it be a fire or overcrowding, casualties will result. The Taylor Report made recommendations for maximum heights of fences and the widths of emergency exit gates, but Lord Taylor's view was that fences had to remain. Behaviour has improved immensely since the 1980s and not only are fences no longer required, they would not be tolerated by supporters. We have learned from Hillsborough that never again must too many people be allowed into an area from which there is no escape.

CHAPTER NINETEEN

COMFORT AND DIVERSITY

Comfort and diversity seem to be strange arguments as to why standing shouldn't be permitted in the top two English leagues. On both issues one can debate the differences between standing and sitting, but surely the key is that no one is proposing to take away the choice to sit. If say 15% of a ground is converted to standing, does it matter that supporters who choose this area may be less comfortable or diverse than in the rest of the stadium?

Of course many people find it more comfortable to sit, but others prefer, and it could be argued find it more comfortable, to stand. As the Rochdale supporter told me at Spotlands, he finds it more comfortable to stand than to sit in the cramped seats at many away grounds. If to stand up is their preference how can it reasonably be argued that this should not be permitted because others say that they may find it less comfortable?

Many seats in football grounds are far from comfortable anyway, but are the FLA suggesting they should all be padded like those at Arsenal? Economy class seats on planes are less comfortable than Business Class, but does the Government ban the cheaper option? It would be more comfortable to have plenty of seats provided when waiting for a bus or train, but there's no compulsion for transport providers to do so. It's hardly comfortable being packed into a boiling hot underground train, but for a lot of people there's little choice but to travel this way. If football supporters don't feel comfortable on a terrace, they however have a choice – they can sit down. What a ridiculous argument it is to use comfort as part of the justification against standing.

It is true that as Ruth Shaw says, seating can provide a more defensible space for those who need or want it, including children, elderly people and those with disabilities. There is however no need for anyone who wants or needs to have this space to stand up – they can use the rest of the ground which is seated.

If diversity is used as an argument for the Government to dictate the type of spectator accommodation permissible for football supporters, why don't they do the same elsewhere? If diversity is a reason for regulation in football, why is it not in other sports, or perhaps the theatre or churches?

We want a wide range of people to be able to watch football, but why is it important that there is such a range in a particular area of a stadium? Does it matter if the majority of older people and young children choose not to use one section of a ground? If diversity is important for standing areas one could probably make a greater argument for the best seats at Premier League grounds. How many lower income families or groups of teenagers does one see in the prime seats? Less than there are women and children on terraces I would suggest.

Ruth Shaw asked whether any research had been carried out on the diversity of spectators using rail seats in Germany. My response was to suggest that we look closer to home – at the 23 Football League grounds that still have standing areas. As we have seen, these terraces are popular with young people and families, and both male and female supporters of all ages can be found standing on them. The proportion of older supporters and women who wish to stand is lower than it is of young males, but significant numbers do prefer to stand.

On the whole most disabled supporters probably prefer or need to sit, although this is not always the case. I've seen blind supporters standing both on a terrace and in a seated area. Just because they are unable or prefer not to stand, however does not mean that disabled supporters wish to deny others the choice to do so. Level Playing Field (the trading name of the National Association of Disabled Supporters), gave me the following official statement in November 2011:

'Level Playing Field has a neutral position on the Safe Standing campaign. In principle, we have no objection to safe standing areas per se providing that they do not impact on facilities/services for disabled fans or hinder their associated views and sightlines (both to the front and to the side). However, we also feel that any future or existing safe standing areas should be fully inclusive with equal accommodation provided within such areas for wheelchair users and fans that require easy access or amenity seating. Finally, the introduction of any safe standing areas should not bring about differential ticket pricing and seating allocations that were not equally available to disabled fans and the overall allocation of wheelchair user spaces and easy access and amenity seats within a stadium (in relation to the stadium capacity) should not be reduced.

Level Playing Field is also concerned about the increasing amount of persistent standing that is currently taking place across the game which is often to the detriment of disabled fans and other fans such as children and people of shorter stature. Furthermore, we remain concerned about ad-hoc standing (i.e. at moments of excitement); the latter is particularly disruptive given that these are the moments of a game that everyone wants to see; we are campaigning for all elevated positions to overcome these issues by the use of proper and smart design and improvements (either new or retrospective) or through the utilisation of 'super-risers' or 'seat kills' where appropriate and we'd appreciate everyone's support of these aims.'

Supporters of short stature or who find it hard to stand are those most affected by persistent standing in seated areas, and some people are unable to attend away matches when they know everyone will stand. Providing designated standing areas almost always stops persistent standing, thereby helping these supporters and adding to diversity.

If the diversity argument is relevant, it is more so in favour of the choice to stand. Standing is preferred by many younger supporters, some who do not attend matches where they will have to sit. The average age of those attending Premier League matches is now mid forties, something that should be of concern to those who run the game. There are plenty of children at matches, but far fewer teenagers and young adults than used to be seen. Many simply can't afford the prices, or are put off by the more sterile atmosphere, so become lost to the game.

Standing is usually cheaper than sitting, and hence can make football available to young people and others of lower income, who may not be able to afford seat tickets. For example, Scunthorpe United appreciate that they are in not in an affluent area and offer cheaper terrace tickets to help enable the less well off to come to games. We all want diversity of football supporters, but this can be best achieved by offering affordable tickets with options to either sit or stand. My observations have found no less, and quite possibly greater diversity of supporters at those grounds with terraces than one finds in Premier League grounds. Surely providing choice must increase not reduce diversity.

CHAPTER TWENTY

CROWD MANAGEMENT & DISORDER

A key argument from those who oppose the choice to stand is that all-seated stadia have helped to improve crowd management and behaviour. It is said that to permit standing could have a detrimental impact on control of supporters and lead to disorder.

The Football Association stated that it is far easier to deal with a potential disturbance in a seated area, as CCTV with numbered seats and tickets can identify those causing the trouble. The Taylor Report makes the same comments as part of its justification for all-seating. These however are the only specific examples I have been able to find as to why all-seating may improve crowd control and behaviour.

It is debatable both as to whether a disturbance is more likely to occur in a standing than a seated area, and in which type of accomodation it is easiest to deal with it. While Taylor states that CCTV and numbered seats make it easier in a seated area, the common view of the safety officers who I questioned in my visits around the clubs with terracing was that it is harder to eject supporters from the seats. To overcome the dificulties in removing supporters from seats, it is common for police or stewards to wait until a supporter goes to the concourse at half time and deal with them there, something that can be done equally well in a standing as a seated area.

The argument that numbered seats and tickets facilitate

identification of offenders breaks down if supporters do not sit in designated seats. This may happen where supporters choose to sit elsewhere, or where seating is unallocated as commonly happens at grounds across the country. If it were a true concern would the police permit unallocated seating?

The Football League's statement that the current legislation relating to all-seater stadia in the top two divisions has led to clubs working with the safety authorities to deliver a strong record of improvement in crowd management and behaviour, does *not* say that it is all-seating that has been beneficial. It is the licensing system and Safety Advisory Groups that have led to clubs working closely with safety authorities, not the all-seater ruling. The licensing system applies to all four divisions, not just the top two, and there has been a similar improvement in behaviour in Leagues One and Two, where more than twenty clubs still have terraces. The wording from the Football League is another example of a statement that initially appears to support the anti standing argument, but on closer examination does not.

Whilst I don't doubt that some people believe that all-seating has led to improved crowd control and behaviour, there seems to be little if any firm evidence to support this argument. It is thankfully true that the behaviour of football supporters (or more accurately the minority who caused problems) has improved since the mid 1980s. However, as already discussed, this improvement was occurring prior to Hillsborough and even more so prior to grounds in the top two divisions becoming all-seated. It should also be considered that many supporters still stand, either on terraces or in front of seats, and that the improvement in behaviour has occurred despite this.

With the lack of any firm evidence that all-seating leads to improved behaviour, I investigated the Home Office arrest figures, comparing the arrest rates for League One and Two clubs with terraces and those that are all-seated. Restricting analysis to the lower two leagues makes a fairer comparison than attempting to compare clubs may average gates of not much more than couple of thousand with the Premier League clubs who attract up to 75,000.

The following tables compare arrest rates of home supporters per 100,000 total attendance at League One and Two clubs. The figures should only be taken as approximate as they are based on total league match attendances including away supporters, with a nominal 10% added to cover cup matches.

Season 2008/9

ALL-SEATED GROUNDS	Arrests Home Fans	Arrests per 100,000	CLUBS WITH TERRACES	Arrests Home Fans	Arrests per 100,000
Darlington	15	24.47	Aldershot	21	30.62
Millwall	42	22.47	Lincoln City	13	15.78
Leeds United	85	17.07	Barnet	5	11.11
Huddersfield Town	45	16.73	Rochdale	7	10.39
Tranmere Rovers	22	16.00	Carlisle	10	7.65
AFC Bournemouth	12	11.64	Macclesfield	3	7.56
Colchester United	12	11.29	Chesterfield	5	6.93
Luton Town	13	10.33	Scunthorpe	7	6.68
Grimsby Town	9	9.62	Brentford	7	5.87
Gillingham	9	8.11	Hereford	4	5.85
Rotherham United	5	6.99	Bristol Rovers	7	4.67
Crewe Alexandra	5	5.33	Morecambe	2	4.44
Brighton & Hove A.	6	4.71	Hartlepool	3	3.74

ALL-SEATED GROUNDS			CLUBS WITH TERRACES		
	Arrests Home Fans	Arrests per 100,000		Arrests Home Fans	Arrests per 100,000
Leicester City	19	4.49	Cheltenham	2	2.48
Bury	3	4.29	Dagenham	1	2.34
Walsall	4	4.18	Exeter City	1	1.94
Notts County	3	3.23	Peterborough	1	0.63
Oldham Athletic	3	2.55	Accrington	0	0
MK Dons	5	2.27	Wycombe	0	0
Swindon Town	3	1.91	Yeovil Town	0	0
Bradford City	5	1.88			
Port Vale	2	1.73			
Southend United	2	1.22			
Northampton Town	1	0.92			
Shrewsbury Town	1	0.84			
Stockport County	1	0.78			
Chester	0	0			
Leyton Orient	0	0			

Season 2009/10

ALL-SEATED GROUNDS			CLUBS WITH TERRACES		
	Arrests Home Fans	Arrests per 100,000		Arrests Home Fans	Arrests per 100,000
Port Vale	34	32.01	Barnet	4	9.29
Tranmere	35	29.52	Lincoln City	7	9.12
Leeds United	72	13.88	Rochdale	5	6.93
Grimsby Town	11	11.88	Aldershot	4	6.22
AFC Bournemouth	12	10.03	Carlisle Utd.	5	4.59
Swindon Town	15	8.55	Chesterfield	3	3.73
Millwall	16	7.06	Brentford	4	3.18
Gillingham	9	6.79	Wycombe	1	0.86
Colchester United	7	6.05	Bristol Rovers	0	0
Southampton	24	5.47	Exeter City	0	0
Stockport County	5	5.41	Yeovil Town	0	0
Darlington	2	4.92	Hartlepool	0	0
Notts County	7	4.55	Burton A.	0	0
Charlton Athletic	13	3.57	Cheltenham	0	0
Crewe Alexandra	3	3.52	Torquay	0	0
Shrewsbury Town	3	2.62	Morecambe	0	0
Southend United	4	2.48	Hereford	0	0
Walsall	2	2.38	Dagenham	0	0

ALL-SEATED GROUNDS			CLUBS WITH TERRACES		
	Arrests Home Fans	Arrests per 100,000		Arrests Home Fans	Arrests per 100,000
Northampton Town	2	2.16	Accrington	0	0
Norwich City	9	1.75	Macclesfield	0	0
Huddersfield Town	5	1.66			
Bradford City	3	1.26			
Oldham Athletic	1	1.03			
Leyton Orient	1	0.97			
MK Dons	2	0.93			
Brighton & Hove A.	1	0.74			
Rotherham United	0	0			
Bury	0	0			

These figures can be summarised as follows:

	ALL-SEATED GROUNDS	GROUNDS WITH TERRACES
	Arrests per 100,000	Arrests per 100,000
2008/9	7.18	5.39
2009/10	5.44	1.95
AVERAGE	6.24	3.74

This data not only contradicts the claim that to allow standing areas will increase disorder, but actually appears to suggest the opposite, there being more arrests of home supporters at clubs with all-seated grounds. It is accepted that the figures quoted are not exact and that there are differences between supporters of individual clubs, but in seeking to make evidence based arguments we can go only on the data available. This shows that terraces do not lead to increased arrests.

The claim that all-seating has led to improved crowd behaviour is also refuted by overall arrest figures. The following graph shows arrests inside and immediately outside grounds at league matches per 100,000 attendances, for all clubs over the period 1984 to 1998.

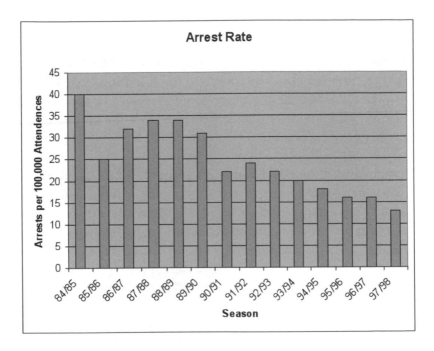

The graph clearly shows a drop from 40 arrests per 100,000 in 1984/5, to 34 in 1988/89 (the season of Hillsborough), then an almost steady drop to 1997/98. Total arrests fell from 7,140 in 1984/5 to 3,307 in 1997/8. By 2009/10 the arrest rate had fallen to around 9 per 100,000, less than 60% of the average for the four years after Taylor's all-seating deadline.

What is most interesting is that all-seating did not become a requirement in the top two divisions until the 1994/5 season, by which time arrests rates had already fallen to half the 1984/85 peak. Although the amount of terracing was reducing a year or two before Taylor's deadline, it is clear that the arrest rate was falling before the Football Spectators Act came into force in April 1990 and well before stadia had become all-seated. Arrests continued to fall after most grounds because all-seated. This reduction in arrests is despite additional offences such as pitch incursion and racist chanting being introduced, and the policy of prosecution wherever possible. Again the figures do not support the claim that all-seater stadia reduce disorder.

It is interesting to consider the experience of Coventry City, whose Highfield Road ground was converted to all-seating from 1981 to 1983, but then reverted to part terracing. A report for the Football Trust by Williams, Dunning & Murphy from the University of Leicester provides much useful information.

A month after Jimmy Hill's announcement that the ground was to be all-seated protest banners started to appear at home games, but Coventry went ahead with conversion in the summer of 1981. The club's aim was to eliminate hooliganism, regain lost support and appeal to a family audience. Prices were increased and matches made all ticket, to deter trouble makers and move 'up market'. High prices were set for away fans in order to deter them from attending.

Although increased prices reduced numbers of away supporters, disorder still occurred. Most notably, serious disturbances with over 100 seats damaged and a policeman receiving serious facial injuries after being struck by a seat at the match against Leeds, and 43 arrests after widespread fighting and vandalism against Oxford United. Average attendances reduced by over 25% in the first season of all-seating and season ticket sales for the following season fell by a third.

A survey of fans at a match against Luton Town in November 1982 elicited over 3,000 responses and provided data on the make up of the crowd. Asked whether they attended matches with relatives, 38% said that they had done so prior to all-seating and the same percentage that they did now the ground was all-seated, suggesting that conversion had failed to increase the number of families. The survey found little evidence that all-seating had increased the number of females, 12% of respondents being female, a similar proportion to a survey at Leicester and less than the 25% of females who had responded to a survey at Brentford. Over a third of females responding had watched from the terraces prior to conversion. The survey concluded that there was little evidence that all-seating had attracted proportionally more females or families to Highfield Road.

Asked if they thought Coventry City were right to invest in the all-seater scheme, only 30% of supporters (29.9% male, 31.3% female) said yes. Only 21% of the visiting Luton supporters said that they would like to see their club introduce such a scheme.

Coventry's unpopular and unsuccessful all-seating scheme lasted just three years before seats were taken out to restore some terrace areas. It had not only failed to stop hooliganism, but it hadn't resulted in the expected increase in female and family supporters.

Thirty years after Coventry's experience there are now more families and very rarely any disorder in football grounds. That this trend has occurred at grounds with and without terracing, but did not happen at Coventry in the 1980s, strongly suggests that the changes in behaviour are due to factors other than all-seating.

Lord Taylor is correct that 'safety and crowd control are inter-dependant', however there appears to be no evidence that permitting supporters to stand up as they watch football means that the crowd cannot be controlled. It is often said, and from my discussions with safety officers I would agree can be true, that it is easier to control a crowd that is seated than one that is standing. However, as I have been told by clubs and seen first hand, most standing crowds present no problem and with adequate stewarding standing supporters can be safely managed. Simply because it is less easy to steward does not mean that something should be prohibited.

CHAPTER TWENTY ONE

STANDING IN SEATED AREAS

In 2002 the FLA published a paper entitled '*Standing in Seated Areas at Football Grounds*', which examined the nature and causes of spectators standing in seated areas at Premier and Football League grounds. It concluded that, '*this is unacceptable from the point of view not merely of the clubs and the authorities but also for many spectators*' and identified '*various possible measures to tackle this matter*'. The report was produced in association with a number of bodies, but notably the only supporter representation was the National Association of Disabled Supporters. In September 2011 Ruth Shaw told me that the FLA were currently in the process of reviewing the joint statement.

The report lists five reasons why supporters may stand persistently:

1. They stand because inadequate sightlines obstruct their view or the seats are uncomfortable.

2. They cannot see because other spectators are standing.

3. They see supporters of the other team standing.

4. They positively prefer to stand.

5. They are demonstrating their opposition to the policies of the club or the Government.

My observation from many years of watching football and from talking to other supporters, is that by far the greatest reason that supporters stand is a strong positive preference. By standing they feel more involved in the event. It is natural to stand to sing to develop the atmosphere that many consider greatly enhances their enjoyment of watching football. There is much concern from fans that the atmosphere at British football matches is far less exciting than it was prior to all-seated stadia. The feeling of most supporters is that this is mainly as a consequence of the loss of standing areas. It's not just the sitting down, but the logistics of seating that make it harder for like minded supporters to gather together. Hence it is now normal for away supporters, a large proportion of whom tend to want to sing, to make more noise than the home fans.

It is true that some people have to stand because those in front are doing so, and that some stand for short periods to demonstrate solidarity with fellow supporters (Stand up for the champions etc). It should also be noted that persistent standing occurs not only in the UK, but that where there are no designated standing areas, is regularly observed across Europe. However it is very significant that at grounds in Football Leagues One and Two where a choice to use terracing is available, standing in seated areas rarely occurs.

The FLA's report addresses the reasons requiring spectators to sit at all-seated grounds under three headings; safety, crowd management and customer care.

Safety

'Spectators standing in these circumstances are not protected by any crush barriers. Instead they have a seat back in front of their legs. In the event of an incident, there would be nothing to prevent them from falling forwards onto the heads and upper bodies of the spectators in front. The falling spectators could themselves incur

lower limb injuries from the seats. The risk is exacerbated if spectators stand on the seats themselves.

The risk of such falls and the likelihood of a cascading effect increase along with the gradient of the seating deck. The majority of upper tiers and many single and lower tiers have gradients above the 25° that the Guide to Safety at Sports Grounds considers safe for any standing accommodation, even where this is equipped with crush barriers to the highest standard. Indeed many seating decks, particularly on upper tiers, have gradients close to the recommended safety maximum for seating of 34°. Standing in a seated area with such a gradient must by definition be treated as unsafe.

A further significant safety hazard arises if spectators stand on an upper or elevated tier. The front barrier or parapet in front of the seated spectators will normally be at a height of 800mm, rising to 1100mm at the foot of each gangway. The Green Guide recommends that 800mm is sufficiently high to protect spectators entering and leaving, but may not prevent a standing spectator from toppling forward. Raising the barrier would in many cases create a restricted view and might even encourage spectators to stand.'

Whilst persistent standing presents a theoretical risk, examination in fact shows it to be negligible in all but the steepest stands. Passive standing in seated areas has occurred to varying degrees in most grounds since the advent of all-seated stadia. In this time there has not been a serious accident involving those standing in front of their seats, no cascade effect has occurred, and no one has fallen over the edge of an upper tier (other than a Cardiff supporter who decided to stand on the front wall at Millwall, an action that no one can legislate for).

Whilst there having been no previous accident does not necessarily mean that a situation is safe, it must add weight to the case that the risk is low. Indeed as there have been thousands of games played where supporters have stood, with no significant incident occurring as a result, it must be concluded that the risk is very small. It should be noted that the Hillsborough disaster was preceded by a number of 'near misses', such as that described at QPR, where only the lack of fences prevented overcrowding leading to a potentially serious accident, but there have been no 'near misses' relating to standing in seated areas.

Furthermore, even prior to the all-seated ruling, spectators in seated areas have stood up at moments of excitement for many years, and there have been no significant accidents due to a cascade effect. In the last 50 years there have been around 40,000 games played in the top two divisions, and at an average of say 2.5 goals per game, there would have been 100,000 goals. With no major incident occurring as a result of 100,000 goal celebrations, the risk of such an event occurring must be extremely small. These figures relate to moments of excitement, which is the most dangerous time, so the risk of an accident occurring due to spectators standing passively behind their seats must be even less.

The degree of risk, such as it is, must vary considerably between stadia and within different areas of each stadium. Most grounds have at least some areas of single or lower tier, of reasonably low rake, where the risk of a cascade effect must be very small indeed. As there have been tens of thousands of goal celebrations in stands with steeper gradients, without a cascade occurring, the chances of this happening in a shallow stand during passive standing must be minute.

The FLA have never provided any statistics to support their concern that supporters are, or could be injured by falling onto seats or those in front. Discussion with several safety officers suggests that the injury rate is the same whether supporters stand or sit in seated areas. The concern about supporters falling onto the heads of those in front is only relevant if the person in front is sitting, so would not be a hazard in a designated standing area. The greatest measure of the degree of risk must surely be common sense. In most grounds it is very difficult to conceive that a significant accident could occur as a result of supporters standing passively in front of their seats. This view is privately held by many safety officers, although few are willing to state it publicly as this may undermine their club's attempts to stop the standing.

It is accepted that supporters can stand at moments of excitement, such as goals, and of course to enter and leave the ground, but standing passively throughout the game is not permitted. A report on safety at Old Trafford commissioned by Trafford Borough Council, and undertaken by the Warrington based independent consultants WS Atkins, examined the safety of supporters standing in seated areas. It concluded, not surprisingly, that the most dangerous time is at moments of excitement, such as when a goal is scored. The next most dangerous time is when fans are leaving the stadium, and the least dangerous time is passive standing during normal play.

The FLA report states that if supporters do not occupy their allocated positions spectator density may exceed recommended levels for seated and even for standing areas. It also says that, *'spectators standing side by side will, if they can, tend to occupy a greater lateral space (typically 550mm) than those who remain seated (typically 460mm). If the stand is full, standing spectators are likely to spill out into the gangways'.*

It is clearly important to keep aisles clear, although at many grounds stewards make little attempt to achieve this, and indeed they are often occupied by police or stewards themselves. The tendency of passive standing to cause aisles to be blocked will depend on factors such as seat widths, efficiency of stewards, and discipline of supporters. Observation however has shown that in most cases of widespread persistent standing aisles do not get blocked, but even if they do, with good stewarding it should not be too difficult a problem to overcome.

If it is known from previous experience that supporters are likely to stand and the width of seats means that aisles may become blocked, this could be overcome by not selling the end seat(s) on each row. In general however supporters have adequate room to stand side by side, or occasionally form a slightly staggered pattern.

Supporters standing in the aisles the previous season was quoted by Liverpool FC as the reason why Manchester United's allocation at Anfield was reduced by 1,000 in October 2011. Rather than reducing the number of seats sold per row, which would have alleviated the problem, the reduced number of supporters were simply given a smaller area, but at the same spectator density. The extra seats which normally are allocated to away fans were sold to Liverpool supporters. Similarly when West Ham's allocation was reduced at Nottingham Forest in 2004, away supporters were restricted to blocks in the centre of the terrace, with at least a thousand empty seats either side. Surely if it is considered that persistent standing is such a safety hazard as to merit cutting away allocations, the density of supporters should be reduced to alleviate the risk.

Finally under the heading of safety, the FLA say, '*Spectators purchase a seat in the reasonable expectation that they will be able to see the match. If those in front are standing, smaller spectators, in particular children, may be unable to see unless they stand on the seat. This constitutes a significant safety hazard.*'

It is of course right that those wishing to sit should be able to do so, but if every ground had advertised designated standing areas this would not be a problem. Supporters would simply purchase tickets for their preferred area. Children do sometimes stand on seats in order to see, which is a safety hazard, but again this could easily be resolved by providing choice to separate those who wish to stand from those who prefer to sit.

Crowd Management

The FLA report gives the following examples of why, *'standing in seated areas can have a number of potentially serious consequences'.*

'A seated crowd is easier to monitor in the interests of both safety and public order. It is easier for the ground management and police to identify potential problems in advance and respond before they become serious. Known troublemakers can be kept under observation. This becomes harder if spectators are standing.

Spectators who deliberately choose to stand for prolonged periods in seated areas are effectively refusing to accept the authority of the ground management and the stewards. While there is no automatic correlation between standing in seated areas and misbehaviour, there is evidence that some groups of standing spectators regularly adopt a hostile attitude to stewards and to the authorities generally. This can make it harder to tackle offensive conduct such as racist chanting or obscene language. Even where this does not lead to misbehaviour, standing spectators may not be in the mood to comply with reasonable requests (in particular to keep the gangways and exits clear) that may be for their own safety.'

It is claimed that a seated crowd is easier to manage than if spectators are standing. Whilst it is true, that for example observation of individual supporters may be less easy in a terrace situation, if supporters are simply standing passively in front of their allocated seats, this should be little different from a seated crowd. Whether supporters sit or stand there is no guarantee that they will occupy a particular seat, and unallocated seating is commonly used at many grounds. In 2004 when West Ham played at Millwall the police chose to make West Ham's tickets unallocated, allowing fans to sit where they chose. If the need to observe individual supporters is a justification for making them sit, why did the police choose to forego this 'benefit' at such a high risk fixture? In the lower divisions standing crowds on terracing are of course still managed perfectly adequately.

It has been argued that supporters are more likely to throw missiles if standing, but this does not relate to persistent standing. Any disorder would almost certainly occur at a time of controversy or excitement, when supporters would already be expected to be standing. A ground regulation banning standing is not likely to stop anyone who is sufficiently agitated as to cause trouble from getting out of their seat. As disorder is so rare, why the need to observe supporters so closely?

The FLA express concern that spectators who stand are effectively refusing to accept the authority of stewards, and that this can lead to confrontations. It could however be said that the problem is that supporters believe that there is no real safety risk in standing, and that the confrontation arises from stewards trying to enforce an unworkable regulation.

As we have seen, instances of disorder in grounds are now rare and the number of arrests is continuing to fall. There is widespread persistent standing in seated areas, but it seems no evidence to show that this results in disorder, or the 'potentially serious consequences' suggested by the FLA.

Customer Care

The FLA report states that:

'Once the spectators at the front of a seating deck stand, those behind them have no alternative but to do likewise, whether they wish to or not. Those who are unable to stand for prolonged periods, or who prefer not to are likely to suffer a significant loss of enjoyment. They cannot remedy this themselves.

Over the past ten years, there have been significant increases in the number of women, children and older people attending matches. If these are prevented from enjoying matches in popular areas, they may choose to stop coming rather than move to other areas, and hence may be lost to the game.'

All the customer care issues listed by the FLA relate to problems where some supporters wish to stand, and others do not. Clearly this does cause problems and needs to be resolved, but it should be easy to resolve by separating those who want to stand and those who don't. To some extent this should have already occurred, as the areas where supporters stand are well known to regular supporters, so those wishing to avoid them can simply purchase tickets elsewhere. The FLA comments however highlight a disadvantage of seats. On a terrace someone can move if unhappy with their position, but in a full seated stand one cannot.

Concluding that persistent standing in seated areas is against the public interest and should be eradicated as far as is reasonably practical, the FLA outlined possible measures to achieve this and who should be responsible for them. Whilst stating that, *'it would be preferable for standing in seated areas to be addressed primarily through the education, persuasion and positive management of spectators'*, the report accepted that other methods may be necessary, such as cutting capacities, reducing away allocations and withdrawing season tickets.

Almost ten years after the report was published we have seen all of these suggested methods attempted, but still supporters stand, and often in larger numbers. Allocations have been cut, supporters ejected and there has been much conflict between supporters and stewards, but with no lasting effect on the numbers standing. The FLA set as one of its objectives to, *'secure elimination of large-scale persistent standing by home supporters and a reduction in standing by visitors during the 2003/04 season'*. It has however proved impossible to stop.

Ruth Shaw's letter to me listed the same measures as the 2002 report suggested for addressing persistent standing. They have not worked until now, and there is no indication that they will start to do so. The FLA point out that ground management is responsible for the safety of spectators, and are looking to the clubs, local authorities and police to deal with persistent standing. The police have however said that it is not a matter for them, and increasingly clubs are turning a blind eye to standing in lower tiers, as they do not agree that this is unsafe.

John de Quidt, when FLA Chief Executive, said that it if a stand were to be closed due to standing it is very likely that the club would challenge the decision in the courts. He said it would be necessary to show that such action was proportional (to the risk) and that the FLA could not be sure of winning. That in the face of continued standing neither the FLA or any local authority have chosen to implement threats to close part of a ground and elicit a court hearing, suggests that perhaps even they accept that the safety risk would not justify such action.

Ruth Shaw's letter raised the question as to whether conversion of relatively small areas to standing would prevent persistent standing in seated areas and asked whether there was evidence available from other countries. I would suggest looking closer to home, to the 23 grounds with terraces where standing in seated areas rarely occurs, other than in the case of away supporters who are allocated only seating areas. It is a case of matching the demand and will vary according to the club and its support. This I would estimate to range from 10 to 25% of capacity, but could easily be determined by supporter surveys at each club.

The FLA say that they see persistent standing as a matter primarily for enforcement, rather than a reason to change the regulations, but the regulation is unworkable. They proposed nothing new to stop the standing and there seems no prospect of it diminishing. Supporters want to stand, consider it safe, and will continue to do so. A more realistic solution is required.

There is no doubt that persistent standing can cause a customer care issue, particularly where an entire away following stands, or for casual supporters who may not know which part of the ground to avoid if they want to sit. There is also a degree of safety risk if supporters stand in steep upper tiers, although this risk is greater at moments of excitement and when supporters leave the ground.

A solution is required, but this needs to be based on the realistic situation that supporters will stand in seated areas unless designated standing areas are provided. Supporters want choice and if it is not provided many will stand, although not necessarily in the most suitable areas of a ground. Permitting a reasonable proportion of safe terraces at all grounds would provide this choice and as is seen at the 23 grounds with standing accommodation, prevent standing in seated areas. Until safe terracing, rail or other convertible seats are provided, the common sense solution is to manage what already occurs by designating certain areas of all-seated grounds as allocated standing areas, where supporters may stand in front of their seat.

CHAPTER TWENTY TWO

FURTHER ARGUMENTS

We shall start looking at the remaining arguments against extending the choice to stand by considering another piece of misleading information, this time from the DCMS.

'As well as all grounds in the Premier League now being all-seater many of the clubs in Leagues 1 and 2 are also all-seater. This indicates that a number of clubs are content to provide all-seater accommodation even when not legally required.'

This statement ignores three crucial factors.

Firstly, the Football Foundation, a body that was set up to provide grants to all levels of football, has consistently refused to provide funds for standing areas at league grounds. Their reasoning is that should a club be required to become all-seated at a later date due to promotion, they may then require further funds for conversion. Some however believe that the underlying reason is a hidden government agenda of moving as many clubs as possible to all-seating. They won't provide funds for terraces even if clubs say that they understand that this would preclude them from future grants for possible conversion.

Football Foundation grants have been the major source of funding for many clubs as they have redeveloped or moved stadia, and given the choice of no money or all-seating, they have chosen the latter. It is rare that a lower league club is in a position where it can afford to turn down funding, but often it has been the Football Foundation policy rather than the club's preference that has resulted in grounds becoming all-seated. Clubs such as Burton Albion and Morecambe chose to have terraces on three sides of their new grounds, as they were self-funded and didn't rely on grants.

Secondly, all football clubs are ambitious and although for some simply surviving could be deemed as success, from directors to supporters everyone harbours a belief that one day their team can move up the leagues. Wigan, Oxford United and Wimbledon showed that the leap from non league to top flight football is possible, and seeing the likes of Swansea, Blackpool and Hull in the Premier League gives hope to many others. Smaller clubs such as Colchester, Scunthorpe and Doncaster, who played for many years in the lower leagues, have reached the Championship, giving every club the belief that one day they can achieve the same. With the hope that they will achieve Championship level football, some clubs have moved towards all-seating, so that they are ready for promotion and to avoid two sets of conversion costs.

Thirdly, some clubs in Leagues One and Two have previously played at Premier League or Championship level for at least three years, meaning that regulations required they were all-seated. The regulation does not permit clubs that have been all-seated to reintroduce standing, so even if they wanted to they have to remain all-seated. Contrary to the DCMS statement, they are all-seated because they are legally required.

Although the DCMS statement is correct in that some clubs have chosen to go all-seated, it is misleading as for many being all-seated has been their only realistic option.

It has been claimed that access for paramedics to deal with any casualties is more difficult in standing areas. In the old days of 10,000 plus supporters densely packed on fenced terraces with few gangways, this was a valid argument. Proposed new standing areas would be far smaller and have adequate aisles as outlined in the Green Guide. Common sense says that it must be easier to remove a casualty from a modern terrace than from amongst seats, which are often steeper and may be on a second or even third tier. Comments from the safety officers at clubs with terraces and my own observations, concur that it is in fact usually easier to deal with a casualty on a terrace than in seats.

The FA and Football League referred to changes in the game that have made it successful. It is true that the matchday environment has changed and the absence of hooligan behaviour is one reason for increased crowds. A major factor too is the television contracts, which generate the huge sums used to attract top players from around the world and take the game into living rooms across the country. Improved stadia have helped to increase crowds and to a less conformational atmosphere, as has the change towards treating supporters as customers, not hooligans. But where is the evidence that these improvements are due to the abolition of standing?

The FA's statement that, 'A *return to standing at football matches would be a retrograde step and would reverse a number of the advances that have made the game as accessible and successful as it is today'*, merits closer analysis. It forgets that we already have 23 league grounds with terraces, so it is not a return to, but an extension of standing that is being requested. It ignores the widespread standing in seated areas that effectively means we already have standing at Premiership and Championship grounds. How can it be a retrogade step to return to what we already have. Quite what the *'number of advances'* are I have no idea. It is yet another statement that on initial reading sounds like a convincing argument against the choice to stand, but on closer examination turns out to be pretty well meaningless.

The changes in diversity, behaviour and atmosphere that are seemingly linked with all-seater stadia have also occurred at those grounds with terraces. As I found, the matchday experience at these clubs is friendly, safe and enjoyable, often more so than at top league matches. In many all-seated grounds where these changes have taken place thousands supporters still stand. There has been no evidence presented to support the claim that to permit a proportion of supporters to stand at every match would reverse the 'advances' of the recent years.

And finally, customer care, the concept of how to treat a customer. Plainly a supporter who attends a match and finds they can't see because others are standing isn't being treated with care. Customer care therefore requires finding a realistic solution to persistent standing, but it also requires talking to all customers and trying to accommodate their requests. Both objectives could be met by providing a choice to either sit or stand at every ground.

PART FOUR

CAMPAIGNS FOR CHOICE

CHAPTER FOURTEEN

SAFE

The various campaigns for the choice to stand could fill in a book in themselves. In the next three chapters I have attempted to give just a brief history of the main campaigns, to highlight what has been achieved and the obstacles they faced.

After publication of the Taylor Report there had been opposition to the all-seater recommendation from supporters, and many clubs still felt the ruling unnecessary, but the policy was not going to be stopped. The Football Supporters Association (FSA) opposed all-seating, but no concerted campaign was mounted. As FA Secretary Graham Kelly told me on a radio phone-in, with Hillsborough so recent there was no appetite to oppose Taylor's recommendations. Kelly clearly believed that safe standing areas could have been retained, but that it would appear insensitive to oppose the Taylor Report. Tom Finn, West Ham's Secretary, told me a similar story when I met with him on behalf of the FSA. His view was that the terraces at Upton Park were safe (it was one of the few First Division grounds that had never installed fences), but that there was no way the ruling could be overturned.

My meeting with Tom Finn however highlighted the insular nature of many football supporters, something which often makes united campaigning difficult. I had written an article for a West Ham fanzine, for which the editor decided to entitle me as 'Chairman of West Ham Supporters Against All Seating'. Several supporters desperate to save the Upton Park terraces wrote to me, but having recently started a business I didn't have the time required to front a campaign. Furthermore, my initial investigations had shown that there was no prospect of the ruling being overturned. After meeting with Tom Finn I wrote a carefully worded report, which after several amendments he cleared for publication (as I was to find, many within the game hold views on standing that for various reasons they do not wish to make public). Instead of printing this, the fanzine editorial complained of the Football Supporters Association sticking their noses in and how we fight our own battles in the East End, a hopelessly unrealistic attitude that had no chance of saving the Upton Park terraces.

There was however a minor victory for the fans at Upton Park. It was announced that the East Terrace, commonly known as the Chicken Run, was to have seats installed during the 1993 close season. Fans were not happy and on the club's end of season video strains of 'Stick your f**king seats up your arse' could be heard coming from the Chicken Run! Responding to a demonstration by supporters the club asked then manager Billy Bonds to speak to the fans. Bonds told us he was 'gutted' that the terrace was to go and recalled his days of bombing down the wing with fans breathing down his neck. Vinnie Jones had enjoyed banter with the famous Chicken Run, the most celebrated occasion involving an inflatable sheep, but perhaps Paul Ince who kept well clear of the touchline on his first return to Upton Park, might have been happier to see it go. Pressure from the fans, backed by the club, persuaded Newham Council to give the terrace a stay of execution, until implementation of the new regulation meant there was no choice but for it to go all-seated.

Although there was no concerted campaign, across the country many supporters bitterly opposed the imposition of all-seating. Dougie Brimson's book *Rebellion* tells of red card protests at Old Trafford, Maine Road and Highfield Road, and just two years after Hillsborough of Liverpool supporters signing, '*You'll never seat the Kop*'.

At West Ham it wasn't just all-seating, but the way the club's board expected fans to pay for conversion that caused uproar. When supporters were told that they had to purchase bonds of £500 to £975 (equivalent £1900 in 2011) simply in order to have the right to buy a season ticket, rebellion ensued. Many refused to attend matches, some never to return, and a series of protests were organised by the newly formed Hammers' Independent Supporters' Association.

At the start of one game we saw the surreal sight of a man dressed as a chicken orchestrating a stand up sit down protest, where the entire terraces sat and all those in the seats stood. During a break in play in a dismal match with Everton a single fan ran onto the pitch, grabbed a corner flag, placed it on the centre spot and sat down. Others followed and the players had to be taken off as hundreds of supporters chanted for the board to be sacked. This was not hooliganism, but what most saw as legitimate protest against supporters being told they had to pay for a stadium that they didn't even want. Eventually the scheme was scrapped, the few hundred bonds that were sold failing to raise even the cost of advertising. Perhaps I shouldn't admit that I'm proud to have been one of those who ran onto the pitch and to have played my part in the downfall of the Hammers Bond Scheme.

One by one terraces across the country were knocked down or had seats installed, as clubs redeveloped or moved grounds. Whilst supporters were sad to see much loved grounds bulldozed and unhappy both at the loss of their traditional terraces and the option to stand, there was little they could do. It was not until 1999 that we had a proper campaign for the choice to stand.

In October 1999, Phill Gatenby, a Manchester City supporter, was on holiday in Portugal. He went to the local stadium on advice of the hotel manager (who said it was all-seated), but on arrival found there wasn't a single seat in the ground, just concrete that people sat on, with seat numbers painted on it. This got Phill thinking, what constitutes a seat? With City moving from Maine Road he wondered if such an area could be included in their new stadium.

Phill contacted a journalist at *The Independent* who had made a comment about 'the return of terracing'. He rang to say he'd put a little piece in the paper and see what support it received. In response Phill received a few phone calls from supportive fans and a campaign was born: SAFE – Standing Areas For Eastlands.

Soon afterwards the journalist called again and said UEFA were banning the 'seating' style seen in Portugal. Now each seat had to be a set measurement off the step and made from non-flammable material. Two days later he rang again, this time with positive news. A friend of his had just got back from Germany and was raving about the convertible standing areas there. Acquiring a computer from work and discovering the wonderful world of email and internet, Phill fired off a succession of newsletters to interested fans.

He contacted the then Minister for Sport, Kate Hoey, asking if such areas could be looked at for use here. Her reply was that she had been advised that they were decrepit and being phased out, and that the stadia being built to host the 2006 World Cup would be all-seated. She added that no way could England go back to 'terraces' because according to Tony Banks, the former sports minister heading England's 2006 bid, no grounds with standing could host the World Cup games. Of course not only did England fail to win the 2006 bid, but lost out to Germany, where 9 of the 10 grounds used had areas with convertible standing / seated systems.

After contacting a Hamburg fan group, Phill found that Hoey's reply was not correct. Hamburg's ground had just been redeveloped and included a convertible standing / seating area. All the grounds being used in the World Cup would have such areas built into the design (as it happened, all but Berlin had convertible areas). Armed with this information, Phill replied to Kate Hoey and was invited to meet her. She was genuinely interested and went to the FLA (who had given her the false information) suggesting they did their homework!

Phill made contact with the FSA, asking them to back the campaign. At a meeting in a Stockport pub it was agreed that the campaign would remain independent, but would have their support. SAFE then became Standing Areas for England and grew in numbers by the week, with word getting out in FSA publications and articles in *When Saturday Comes*.

In December 2000 the FSA funded a trip to Germany when Phill Gatenby with Mark Longden and Kevin Miles went to see stadiums at Werder Bremen, Schalke 04 and SV Hamburg. The three came away with considerable information on the different methods of standing areas in use by various clubs. A report was produced and copies sent to the Minister for Sport and other parties. As a result, Kate Hoey instructed the FLA to go to Hamburg and investigate the standing / seated area. Apparently the FLA were not keen and in the end were 'told' to go.

Adrian Goldberg, a presenter on BBC's *Watchdog*, contacted the campaign and a short piece was produced for the programme, with filming at Hamburg. It included an interview with Kate Hoey (unbeknown to her boss, Culture Secretary Chris Smith), who suggested that here was new technology that we should look at. The programme made headline news on the back pages of national newspapers, although the main focus of reporting was Hoey's comments rather than the issue itself. Some were very scathing towards her for wanting to bring standing back. Members of The Hillsborough Families Group were highly critical and many papers gave column inches recounting that tragic day in 1989 and interviewing families of those who died. Hoey had not however said that we should bring back standing, but merely that she had a duty to investigate new evidence brought to her about a new design of standing / seated areas.

In February 2001 Phill was asked to appear on the Discovery Channel in a debate about the return of standing. At his hotel in London the night before the show he received a phone call from Kate Hoey, telling him that the FLA had returned from Hamburg and had been asked to report back to her with their findings. Her boss, Chris Smith, had however intervened and requested the report went to him. Hoey had now seen copy of the FLA's report and the Government's response, which she was clearly not happy about. She faxed a copy to Phill, although officially the report wasn't to be released until the following morning.

Talk Sport had also contacted Phill, asking him to go on the show in the morning to discuss the report. A favourable Alan Brazil discussed the issue with Phill, who had to act as if he hadn't seen the report, yet teasingly asked if it had come from the Minister for Sport or someone else. Brazil took the bait and doubted it had come from Hoey, adding that he felt she had been pushed aside. In truth, the report had been prepared by Andy Burnham MP, Chris Smith's Private Parliamentary Secretary, and a rising star in the new Labour Government. Publicly, Burnham had been claiming to support the standing campaign in letters to supporters in his constituency, a contradiction that didn't go un-noticed with the FSF.

As soon as his TV recording ended, Phill made his way to Hoey's office. She was fuming that Smith had intervened and between them they produced a press release criticising the Culture Secretary. She got her secretary to type up the finished article and then printed off the piece for Phill to fax to the press associations – from an internet café the other side of the square, not her office!

Kate Hoey must have known that she was on borrowed time as Minister for Sport. I had heard her speak at an FSA meeting while she was still Shadow Sports Minister and it was clear that she both understood football supporters and was prepared to speak up for them. On her website Hoey writes that she is *'proudly independent minded'*. Such a philosophy does not go down well in Whitehall. In

April 2001, with Labour winning a second term in office, she was replaced by Richard Caborn. Whether her questioning of the Government line on standing areas in football grounds contributed to this decision we shall never know.

Caborn was a Sheffield MP. His response to any correspondence regarding standing, started with the words, '*I visited Hillsborough the day after the disaster…*' The campaign continued but progress was not easy.

The following month at the FSA's AGM the historic joining of two supporters' organisations took place. The FSA and the National Federation of Football Supporters Clubs merged, forming the Football Supporters' Federation (FSF). Phill spoke about the campaign and the meeting voted in favour of the safe standing campaign being supported by the FSF. At the following year's AGM at Highbury Phill was elected onto the National Council and Safe Standing became an official FSF campaign.

CHAPTER TWENTY FOUR

STAND UP SIT DOWN

It was during a particularly dull Championship match at Upton Park in early 2004 that I decided I could no longer just moan, but had to do something. Newham Council, under pressure from the FLA, were threatening to close the Bobby Moore Stand Lower Tier due to persistent standing. The club had sent out letters threatening to ban supporters and with the recently relegated team, bereft of the likes of Paulo Di Canio, Joe Cole and David James, struggling to make even the play offs, the Upton Park atmosphere was not good. A group of lads stood to try to get fans to sing. Soon stewards moved in and they were ejected from the ground. Something had to be done.

First I needed to gain greater understanding of the whole issue and to find a workable solution. After much research I produced a report which concluded:

'A significant proportion of supporters wish to watch football whilst standing, and as terraced areas are no longer permitted in the top two divisions, many choose to stand in seated areas. The desire of these supporters to stand is very high, and it will be very difficult to stop the persistent standing.

Unless some compromise can be reached there will be increasing conflict, which will have a negative impact on supporters and clubs, and occupy resources which the safety authorities could use to deal with more serious issues.

A common sense approach is required, with the parties concerned working together, and a realistic approach to safety management.

It is suggested that for a trial period, one or more areas of each ground should be selected as giving the least risk, and supporters in these areas permitted to stand in front of their seats.

A new initiative is required to reach a solution and football clubs should be encouraged to become involved in seeking a compromise solution.'

I had concluded that a new campaign was needed with the aim to work with all those involved, to gain agreement for supporters to stand in front of their seats in specified areas of all-seated grounds. This solution would manage what was already happening across the country, benefiting both supporters who prefer to stand and those who want to sit, and stopping the ongoing conflict with stewards. It would improve safety by allocating the most suitable areas of grounds for standing, and therefore preventing it occurring in steep upper tiers. In essence, it was a common sense solution to solve a problem to the benefit of all concerned. If only things were that simple!

A campaign needs a name and after several weeks of playing around with words and initials it suddenly hit me – 'Stand Up Sit Down' (SUSD). The name reflected that this was not just a campaign for those who want to stand, but to allow choice for all supporters. It was as much for people like my young niece who couldn't see if people stood, and a friend in his seventies who was unable to stand for ninety minutes, both of whom couldn't watch West Ham away, as it was for those who wanted to stand.

The campaign would be internet based and have two main lines of approach. The first was to show the strength of feeling about standing and raise the issue's profile, and the second to work behind the scenes with the various parties involved.

I was invited to present the campaign's proposals to the FSF National Council, who gave Stand Up Sit Down their unanimous support. We agreed that SUSD, with its specific aim of achieving managed standing in front of seats, should continue as a separate campaign, although we would work closely together. We also contacted Supporters Direct, a Government backed body involved in setting up supporters trusts, for whom Dave Boyle, Deputy Manager, told us, '*We need to have a debate on this issue and current policies simply aren't working*', adding the wise but often ignored words, '*supporters are the moral owners of the game of football*'.

Answering an appeal for help on the West Ham forum KUMB, a fellow supporter designed a website and an online petition was set up. On the launch date of 1st July 2004 I posted on a number of internet forums, finding much support. Fans were asked to sign the petition and enrol as members. There was no fee to join, but they would receive regular email updates and were showing their backing for the campaign's aims.

Members flooded in from across the country, the information they submitted showing a wide range of ages (average 30), a significant proportion of women and that around 10% expressed a preference to sit. Some members of both sexes in their fifties and sixties said they wanted to stand as they had done for many years, whilst some teenagers preferred to sit.

Several fanzines carried articles about Stand Up Sit Down and there was local radio and national press coverage. A few weeks after the launch I was interviewed on BBC Radio Five Live, along with John de Quidt, the Chief Executive of the FLA. De Quidt was very dismissive, saying that these campaigns come and go every so often, but that there was no real demand for standing areas. As the FLA was to find, Stand Up Sit Down did not go away, and nor did the desire of supporters to stand.

My aim was to get support from fans, for them to put pressure on their clubs and the clubs do the same with the football authorities. The Government would not listen to supporters and was saying that 'football' didn't want standing, so it was important to get those running the game to back the choice to stand.

Copies of my report were sent to all clubs in the top two English leagues and the football authorities in both England and Scotland. Replies were received from twelve clubs. Leicester City and Crewe Alexandra expressed support for our objectives as did two other Championship clubs who didn't wish to put this in writing. Encouraging replies were also received from Cardiff City, Portsmouth, Southampton and Manchester City.

Cardiff City Stadium Manager Wayne Nash wrote in November 2004, '*Your arguments are well placed and I think that by accepting that there are many areas where standing does cause safety concerns you have made a balanced and judged opinion. We at Cardiff City agree that orderly standing in front of seats is an option that could work in some areas and needs to be investigated. We believe this largely passive method of standing should be considered as low risk and would provide reasonable safety for fans.*'

Manchester City Chief Executive Alistair Mackintosh wrote, '*We have reviewed your document with interest. It is clearly a comprehensive and well prepared review which takes a balanced view of the standing issue. Whilst individuals within this organisation may have a number of views on this subject, the Club is constrained by the fact that at this time the view is not supported by the football authorities and indeed the Football Licensing Authority. We will clearly be watching this debate continue with great interest*'.

Replies from Sunderland, Bristol City, Derby and Manchester United advised that they didn't support *Stand Up Sit Down*'s proposals.

Bristol City Operations Manager Keith Draisey wrote, *'We cannot support your proposals, as we do not consider it to be a safe environment for supporters to stand in front of seats. Any movement of people may result in them falling over seats and causing injury to themselves or others'.*

The other three clubs didn't give specific objections other than to say that they had all-seater stadia and were putting out the message to supporters that they should remain seated.

Correspondence from Leicester City Chief Executive Tim Davies was of particular interest, as City were at that time in negotiation with Leicester Rugby Club with a view to possible ground sharing. A proportion of City fans wished to stand and many rugby supporters didn't want to move to a ground where they would have to sit. On 26th July 2004 he wrote saying:

'We are keen, as a club, to allow as much standing as our 'Health & Safety' certificate allows. We will work with supporters for a solution.'

'One has to bear in mind the cost of converting all seater stadiums to part-safe standing, thus the beauty of your proposal if the legislation issue can be overcome. We want to give our supporters what they want but are also aware of our need and duty to conform to all stadium legislation'.

At a Supporters Trust meeting on 2nd December 2004 Tim Davies announced his support for the return of 'Safe Standing' to the Walkers Stadium. He urged fans groups to lobby MPs, and get in touch with the Stand Up Sit Down campaign. Davies said he hoped the dual usage of the Stadium might lead to it being used a trial to see if this was viable.

Tim Davies was quoted in the Leicester Mercury on 4th December 2004:

'We are one of a number of clubs who are behind the Stand Up Sit Down campaign and have been looking into the idea for a while now, even before the ground-share proposal came to the fore. I have written to Sports Minister Richard Caborn and met Leicester East MP Keith Vaz in an attempt to try to get the Government together with the football authorities to overturn their decision about standing and sitting. But it is early days. I believe that if people want to stand and it is safe then they should be allowed to do so in areas which would not obstruct the view of those wishing to sit.*

*The idea must be financially practical as well, but if we were given the go-ahead, then as a football club we would introduce an area of the ground where supporters would be permitted to stand in front of their allocated seats. It could only help add to the atmosphere on match day'

Just a month later, writing to Stand Up Sit Down on 6th January Tim Davies's support was somewhat less emphatic:

'At Leicester City we believe in safety and in providing our fans with a matchday experience that they want. We also wish to follow all the legal requirements that we operate under. In our view, in an ideal world, we consider that in the 21st Century it must be possible to design a safe standing area at football grounds. Once this safe standing area has been designed, and if it is cost effective, we would request that the FLA would consider allowing safe standing, even if it is initially on a pilot basis'.

His toned down support for standing strongly suggested that he had been 'got at'. Someone had told him or Leicester City that their open support for standing was not welcome.

The Premier League invited me to talk to them, and I met with Cathy Long and a representative from the Football League, at their offices in Connaught Place. Both seemed supportive of our proposals, but as I was to find, what is said in private is often not repeated in public.

Neil Doncaster, Chief Executive of Norwich City, who were newly promoted to the Premier League, asked me to visit him as they had problems with the FLA Inspector threatening to close the Barclay Stand due to standing.

The club had met with supporters, who saw no problem with standing at the back of the stand, a view that Mr Doncaster clearly concurred with. There was disagreement as to whether the standing was 'persistent', and to show the FLA that supporters didn't stand for the whole game, the club arranged to get supporters to sit for a short time during one match so a photograph could be taken. I was told by an SUSD member that fans duly sat, singing, 'Sit down for the photograph' and the picture was sent to the inspector showing him that the City fans did not stand all the time.

Neil Doncaster drafted a statement of support for SUSD, but just before I left said he'd better check it with his press officer. Doncaster was quickly told that he could not so openly back a campaign for standing (it was considered that the FLA would take a dim view as it would undermine the club's claim that they were doing all they could to get supporters to sit). Instead he redrafted the following watered down statement.

'We recognise that a small number of our supporters prefer to stand at football matches, but are not allowed to do so under current rules.

We would fully support a thorough national re-investigation into the issue of standing at matches and the possibility of standing being allowed in certain seated areas where this is safe.'

West Ham Managing Director Paul Aldridge called me and plainly considered that standing in lower tiers as was occurring at Upton

Park was not a safety issue. I then spoke at length with the club's safety officer, John Ball, a likeable man who had joined West Ham after retiring from the police force. He told me that standing in seated areas was his biggest headache. He was receiving letters from supporters complaining that those standing were blocking their view and writing to those who stood threatening to ban them from Upton Park. Newham Council, who pushed by the FLA Inspector, were putting the club under constant pressure, saying they would revert the safety certificate for the Bobby Moore Lower Tier, forcing the club to close it. John Ball told me that he didn't consider standing in the lower tier to be unsafe, but that the club had to do all it could to ensure that the capacity wasn't cut, with the resulting loss of income.

My next port of call was therefore Newham Council and Steve Miller, the Chairman of the Safety Group – the man who signed the certificate for Upton Park. A West Ham supporter himself, the person blamed by the club for threatening to close the Bobby Moore Lower, was surprisingly realistic about the standing issue. He blamed it on pressure from the FLA to get people to sit and said the council have to do as they ask. As was becoming the norm, the story he told me and what he would put in writing were somewhat different.

Miller said that he cannot choose which laws he has to enforce, but suggested that the law relating to seating was ill thought out, and while stating that stadia must be all seated, it does not deal with people standing in seated areas. He said that it is a matter of interpretation and there is no case law relating to standing in the seats. Miller said that the council and West Ham were trying to reach a happy medium, and that the club were fed up with the problem. There had been some quite heated discussions on the subject, but he clearly had a lot of sympathy for my point of view.

As chair of West Ham's Safety Advisory Group, Miller invited me to one of their monthly meetings to outline SUSD's proposals. Also in attendance were the FLA Inspector Louisa Elliston, Paul Aldridge and John Ball, plus representatives from the Fire, Police and Ambulance services. I understand that one member of the group was most unhappy that I was present.

In Louisa Elliston, another ex police officer, I finally met someone who actually said they opposed standing, rather than seemingly just having to say they did in public. Responding to my presentation she said that we were asking them to accept a lower safety standard. I pointed out that very few people appeared to consider that standing in lower tiers causes a significant safety risk, and that in any case, there's no objection to supporters standing at moments of excitement, which has been shown to be the most dangerous time. She countered by saying that there has been a football disaster every ten years and feared that allowing standing would cause a return to 'terrace behaviour'. It was clear that Louisa Elliston felt very strongly on the issue, and that it was not only the safety of standing that concerned her, but her view that it would result in unruly behaviour. I found it hard to understand how simply legitimising what was already happening would lead to hooliganism.

The Police representative said that they do not have a view as such and don't have a specific safety role, other than to assist the club or deal with major incidents. The police he said, do not eject supporters for standing and only intervene in cases of disorderly behaviour.

I must have made an impression on the officer because the next season while walking back from St James' Park, I asked a policeman the way to Newcastle station. He told us the way, finishing with 'Mr Caton'. My son told me that with the shock of being addressed in name by a police officer 300 miles from home my face was a picture. He then introduced himself, but I hope wasn't too offended by my comment that they all look the same under those hats!

My plan for SUSD had been to get a small group of active members at each club, who would then liaise with the club to put forward our proposals. Unfortunately although membership was still growing, most were unwilling to do more than sign the petition, which reached over 13,000 names. Some wrote to their MPs and clubs, but few were prepared to do more. SUSD had been started and led by me, and although it had much support, there was only so much that one person could do, especially with a family to keep happy, a business to run, and of course a football team to follow! Then I started getting emails from Amanda (then Matthews, now Jacks). An articulate and intelligent lady living in East London, she shared my strong feelings on injustices and threw her enthusiasm and tenacity into SUSD. In January 2005 the two of us met with the FLA at their plush London offices.

Chief Executive John de Quidt, Louisa Elliston and Keith Sears made us very welcome, allowing us as much time as we required to put forward our case, contained in a 292 page dossier that we asked to be presented to the Minister for Sport. Naturally they didn't agree with our proposals, and told us that in their view standing in seated areas was worse than traditional standing areas. We didn't disagree, but of course standing areas are not available at the majority of grounds. The meeting covered many aspects of the issue, but the main area of discussion was safety.

The FLA considered that standing in seated areas constitutes an unacceptable safety risk, and that appropriate measures should be taken to stop it. We agreed that standing in steep upper tiers can cause a safety risk, but pointed out that by managing standing so it is in lower tiers, our proposals would actually improve safety over the current situation of uncontrolled standing.

We asked the FLA's opinion with regard to standing in seated areas at other events held in football grounds such as concerts and in particular, whether they considered that music fans who refuse to remain in their seats and dance through the performance are causing a safety hazard. The FLA said that safety assessment has to take account of the 'profile' of those attending an event and that this was different for a rock concert to a football match. They told us that there is a difference, because at a concert there is a single point of focus, whereas for football the action moves. They said that the side to side and bobbing movements that standing supporters may make in order to follow play, could lead them to overbalance onto spectators in front and a possible cascade effect.

It was at this point that we began to wonder whether the FLA officials truly believed what they were telling us, or if they simply had to concoct arguments to defend Government policy. Surely they could not seriously believe that it was OK to dance at a concert because the stage made a single point of focus, whereas someone moving the top part of the body slightly to follow play at football could cause a cascade effect?

We had an interesting discussion as to whether it is safer to celebrate a goal when already standing, or by jumping from one's seat. The FLA said that is based on many years of observing supporters, plus the fact that someone cannot jump out of a seat without leaving their feet on the ground, it is safer to be seated as this reduces the likelihood of people falling over. John de Quidt declined Amanda's invitation to demonstrate this, saying he wasn't getting involved in 'street theatre'.

We raised the point that some clubs had privately told us that they don't object to standing in certain seated areas, but that they cannot say this publicly, either because it would give mixed messages to supporters, or because they felt it would meet with disapproval by the FLA. This they feared would increase the chances of reduced ticket allocations or stand closures being imposed. Mr de Quidt responded that the FLA are quite accustomed to being used as a scapegoat by those who want to give the impression that they are being forced to take unpopular action, but that any suggestion that they would increase sanctions on a club that criticised it is outrageous.

I wrote comprehensive notes of the meeting and sent these to Mr de Quidt for approval. It was then that we realised quite how far apart our respective views were. I'd written the summary in such a way that showed areas where we agreed and the two party's respective opinions where we differed, but he was quite unhappy with some of this.

For example, we'd taken it as read that the FLA accepted that a significant proportion of supporters preferred to stand and I wrote this as a point of agreement. I had assumed that any disagreement would have been about numbers, not whether some supporters wish to stand. Mr de Quidt said that we had misrepresented the FLA and suggested that my wording was an attempt to fudge. Perhaps we should have asked the question and not assumed that although supporters stand on terraces and in front of seats, the FLA might think that this was not through preference.

Our discussions had mainly been about the SUSD proposal of managed standing in front of seats, but we also asked what would have been the FLA's response had we been asking for small terraces, such as those still permitted in the lower divisions, to be allowed at all grounds. The FLA view was that they would not have supported such proposals either and that they would like to see standing areas phased out from all league grounds.

John de Quidt spent a good deal of time reading our dossier, answering our questions and proposing amendments to my report of the meeting, for which we were grateful. The FLA submitted our dossier and proposals to Richard Caborn, the Minister for Sport, but with a recommendation that he did not accept them. Mr Caborn, a staunch opponent of standing, of course did just that.

The FLA told us that the issue has been well debated and saw little point in repeatedly covering the same arguments, although they were very happy to discuss any new ideas or initiatives – hence the meeting with SUSD. I continued to correspond with Mr de Quidt, but it was patently obvious that there was no prospect of him changing his view and advising the Government that regulations on standing should be relaxed.

We seemed to be facing a brick wall. The Government said that they were advised by the FLA that the regulations on standing should not be changed, and the FLA said that Government policy was not to change the regulation! The FLA had told us that they could not support our proposals because they amounted to, '*reintroduction of standing, moreover without the design safeguards that are now required on all standing terraces*'. They now accepted that persistent standing in front of seats was occurring, but said they were confident that this could be stopped. Mr de Quidt had said that, '*wherever possible, persistent standing should be tackled by a process of education and encouragement*', to which we had pointed out there was precious little education from stewards as they ejected supporters. Ejections, reduced away allocations and threats to close areas of grounds continued.

I had sent copies of my original report to all the main political parties in England, Wales and Scotland. Richard Caborn replied that Government policy remains that grounds in the top two divisions should be all seated. Lord Moynihan (Conservative Shadow Minister for Sport, but often referred to by supporters as that well known hockey hooligan after he ran on the pitch when Great Britain won the gold medal at the Seoul Olympics) said that he saw no real cause to reconsider the recommendations of the Taylor Report. More encouraging was Bob Russell MP, Liberal Democrat Sports Spokesman, who stated that he was a strong supporter of the right of football supporters to be able to stand during matches, and that within the Liberal Democrats we had strong support. Patricia Ferguson MSP, Scottish Minister for Tourism, Culture and Sport (Labour) stated that the Scottish Executive's position remained that stadia for SPL clubs should be all-seated and covered. Only the Lib Dems showed any support for standing.

We asked SUSD members to write to their MPs asking for support for our proposals. Generally those with no interest in football either wrote back saying we could not have standing because of Hillsborough, or sent the standard DCMS reply. A few however wrote letters of support, most notably:

Mike Hancock MP (Lib Dem) who said, '*I am backing this campaign and will do everything I can both inside and outside of Parliament to continue to support it. I will do everything possible to help your campaign.*'

Kate Hoey MP (Labour), '*I am a supporter of the right to stand safely at football matches and have always done so. When Minister I tried to move things forward but was thwarted by the Secretary of State and Downing Street. I agree with you that the Government has not even entered into reasonable dialogue. I will continue to do what I can to ensure that those in charge of football change their thinking on this issue*'.

Bob Russell MP (Lib Dem) said, '*As a Colchester United season ticket holder – who has resisted the invitation to sit in the Directors' Box as a guest because I prefer to stand with the fans on the terraces at Layer Road, which I have done for 48 years! – I fully support the concept of "safe standing areas". I am hoping that such provision will be included as part of the new Community Stadium which is being planned in Colchester. Good luck with your efforts.*'

David Clelland MP (Labour) wrote, '*I have considerable support for this particular campaign and I am enclosing a copy of an Early Day Motion that I tabled in the House of Commons in January 1990 on this very subject. I share your hope that a sensible compromise can be worked out and I will continue to express my view to the appropriate authorities.*'

Most of the support was from Labour and Lib Dem MPs, which was illustrated by an Early Day Motion asking the Government to reexamine the case for small sections of safe standing areas at football grounds. Of the 24 signatories, only 2 were Conservative MPs.

Taking note of the objections to our proposals by the FLA and the increasing reports from our members of heavy handed treatment by stewards, I wrote a further report, this time concentrating on the safety argument. The report concluded:

'There appears to be little prospect of the authorities stopping many supporters from continuing to stand for prolonged periods, with resulting customer care and in some cases, safety implications.

It is time to accept that the current regulations are unworkable and to allow managed standing in the most suitable areas, where most people, including (some) Safety Officers, find it hard to see that this causes a safety risk.

Such a solution will provide safety and customer care benefits for all concerned and stop the escalating conflict between supporters and stewards.'

By now SUSD was putting forward not only its proposals for standing in front of seats, but also for 'safe standing' areas to be permitted at all grounds. We started to look at those clubs who already had terraces and what could be done to protect these. A 'Safe Standing Day' was organised in conjunction with Wycombe Wanderers and a banner shown on Sky TV being held on the pitch by representatives of the club, supporters, the FSF and SUSD. Red or yellow card protests were organised at a number of grounds including Manchester City, Norwich and West Ham, the strength of feeling being illustrated by generous donations made to cover the printing costs.

A West Ham fan who had been ejected for standing made contact with Russell Brand, who used to stand with the fans until fame forced him into the posh seats. Brand agreed to be photographed handcuffed to the Upton Park gates in protest, but although a man from *The Sun* took an excellent picture, it was never published. Brand mentioned Stand Up Sit Down in his *Guardian* column, saying:

'Roy Keane famously bemoaned the culture of prawn sandwiches and indifferent fans in executive boxes. The constant renewal of strips, the spiralling ticket prices are expenses faithfully tolerated by football's hardcore support, but being forced to remain sedentary, it seems, is one restriction too many.'

A discussion forum was set up on the website that attracted much debate and got more supporters involved in the campaign. One of these, Barnet fan Chris Nash, joined Amanda and myself as leaders of SUSD. As seen in Chapter Seventeen, Chris's analytical accountant's mind proved to be a great asset, particularly in challenging injury statistics published by the FLA.

Amanda, Chris and I met every so often at the White Hart pub outside Liverpool Street station. It was always referred to as 'the pub where Amanda sent her eggs back', after she rejected her lunch there as overcooked on our first visit. A meeting of SUSD members held in Birmingham showed there was much enthusiasm, but it was hard to know where to take the campaign. We had gained media coverage, including a piece in *The Guardian* where Richard Caborn and I had presented the cases for and against standing, but fan pressure was not going to change the Government's policy. It was becoming clear that this was a battle that had to be won behind the scenes, albeit it with the assistance of fans to show the demand for a change.

The FSF Safe Standing campaign was ongoing and they had many contacts with a degree of influence. In Malcolm Clarke, a highly intelligent, likeable and well respected chairman, who had a place on the FA Council, they had someone well placed to articulate to both the media and decision makers on behalf of supporters. For some time Amanda, Chris and I debated as to whether we should approach the FSF with a view to merging the two campaigns. Amanda was busy with her job, plus had got involved on policing issues with the FSF, Chris with exams, and me with work, family and latterly writing, so none of us had the time we would have liked to devote to SUSD. The sticking point was however the FSF's campaign focussing almost entirely on the German style convertible seats and their unwillingness to openly campaign for managed standing in seated areas as a solution. They felt that the FSF could not be seen to be encouraging supporters to break the ground regulation, although like SUSD, neither would they tell supporters that they should sit. This we both agreed was not our role.

Eventually we decided that if the FSF would encompass our proposals for managed standing in front of seats as an interim solution and devote some resources to trying to prevent further loss of existing terraces, we would agree to a merger. It would have to be a merger though – I was not going to allow those words of John de Quidt a few weeks after the campaign started that, 'these campaigns come and go', apply to Stand Up Sit Down.

In September 2009 we met in the Sadler's Club at Walsall FC. Representing SUSD were myself, Amanda, Chris, plus Stuart Wood, a Manchester United fan living in Doncaster who had effectively run our online forum. Colin Hendrie, then leader of the FSF Safe Standing campaign, chaired the meeting. Agreement was reached and after five years Stand Up Sit Down ceased to exist as a separate campaign, although the forum continued to run on the Vitals Football website. We had however most certainly not given up and it was expected that the new merged campaign would go forward with renewed vigour.

CHAPTER TWENTY FIVE

SAFE STANDING

For some years the Football Supporters' Federation and Stand Up Sit Down campaigns had run side by side, often working together but with separate leadership and members. We both continued to lobby MPs and the FLA, Phill Gatenby becoming a particular thorn in John de Quidt's side as he tenaciously pursued reasonable answers.

I met with FSF Chairman Malcolm Clarke after our respective teams had played at the Britannia Stadium and we agreed that a new report should be produced outlining the case for safe standing. I compiled an initial report which was expanded by the FSF's Peter Daykin, and produced in a highly professional manner that would have been beyond the resources of SUSD. The foreword by Dr Anne Eyre, a Hillsborough survivor, included the sentence:

'I believe that the case for safe standing to be introduced at our major grounds needs to be carefully weighed and considered. This report is a reasoned contribution to that debate.'

In June 2007 the report was sent to football authorities, clubs, politicians and the media, but predictably was largely ignored by decision makers.

A month later a report commissioned by the Premier League into standing, for which Phill Gatenby had been interviewed on behalf of the FSF, was due to be launched on 7th July 2007, the day of the

London Bombings. The chaos in London meant that this had to be postponed, but it was never rescheduled. It has been strongly suggested that the report did not say what the Premier League wanted to hear, which is why it was quietly swept under the carpet.

In 2006, Kate Hoey had contacted the FSF, introducing them to Drivers Jonas, a company offering construction consultancy. They had seen the potential for safe standing areas in the UK and wanted to be ahead of the field in working with stadium designers should legislation change.

Drivers Jonas wanted to host a conference on the issue, bringing all key stakeholders together. This took place at Portcullis House, opposite the Houses of Parliament and coincided with the release of the FSF's Safe Standing Report. The DCMS, FLA, Premier League and others within 'the football community', MPs, media representatives and the FSF were invited to attend. The conference was well attended, although the DCMS and FLA declined to participate. The FLA had already declared their lack of attendance in that day's media, John de Quidt saying, *'The government has made its position clear, that is why we will not be attending. It is a forum designed to generate more heat than light. There is a difference between entering into a debate and participating in a circus.'*

However, the event became major news on the sports pages after Everton's Chief Executive Keith Wyness surprised those present by openly declaring that his club would be interested in looking at the possibility of a standing area for their proposed new stadium in Kirkby. Wyness asked for the issue to be kept private for now, but his comments were shown on Sky Sports News that evening and in the following day's papers. Condemnation came from various corners, most notably The Hillsborough Family Group. In the same way that Kate Hoey had been vilified for suggesting the issue be looked at, Wyness and Everton were strongly criticised, not for advocating standing, but for expressing a view that the issue was one that should be considered along with all other aspects of building a new stadium. Wyness retreated under such criticism and the possibility of standing areas was not mentioned publicly by Everton again.

Following the Walsall meeting, progress with the new merged campaign was initially slower than hoped and it was only after the FSF Fans' Parliament AGM at Arsenal's Emirates Stadium in July 2010 that things started moving forward as we'd envisaged. Chris Nash and I spoke at a session on standing and there was much support and enthusiasm from those present. A new leader was required and to my relief that I needn't feel guilty at not having the time, Chris and Stuart Wood both volunteered. It was agreed that they would share the post, something I felt would work well with their very different but complementing qualities.

In January 2011 Amanda accepted an offer to work full time for the FSF, concentrating on policing issues. She had already gained a well deserved reputation for helping fans who had been victims of unfair treatment by police, clubs and stewards, most notably Sunderland supporters who were recipients of brutal treatment by Northumbria police at Newcastle station. She however maintained an involvement in the Safe Standing Group.

Safe Standing moved forwards as a well organised and active campaign. Responsibilities for each area were divided amongst members and included publicity, political campaign, standing in seated areas, engineering and rail seats.

I took on 'Protection of Existing Terraces', something which I felt had been neglected as one by one perfectly safe standing areas were being lost when clubs moved or redeveloped. I wrote a report outlining the benefits of clubs retaining standing areas and our proposed solutions of the Morecambe style of modern terraces or convertible rail seats. This I took to the 23 league clubs with terraces, with the aim to identify terraces that were at risk and to work with clubs and supporters to try to keep the choice to stand. The results of these meetings you will have seen in Chapters Ten to Twelve.

Jon Darch, a Bristol City supporter who had lived for some time in Germany, joined the campaign as an expert on rail seats. Working closely with Eheim, a seat manufacture who have installed rail seats at a number of German grounds, plus their UK partner Ferco, Jon had a working demonstration unit made.

Jon set up his own website www.safestandingroadshow.co.uk, complementing the FSF's site and outlining the benefits of rail seats. At the invitation of clubs and supporters he took the road show with its rail seat demonstration unit around the country. Response from as far south as Portsmouth and as far north as Celtic was almost invariably positive. If the regulations permitted it, some would have undoubtedly installed rail seats to gain the benefits of increased capacity, overcome the problems from persistent standing and give their fans the choice they were asking for.

After the roadshow and open meeting was held in Liverpool, the FSF's Martin O'Hara gave interviews for a number of radio stations, explaining the benefits of rail seats and answering the points raised by a lady from Liverpool, who although not representing any particular group, was given considerable airtime to put forward her views. These misguided opinions included that if Safe Standing was to be permitted clubs will no longer need a safety certificate, seven people can stand in the same area as one seat, families and children will be excluded because they won't be able to see anything and Liverpool fans will be too traumatised to attend away games if they're forced to stand. It is a huge job to overcome the misconceptions of some people.

At the 2011 Fans Parliament in London Peter Daykin took over heading the Safe Standing campaign, which continued to be active in a number of areas. An online petition was launched calling for supporters to have the choice to watch football from safe standing areas, and as the book went to press had received over 13,000 signatures.

A strength of the FSF is the behind the scenes lobbying which it carries out. Much of this goes unpublicised, but it is this route that's most likely to lead to eventual success. Meetings are held with the football authorities, police, Safety Officers Association, Government and FLA, plus of course supporters across the country.

Relations with the FLA improved immensely after the appointment of Ruth Shaw as Chief Executive, the transformation in the organisation's outlook being quite amazing. The views of supporters are now actively sought and regular meetings held at the request of the FLA. Ruth Shaw has been both interested and helpful to me in the writing of this book, and gives the impression of someone who is genuinely keen to understand all the issues and form a considered opinion.

In December 2010 Liberal Democrat MP Don Foster put forward a Safe Standing Bill, starting his speech with the words:

'I beg to move that leave be given to bring in a Bill to give all football clubs the freedom to build, or maintain existing, safe standing sections in their stadia if they choose…'.

The FSF worked closely with Don Foster who chaired a meeting to discuss safe standing at which the three football authorities, Association of Safety Officers, FLA and FSF were represented. Encouraging FSF members to contact their MPs helped to gain 145 signatures for an Early Day Motion supporting the choice to stand.

The campaign is ongoing and as this book was completed the FSF had identified six Premier League Club Chief Executives who had all indicated that they would publicly back standing if other clubs would do likewise. Consideration was being given to approaching these clubs to put together a joint statement in support of safe standing. By the time you read this the campaign will have moved further forward and the latest updates can be seen on the FSF's website www.fsf.org.uk.

PART FIVE

CONCLUSIONS

CHAPTER TWENTY SIX

INCONSISTENCIES

Before moving onto conclusions we should consider some of the many examples where the arguments against the choice to stand are inconsistent or simply illogical. Maybe we should start with our country's media driven and highly inconsistent attitude to safety. The litigious society that leads to schools being shut after a couple of inches of snow and kids spending the day tobogganing at far greater risk than they'd have been in the playground. The nanny state that runs a continuous announcement asking people to hold the hand rail as they walk up a short flight of steps at Glasgow Queen Street station.

With regard to football, considerable resources have been directed to dealing with the relatively low risk of supporters standing in seated areas, when far greater hazards receive less attention. The greatest density of people and the most difficulty in moving about that I've experienced for many years, was on the concourse under the Arthur Wait stand at Crystal Palace. Such conditions would not be tolerated on a terrace and were commented on by many supporters, but although the Safety Advisory Group must be aware of them, no action seems to be taken to relieve congestion.

Not only does the movement of fans within the ground at half time and after matches create a greater safety risk than passive standing, but other greater hazards outside the stadium receive far less attention. At many grounds, having had the option only to sit to watch the match, supporters then walk en-mass to the railway station, many in the road, weaving through traffic. They stand queuing to enter the station, and again on crowded platforms, where approaching trains pass, often on electrified tracks, with no protective guarding. They then board crowded trains, with many people again having to stand. Supporters may stand on escalators on the journey to or from matches, and even within a few modern grounds. The risk of a domino effect is far greater than in seated areas of a football ground, but there is no pressure to modify escalator design to incorporate barriers or reduce user density, yet this is an area where accidents including fatalities do occur. In the 12 months to July 2011, thirty four London Underground passengers were injured and one killed in accidents on escalators.

This illogical approach to safety is not confined to football. For example, a series railway of accidents between 1991 and 2000 killed a total of 58 people, an average of six per year. Of course it was right that action was taken to improve safety, but was all of the huge sums spent the best use of funds? In the same period around 40,000 people were killed on British roads, where expenditure in areas such as crash barriers, lighting or by-passes, would give a far greater value in terms of lives saved. The report of the Ladbroke Grove Rail Enquiry observed that the expenditure to prevent a road fatality is around £0.1 million, whereas the cost per fatality prevented by fitting the hugely expensive TPWS rail safety system was 100 times less value at about £10 million. Many more lives could have been saved if this had been spent on road safety or in healthcare. To compound this illogical approach, much of the cost of safety works on the railways has been passed on to rail passengers, with the result that some will now choose to travel by road, and therefore actually face increased dangers.

Simple measures such as insisting all cars are painted in bright colours would save lives, yet there is no pressure to do this. It would be resisted by the consumer, yet with football it seems that customer's opinions are barely considered.

After witnessing a road accident when a motorcyclist wasn't wearing clothing which would have increased both his visibility and protection against injury, I wrote to the Department for Transport, asking whether the principle of safety over choice for football supporters also applied to the Government's policy with regard to transport.

The Department for Transport made some interesting comments:

'The Department continues to remind motorcyclists that they should make themselves as visible as possible when riding. The Highway Code prompts riders to wear fluorescent clothes or a brightly coloured helmet in the daytime and reflective clothing or strips in the dark. The Code also reminds riders that strong boots, gloves and suitable clothing may help to protect riders if they fall off.'

'However, the Government believes that the clothes motorcyclist wear continue to remain a matter of personal choice and there are currently no plans to make protective clothing compulsory'.

One therefore is led to ask why that in allowing personal choice for motorcyclists, the Department of Transport has a very different policy than Richard Caborn, the Minister for Sport, who had told me with regard to standing at football:

'The issue here is one of safety versus choice. While offering spectators a choice is desirable, ensuring their safety is essential and this must be our priority.'

Department of Transport figures for 2008 show that 491 motorcyclists were killed, and 21,057 injured. However, despite standing occurring either legitimately or in front of seats, there are very few injuries at football matches – 1,386 in 2009/10, most of which were minor, with just 83 supporters taken to hospital. In rough figures, a football supporter has a 1 in 25,000 likelihood of being injured at a match, whereas 1 in 50 motorcyclists can expect to receive a significant injury or be killed each year.

It is good that watching football is so safe, and of course injuries should be minimised where reasonably possible, but how can it be justified to allow motorcyclists the freedom to choose whether they use protective clothing that undoubtedly reduces casualties, while giving football fans no choice as to how they watch matches. An inconsistency which of course is heightened because modern standing has not even been demonstrated to be less safe than sitting.

The response to an accident in which many people die at once is an inquiry and huge sums spent on preventing a recurrence. Whilst this is not wrong, if a greater total are killed in ones and twos, there is less publicity or pressure to improve safety. Certain activities, including football, public transport and medical matters, attract disproportionate attention than for example, car accidents. However, surely safety should be assessed on objective factors, and not driven by emotion or the media.

The FLA's major concern with regard to standing in seated areas is that a cascade effect could occur, but common sense and the report by the independent consultants Atkins conclude the most hazardous time is at a moment of excitement, such as a goal. Many of the stands in which the FLA are concerned this domino effect could occur have been built in the last fifteen years, often with steep upper tiers, but to comply with existing regulations. The Taylor Report accepted that spectators will stand at moments of excitement, a fact which was therefore known when these stands were built. If the safety risk caused by persistent standing is such that sanctions have to be taken against clubs and supporters, surely the far greater risk from an accident occurring at a moment of excitement should mean that these steep stands should never have been allowed to be built.

In his programme notes for the home game against Newcastle in

March 2011, the Stoke City Chief Executive Tony Scholes wrote:

'Another glowing example of how far the club has progressed, both on and off the field, was provided by the outcome of a visit which we received from members of the Football Licensing Authority to last Sunday's FA Cup quarter final. They were full of praise for our stewarding and policing operation for the game as well as the behaviour of both sets of supporters.'

At the quarter final which the FLA had attended, the whole of West Ham's 4,500 travelling support had stood throughout the game, as did at least 500 City fans. There had been no announcements or attempts by stewards to get them to sit down. It seems strange that whilst elsewhere a handful of standing supporters may be threatened with ejection at a lower league match, when over 5,000 stood at Stoke the FLA chose to praise fans' behaviour.

Another strange inconsistency is the matter of the relative view from sitting or standing. FLA Inspector Louisa Elliston wrote to me with regard to persistent standing in the Bobby Moore Lower Tier at Upton Park, where thousands stand every match, with the comment that:

'there is the very real practical problem that an area designed for seated spectators would not allow standing spectators a clear view of the pitch without major structural changes to the profile of the viewing area'.

On a similar theme from the FLA, John de Quidt told us that sightlines for seated areas are based on the height of a person when they are seated, so that when standing supporters will be forced to stretch and strain to follow play down the wings, thereby increasing the risk of losing balance and falling. I have yet to witness even one supporter topple over as they watch a left winger dribble down the line.

To seek the view of supporters SUSD emailed our members, but not one said that they found the view worse when standing. If the FLA's comments were valid, would supporters still stand? The only examples we were able to find where the standing view is worse than sitting, is at the back of some lower tiers such as the Matthew Harding Stand at Stamford Bridge, where the ceiling is low and a higher position accentuates the 'post box' viewing effect.

However, whilst the FLA were claiming that supporters should stay in their seats to gain the optimum view, we found many examples where fans were being threatened with ejection or future allocation cuts, when they were having to stand, either because seats were too cramped or they couldn't see the whole pitch due to stadium design. SUSD asked our members to tell us about stadia where the supporters tended to stand for reasons of either comfort or view. These came into two categories: grounds such as Southend United and Luton Town where seats bolted onto existing terraces provide minimal legroom, and upper tiers at grounds such as Newcastle United and QPR where the near goal cannot easily be viewed from the seated position.

SUSD took up two examples with the clubs concerned and found that despite their failing attempts to stop fans standing, they had little interest in taking simple actions that would improve the view and hence encourage fans to stay in their seats.

Following West Ham's visit to QPR in October 2004, when leaflets had been distributed advising that if supporters stood the ticket allocation may be reduced for our next visit, I wrote to club Safety Officer Clive Doyle. My letter pointed out that fans had told us that they couldn't see the goal line from a seated position, so it was not surprising that they stood up. Mr Doyle's reply indicated that he was clearly not a supporter of Stand Up Sit Down!

'Obviously you have an open and declared stance on the standing issue which I respect although disagree with. Having monitored

your organisation's input to various national and local football supporter club sites I am aware that you have a number of people who visit those sites and agitate to promote your cause. This again is understandable and part of your strategy, however being an independent and professional employee of the club I look at the same issues from a different stand point.'

All tickets in the School End Upper Tier were marked *'partially obscured view'*, although supporters purchasing them were not aware of this until their tickets arrived in the post. Mr Doyle told us that this was, *'for the reason that some obscure areas of the pitch are not all within view whilst sat down not because it is impossible to see the key areas of the pitch'*, and that there is a *'yard of the edge of pitch that you cannot see but the sight lines do generally allow you to see the goals and goalmouths'*.

We found it hard to understand how one could not see a yard at the *edge* of the pitch, as it was the goal line that was obscured by the wall at the front of the stand. Furthermore, it was not just any yard of pitch and certainly not an 'obscure' one, but the most critical yard that was hidden – the goal!

Mr Doyle explained that his reason for being so against standing in a seated stadium was because some supporters may use this as cover to throw missiles at other fans or onto the pitch. It was however his following paragraph that spurred us on to pursue the issue at QPR.

'I hold the view that issues of obscured views in older grounds may have some legitimacy as indeed our tickets indicate, and if you are urging us to not sell such tickets then you are in effect urging QPR to dramatically reduce the away ticket allocation for West Ham. This I find strange and may upset many West Ham fans who were grateful to be at a local derby. Perhaps we ought to publish the interpretation of your suggestion on West Ham's supporter web sites for comment. Your letter if forwarded to our local authority

and the Football Licensing Authority will without doubt encourage a reduction in ticket allocation to West Ham fans in future seasons. Is this what you want? Are you really trying to stop and or reduce the allocation of tickets to West Ham fans?'

Taking up his suggestion I posted my letter and his reply on two West Ham supporter internet forums. The responses were not exactly complimentary about either the content or tone of his letter, and none were in agreement with what he had said.

I wrote back to Mr Doyle pointing out that one of the Green Guide recommendations is that seat design should ensure that spectators are encouraged to remain seated and do not have to stretch or strain to view an event. We also proposed the simple solution that if the pitch were to be moved forward (shortened) by about two metres, it would no longer be necessary for spectators to stand in order to see the end of the pitch and the whole goal.

Mr Doyle's response was to ask whether SUSD will be encouraging supporters to sit down when this gives a perfectly good view of the pitch. I replied saying that we didn't believe that it is the role of a supporter's organisation to tell people whether they should sit or stand. My letter also pointed out that this stand was one of fourteen that had been highlighted by SUSD members where seats did not appear to meet the Green Guide guidelines and that it was not only West Ham supporters who were complaining about the School End at QPR.

It was clear that we were getting nowhere with Mr Doyle, so a formal complaint that it was not possible to see the goal line while seated in the School End Upper Tier was sent to the Head of Health & Safety at Hammersmith & Fulham Council, the body responsible for licensing Loftus Road. Our letter made the simple suggestion that the pitch be shortened by two metres. We also brought the matter up with the FLA when meeting them later that month and were told that following SUSD's letter to Hammersmith Council, the restricted view seats in School End Upper Tier at Loftus Road would be discussed at the next QPR Safety Advisory Group meeting.

A while later QPR supporters wondered why the pitch had been moved forward. After much persistence SUSD had won a small victory and supporters in the School End Upper Tier could now see the whole pitch whilst seated. What we didn't understand was why a safety officer, who was so against standing, was unwilling to make this simple change that would reduce the need to stand in an upper tier.

At Upton Park it was new goal nets that obstructed views. From seats about half way back (including mine), when seated one has to view most of the pitch through the net, but when standing the different angle means that this proportion is much reduced. It had not been too much of a problem until new nets with a finer mesh were introduced. I wrote to the MD Paul Aldridge pointing out that the new nets were encouraging fans to stand, or at least giving them an excuse to do so. His response was that the nets had been specified by the team manager (Alan Pardew) and rather than the simple option of changing them to assist supporters and potentially reduce standing, he offered to relocate our season tickets. It seemed strange that here was a club under great pressure to reduce persistent standing and threatening to ban supporters, but was allowing the view of the team manager to prevail in a matter supposedly affecting safety of supporters. I wrote to the FLA Inspector and within a few weeks the nets were changed.

At some grounds the areas reserved for disabled supporters are behind blocks of seats. This is fine if they are on a raised platform, but not if their elevation is insufficient to allow those in wheelchairs to see the pitch if others in front stand up. Sometimes there are announcements asking for fans to sit because they are blocking the view of disabled supporters behind them, and this is an argument that has been put forward as to why supporters should not stand in front of their seats.

Obviously disabled supporters should be able to get a full view, but it is accepted that supporters will stand at moments of excitement. This would have been known when the ground was designed. Why then were disabled areas placed where their users, who are likely to be unable to stand, won't be able to see the pitch if their team scores a goal or gets a penalty? This was a particular problem in the away end at The Valley, but Charlton commendably dealt with it by roping off the row of seats immediately in front of the disabled area. Perhaps however it would have been better to have designed this relatively modern stand in such a way that the normal action of at least occasional standing would not stop disabled supporters from enjoying the most exciting parts of a match.

Sometimes the actions of those in charge of safety undermine the very arguments they are supposedly making. When West Ham played at Sheffield United in the FA Cup in February 2005, visiting supporters were allocated the steep upper tier of the Gordon Lamb Stand, with the gently sloping lower tier left empty. Letters were given to supporters requesting that they didn't stand and warning of a possible domino effect. I wrote to the club's safety officer questioning why West Ham supporters, who were known to have a tendency to stand, were allocated the upper tier, where any safety risk from standing was far greater than the lower.

His reply was that each fixture is individually assessed taking account of the possibility of disorder. My response was to express surprise that this assessment leads Sheffield United to allocate the upper tier first to visiting supporters at every match, regardless of the opposition. Whilst there may be occasional matches at which there is a possibility of disorder occurring within the ground, there are others where this risk must be negligible. Of course the club had to take all factors into account, but supporters found it hard to understand that while at other grounds threats have been made to close lower tiers due to the safety risk said to be caused by standing, Sheffield United's assessments led them to put away supporters in a steep upper tier when the lower was empty.

Finally we should look at perhaps the greatest inconsistency of all. Every summer a number of football grounds around the country host music concerts. At these concerts supporters often stand on the pitch, but more significantly no one objects to them standing, drinking and dancing in front of the very seats that football supporters are threatened with ejection if they stand up.

In 2005 Phill Gatenby wrote a report highlighting the inconsistencies between the behaviour of those attending football and concerts at the City of Manchester Stadium. Prior to five concerts by U2 and Oasis, Phill wrote to Manchester City Council's Stadium Licensing Officer asking what action would be taken to ensure that rock fans did not stand persistently throughout the shows. His answer was that no action was necessary as the regulations and guidelines for concerts were different than for football. Manchester City's website however stated that regulations applied 'to all events' and included the standard wording about persistent standing.

At the five concerts every fan in the seated areas stood up unchallenged for the entire shows. This included the second tiers and the very steep third tiers. Unlike at football where standing is mostly passive, concert fans were dancing and moving from side to side. With alcohol on sale inside the stadium for seven hours (as opposed to around two hours for football) and unlike at football being permitted to be taken to seats, many music fans were drunk. Others, despite a warning on the tickets, were openly consuming illegal drugs.

It was noted that people were going to the toilet far more frequently than at a football match, resulting in more movement along the rows. Some others on the pitch and not wanting to lose their positions, urinated into plastic cups, many of which were then thrown into the air to land on other people. The Manchester Evening News carried a letter from an irate mother after her daughter returned home with her clothes 'covered in urine'. Some fans in the seats urinated into containers rather than miss the show, but cups were then spilt onto rows in front, soaking people's bags and jackets. If football supporters were to behave in such a way they would be described as animals.

The combination of standing in upper tiers, intoxication and dancing in the seats resulted in a far greater safety risk than occurs with persistent standing at football matches, yet standing at concerts is accepted. Interestingly, the safety officer of a Premier League club recently said that there is nothing unsafe about standing in front of seats, or concerts wouldn't be allowed.

CHAPTER TWENTY SEVEN

CONCLUSIONS

There is no doubt that the state of football in the mid 1980s meant that something had to be done. For many years there had been little investment in grounds and facilities were frequently poor. Far too often safety was given little consideration, with the emphasis on controlling hooliganism, and the resulting fences made many grounds intrinsically unsafe. The behaviour of a minority of supporters was appalling, but often the way fans were treated by police and clubs set up an atmosphere of conflict.

A series of disasters, culminating in the horrific scenes when 96 people died against the fences of Hillsborough, finally resulted in decisive action. Lord Taylor's report, and the safety culture that now encompasses all aspects of our society, have led to our stadia becoming safe places to watch football. However, all-seating, the best known of Taylor's 76 recommendations, was considered by many at the time to be unnecessary. More than twenty years later, as supporters still refuse to sit, calls grow for all grounds to offer the choice to stand.

Although I started writing this book already holding firm views, I wanted to show and consider all the arguments. I was quite looking forward to wrestling with the pros and cons, and was willing to be swayed or conclude that the argument may be finely balanced. What was however surprising was just how weak almost all the arguments against the choice to stand become under close examination.

There's no doubt of the demand for standing. All the polls show that the vast majority of fans think choice should be provided, a view that significantly is also held by a majority of those who prefer to sit. Where they remain, terraces are often the most popular areas at the grounds, even if the price is little different to sitting, and tens of thousands of supporters stand up in front of their seats at all-seated stadia.

If terraces weren't safe they would not be permitted in Leagues One and Two, at rugby grounds and in Europe. If standing in front of seats was the safety risk that some claim, then music concerts wouldn't be held in football grounds. Although the common perception is that safety is main reason why standing shouldn't be permitted, no specific arguments are put forward as to why modern terraces are unsafe. The Taylor Report is commonly referred to, but it says surprisingly little to explain why the old terraces were unsafe, and of course could not consider modern terraces or convertible standing areas.

What the Taylor Report did do however, was to make recommendations that dealt with the hazards of the old and often ill-maintained terraces of the 1980s. The result of this, plus the removal of fences, is that our terraces are now safe. It is modern terraces or convertible areas that should be considered, not those of over twenty years ago. Supporters are now strictly counted into each area so capacity cannot be exceeded, and crucially the lack of fences means that escape onto the pitch is possible in case of emergency.

It is claimed that injury rates are higher at grounds with terracing than in all-seated stadia, but the data is highly unreliable and there are far too many variables to draw conclusions. Even the FLA admitted the difficulty in getting coherent statistics from clubs and I found one club whose injuries submitted included those incurred by players in a 5 a side tournament. The FLA's figures could equally be used to say that it's safer to watch football at a lower league ground with terracing than it is at all-seated Old Trafford, or that a supporter is twice as likely to be injured at Reading where almost all home fans stay in their seats, than Upton Park where ten thousand typically stand.

I could find little evidence to support the argument that to permit standing would lead to disorder. Thousands already stand on terraces and in front of seats, yet disorder inside grounds is now rare. The rate of arrests in Leagues One and Two is actually lower for those clubs with terraces than it is for all-seated grounds. Overall arrest figures started dropping before top clubs converted to all-seating and have continued to fall since. My conversations with safety officers showed that as general rule a fully seated crowd is easier to control than one which is standing, but that with adequate stewarding a standing crowd can be safely managed. However if no choice to stand is provided, clubs have to deal with the problem of unmanaged standing in seated areas.

It was Hillsborough that led to all-seating, but the disaster was not caused by terracing. A combination of factors resulted in the tragic loss of life, but the key elements were failings by those in charge, most notably South Yorkshire Police, to adequately plan, manage the crowd and learn from previous incidents. Most crucially fences prevented escape that would have relieved the overcrowding. It is right that we should listen to the bereaved families and survivors, but as with other disasters, it must be recognised that their understandable emotional involvement means that it's harder for their views on football grounds to be objective.

Lord Taylor wrote much about the greater comfort of seating, something that is often quoted as a reason why supporters should not be allowed the choice to stand. But choice is the key word – no one is suggesting that anyone should be forced to stand. Comfort is subjective and some people find it more comfortable to stand than to sit, particularly if the seats are cramped as they often are in older grounds. It seems a very strange argument to prohibit standing because some people may find it less comfortable, especially when there is plenty of opportunity for them to sit in other areas of the ground.

The argument that standing should not be permitted because it will reduce the diversity of those attending football, seems equally ridiculous. If it matters that diversity may be less in one part of a ground, then perhaps we should be looking at reducing prices for the most expensive Premier League seats to allow lower income families to enjoy these. Plenty of women, children and older people choose to watch from the terraces in the lower leagues, and with lower prices the diversity of supporters at these grounds is probably greater than at Premiership clubs. There is simply no evidence to suggest that permitting standing (or legitimising what already occurs at all-seated grounds) would stop families from attending matches. It seems more likely that providing choice would increase diversity.

A very valid argument is made as to why the current situation of unregulated persistent standing in front of seats needs to be resolved. It is a customer care issue that means children and supporters who are unable to stand for long periods cannot see the game. This can however be very simply solved by officially designating certain areas for standing, so that those who wish to sit can avoid them. The solution is to provide choice for all, with standing in the most suitable area. It is claimed that standing in front of seats is unsafe, but whilst there may be a degree of risk in steep upper tiers, few people consider standing in relatively low gradient areas to be dangerous. This has taken place without significant incident since our grounds became all-seated, and there seems to be no evidence that it is resulting in additional injuries. An independent report showed that the risks from supporters celebrating goals and leaving the stadium after the match are far greater than them standing passively standing during the game. If standing in front of seats was not safe concerts wouldn't be permitted in football grounds.

It is said that the less confrontational atmosphere at grounds, improved behaviour and greater diversity of spectators is due to all-seating, but I have found no evidence to back this up. There have been many other changes within football and society over the last twenty years, but it is perhaps convenient to credit all-seating with the improvements in our football grounds. If this were the case we would not be seeing the same changes at those grounds which retain terraces, or where many supporters stand in front of seats. Abolishing terraces at Coventry City in the early 1980s failed to solve the problems, and seats were taken out after the experiment failed. If all-seating is the panacea it would have been successful at Coventry.

It is often said that we shouldn't go against the recommendations of the Taylor Report, but these are not sacrosanct. Taylor made 76 recommendations, many of which were not implemented. Successive governments have chosen to allow standing at rugby and other sports, plus in the lower two divisions of the Football League. Lord Taylor's report was written at a time when hooliganism was still a major problem, grounds were in need of modernisation and there was no safety culture in the game. More than twenty years on much has changed and recommendations made against the backdrop of Hillsborough may no longer be necessary.

We should consider four crucial statements in Lord Taylor's final report.

'*I am satisfied that in England and Wales as in Scotland and abroad spectators will become accustomed and educated to sitting*'. Taylor was wrong, they haven't.

'*There is no panacea which will achieve total safety and cure all problems of behaviour and crowd control. But I am satisfied that seating does more to achieve those objectives than any other single measure.*' In this much quoted sentence Taylor clearly says single measure. A combination of a number of other measures could potentially have same effect and in the various controls he recommended for standing areas, this has been achieved.

'The evidence I have received has been overwhelmingly in favour of more seating accommodation'. The evidence favoured more seating, but Lord Taylor recommended all-seating. By going against the evidence that was presented to him Lord Taylor has taken away choice, causing a customer care issue for football supporters.

And finally, *'standing accommodation is not intrinsically unsafe'.* Whilst safety is not the only issue, it is the factor that most concerns the public, media and politicians. Supporters stand at British and European football grounds, at rugby matches and concerts. Various proposals have been put forward for standing areas to be included in all football grounds. They are not unsafe.

As I see it the arguments come into three areas:

Firstly, safety, which the general public believe is the main reason for all-seating, but most of those who understand the issue, whatever their overall views on 'bringing back standing', privately don't consider to be the key issue. On the whole, those on both sides of the argument agree that standing areas which meet the Green Guide are not unsafe.

Secondly, what I call the spurious arguments, such as diversity and comfort, which are easily rebuffed and maybe are primarily put forward in order to try to add to the weight of evidence on the side of those who oppose the choice to stand.

Thirdly, crowd control and disorder. I have seen no evidence to suggest that to permit more standing would result in a return to the football hooliganism that has virtually disappeared from all our grounds. Nor have I been able to find any link with all-seating and the reduction in hooliganism, other than perhaps some effect due to the pricing out of younger supporters. Is this what football, which is so keen to promote diversity, really wants to do?

The one issue where I can understand the argument against standing is that of crowd control. It is true that a standing crowd can be less easy to manage than a seated one, however this does not mean that it cannot be managed or is always more difficult to do so. A fully seated crowd will not migrate into the aisles, but standing supporters may have to be reminded to keep them clear. It should though be noted that some of those who choose to stand on a terrace may well stand in seats if the stadium was all seated, or not come to matches at all if forced to sit. A stadium without choice brings other crowd management issues. Additional monitoring and stewarding techniques may sometimes be needed when supporters stand, but this should not be a reason to deny choice.

Football should be inclusive and cater for the more passionate supporters, who are often those creating the atmosphere that so many enjoy. It might be easier to manage a crowd of sedentary sixty year old ladies, but clubs should want to attract a diverse range of supporters, giving the choice to those of all ages who prefer to stand up. The Albert Hall no doubt finds it easier to steward the Women's Institute AGM than it does a boxing match, but it caters for both, adapting its resources and methods as required. As the 23 clubs have shown, so can football.

Having looked at the arguments for and against the choice to stand, I shall briefly give my own views on how the situation should be taken forward.

The three year rule, whereby clubs must be all-seated after playing at Championship or Premier League level for three seasons, should be scrapped. Instead, on promotion to the Championship, if a club has terraces these should be assessed individually to determine whether any changes, such as capacity reduction or additional stewarding, are necessary to reflect the higher numbers that may be using them. Given that the terrace will have been deemed safe at its current capacity in League One, if a cut is considered necessary this would be expected to be only small.

The rule that prevents any club that has been all-seated from reverting to offering standing areas should be scrapped.

An objective evidence based review, considering the views of all concerned, including supporters, should be undertaken to determine whether the Secretary of State should alter the regulation so that standing areas may be permitted at all football grounds. This review may include trials of various proposed solutions at different clubs and the Secretary of State should permit relaxation of the regulation on individual basis to allow these trials.

While the review is underway, a more relaxed attitude should be taken to some standing in seated areas, provided that this is not in upper tiers and is managed so that those who wish to sit can do so. This can be achieved by giving more open information when tickets are sold, and if stands are not full, by unallocated seating.

There is merit in all the proposed solutions and all should be permitted, with the club, in conjunction with its Safety Advisory Group, allowed the freedom to choose the type of spectator accommodation it wishes to provide, rather than having this dictated by government.

Conventional terraces should be permitted, subject of course to the safeguards suggested by Taylor and currently laid down in the Green Guide. These have been proved to work well and remain the most appropriate solution for clubs who do not expect to play in European competitions.

Rail seats or other convertible standing / seating areas are, as in Europe, the obvious solution for clubs who need be all-seated for some matches. These are ideal for new builds. Whilst conversion of existing seating areas to convertible standing is clearly possible and should be easily achievable at the same capacity, there are potential cost and possibly engineering issues with increasing the capacity. At the time of completing this book further research was being carried out into these issues, which will vary between each stadium. This will give additional information on the likely payback time for typical conversions.

For new builds a maximum capacity of 3,000 should be set for each self contained standing area. There should be no limit on the total capacity of standing accommodation in a stadium, as this should be chosen to reflect demand. Neither should there be a set limit on the maximum proportion of a ground designated for standing, as this would force some smaller clubs to install more seats than they can realistically fill. It is however suggested that, reflecting demand and the evidence which Lord Taylor received, for a Premier League club no more than 35% of a stadium should be designated for standing.

Until such time as every club is permitted purpose built standing areas, and in any stadia that chose not to offer these (I believe it is unlikely that even if they were permitted some clubs would want to convert areas to standing), managed standing in front of seats should be allowed. This would be in clearly designated areas, which would be those of lowest rake. Separation of away supporters who wish to stand from those who want to sit would be achieved by allocating the front of an area (or the upper tier) for sitting and the back for standing. If an area is not expected to be full supporters should be free to self regulate by unallocated seating. The number of standing places for home supporters and the split for away fans, should be determined by customer demand.

So you have read the background, the current situation, the pros and the cons, and finally some conclusions. I accept that I started the book with my own views on standing, although was open to be persuaded by the evidence. Investigation has however served to strengthen my personal view that supporters should have the choice to stand at every football ground. The only argument in favour of all-seating which I can accept as justified, is that a seated crowd can be easier to manage, but not that standing is more likely to cause disorder. However, the vast majority of standing crowds present no problem and with adequate stewarding standing supporters can be managed.

I have presented the arguments – please make your own conclusions.

CHAPTER TWENTY EIGHT

MISINFORMATION, COVER-UP OR CONSPIRACY

My aim in writing this book was to document the reasons why we have all-seater stadia, explain the current situation which many people don't appreciate, and set out the arguments for and against the choice to stand. I have made my own conclusions and hope that setting out the facts will help others to make informed judgements. I'd expected to end the book with the final sentence of the previous chapter, but my investigations seem to have raised as many questions as they may have answered. I cannot end without asking some of these questions.

Why have successive governments refused to allow the full facts about Hillsborough to be made public?

Why did the Hillsborough coroner impose the 3.15pm cut off time when it was clear that there were major concerns about the effectiveness of the rescue and first aid operation, which may have affected the final death toll?

Who took the CCTV tapes from the locked control room at Hillsborough and why?

Why did Lord Taylor recommend all-seating, when he wrote that the evidence he received was overwhelmingly in favour of more seating, his technical working party referred to higher proportions of seating, and he doesn't refer to any evidence that grounds should be totally seated?

Why did Lord Taylor choose to quote selectively and misleadingly from the Norman Chester Centre survey of FSA members, giving the incorrect impression that a majority of supporters backed all-seating if covered and reasonably priced?

Why did the DCMS say that it is critical that debate does not add to the burden of those affected by Hillsborough, then when the influence of survivors and families was questioned, simply say that their original letter was making the point that we must learn lessons from Hillsborough?

Why did the DCMS say that the Government supports the recommendations made in the Taylor Report, then when it was pointed out that many of these have not been implemented, change to referring to just its general support for the Taylor Report?

Why did the DCMS seek to explain why some of Taylor's recommendations were not implemented by saying that they were not all a matter for government, when the report made it clear that the implementation of all-seating for all designated grounds was an action for the Secretary of State?

Why do the DCMS say that many of the grounds in Leagues One and Two being all-seated shows that a number of clubs are content to be all-seated even when not legally required to, when it is the funding restrictions from the Football Foundation and that they hope to or have played in the Championship, that are the primary reason for not offering standing?

Why, contrary to Taylor's recommendation, is standing still permitted at sports such as rugby?

Why is it considered safe for people to stand in all-seated areas of football grounds to watch music concerts, but not even to stand in lower tiers to watch football?

Why do some clubs consider it necessary to reduce away allocations, eject or ban supporters for persistent standing, when others take little or no action to stop it?

Why are stewards not prevented from heavy handed action causing conflict with supporters, and far more risk to safety and of disorder than the act of standing?

What is unsafe about modern terraces?

If a terrace is safe for a given capacity in League One, why does it have to be removed simply because the team is playing a higher standard of football in the Championship?

Why is it not permitted for a club that has been relegated from the Championship to remove seats, when had it not played in the top two divisions it could have kept terraces?

Given that the same changes have occurred at grounds with terracing and those where large numbers stand in front of seats, where is the evidence that the huge reduction in hooliganism, the less confrontational atmosphere and the increase in families in grounds are due to all-seating?

Why does it matter that the demographics of supporters in one part of a ground is less diverse than in others, and if it does, what is being done to increase diversity in the most expensive seats at Premier League grounds?

Why is comfort used as an argument as to why supporters should not have the choice to stand?

Why does the Government continue to suggest that a spectator is less likely to be injured at an all-seated ground, when the statistics are far too varied and unreliable to draw conclusions?

Why do some clubs make a big issue of supporters standing passively in front of seats, but play music after goals which encourages the whole crowd to stand and celebrate?

Why do the authorities seem to want to play down the extent of standing in seated areas?

If the FA and others consider the ability to identify supporters by their seat number as important in dealing with trouble makers, why do they permit unallocated seating at many grounds?

Why when an away allocation is cut on 'safety grounds' due to persistent standing, do clubs not spread the reduced number of supporters over the normal area, so considerably reducing the supposed safety risk, rather than keeping the usual density but in a smaller area?

Why are many club officials unwilling to make public their views that supporters should have a choice to stand?

What made Leicester City Chief Executive Tim Davies change from whole hearted support of Stand Up Sit Down's proposals, to stating very much watered down support for standing just a month later?

Why did a club director send me an email with positive comments about how well the terraces work at his club, then threaten legal action when I asked permission to publish it?

Why does the Premier League no longer ask questions about standing in its annual supporters survey, when it is well aware that this is an issue on which many fans have strong views?

Why do the Premier League and Football Leagues consider it

necessary to make their own rules about standing accommodation?

Why is standing permitted in top European grounds but not in the UK?

Why won't the football authorities and clubs listen to their customers and back the call for the choice to stand?

It seems that whatever the evidence, the powers that be don't want football supporters to be permitted the choice to stand. Unsubstantiated and spurious arguments are used to maintain the status quo, and many people believe that football simply doesn't want the type of supporters that it thinks want to stand up. It has been suggested that all-seating facilitates the social engineering that replaces traditional working class supporters with more affluent customers, who are able to pay high ticket prices and spend more on club merchandise.

It is common for stewards to tell supporters that they must sit because it's 'illegal to stand', perhaps due to either ignorance or over-zealousness on the part of the steward. It can be put down to inadvertent misinformation. If one is generous the same explanation could be used for the Government's change of view when questioned over both the influence given to Hillsborough families and support for Taylor's recommendations. However, when all the anomalies are put together it starts to raise a bigger question.

Lord Taylor received evidence that recommended increasing the proportion of seating and he made recommendations which resulted in terraces becoming safe. But despite the evidence he quotes, he decided that standing should be abolished. The Government implemented his recommendation for football, although later decide to permit terraces in the lower two divisions. It did not implement all-seating for other sports. Despite all the evidence in favour of offering a choice to stand, with the exception of supporters, all the organisations involved present a united front for all-seating. Often much of each organisation's justification for all-seating is to say that other organisations want it. Whatever their private views, few people will publicly break rank. Why is there what seems almost a conspiracy to stop supporters having the choice to stand, whatever the evidence?

I have a theory:

Those who control and legislate the game would like every club to be all-seated, and manipulate the arguments and regulations not only to prevent a return to standing, but to engineer by stealth a position whereby eventually all terraces will disappear.

Governments are scared that they would be held responsible should there be another Hillsborough. They don't really understand the issues, and that the safety controls and removal of fences mean this couldn't happen, but nor do they see any votes in it.

Some local politicians and officials see the prevention of persistent standing as a way to make a name for themselves.

The press (with a few exceptions) aren't interested in the issues, but most papers either think or want to think that football supporters are hooligans.

Sky TV want the passion and atmosphere created by supporters who stand, but would rather pretend that the noise came from families with jester hats and painted faces.

The FLA back Government policy, sometimes it seems no matter how ludicrous the arguments required to defend it, although it must be said that recent changes suggest that they now have a far more reasonable and open attitude.

The police generally don't consider standing unsafe, but want the control of every supporter having their own designated seat (but on the whole they don't mind if they stand up in front of them).

Many safety officers support standing and few consider existing terraces or new safe standing areas to be unsafe, but a number (perhaps as they were police officers at the time) fear a return to supporters running amok as they did thirty years ago if standing is permitted.

The majority of lower league clubs would like to allow standing, but have little influence, their main priority being maximising their share of TV revenue.

Many clubs would like to offer a choice to stand, but won't say so publicly for fear of breaking rank or that it would be seen to encourage persistent standing.

Top clubs can, or until recently could, easily fill their grounds. Most of the more influential clubs would rather have the stadium full of middle class families who spend more on merchandise, than the lower income young males who they see as traditional standers and who don't fit with the 'brand' they want to promote.

The Football Authorities are largely controlled by top clubs, with considerable influence from Sky TV, so reflect what they want. All are hugely influenced by money.

The views of supporters – football's customers – are ignored!

UPDATE

The choice to stand is an ongoing issue and there were further developments between completion of this book and it being sent to press.

In a survey by *Talk Sport* in November 2011, 91% of those voting said we should have '*safe standing zones in football stadia*'.

Almost a third of Cardiff's 300 following at Leeds United walked out in protest at their fellow supporters being ejected for standing, the action stemming from a sense of unfairness at being treated differently to home fans.

Speaking at the International Football Arena Conference in November 2011, John Barrow, a Senior Principal at renowned architects Populous, and who played a key role in designing Wembley Stadium said, '*We as designers have no problem with standing at all. It would clearly need to be legislated for, managed, and safely stewarded, but in terms of safety it can be done without any problems at all in small areas.*'

In December 2011 the Scottish Premier League announced that a meeting of its twelve member clubs had voted to change the rules on all-seating, and that the SPL Board would now have the ability to approve any request made by a club to pilot a standing area. Chief Executive Neil Doncaster said, '*Since I joined the SPL in 2009, there has been widespread support amongst fans to re-introduce safe standing areas. I am delighted that we have been able to respond positively to supporters' views on improving the match day experience*'. Within days, several clubs, including Celtic and

Rangers, announced that they were looking seriously at the possibility of introducing standing areas.

Within hours of the SPL announcement, Dan Johnson, spokesman for the English Premier League, however confirmed their all-seater policy, saying '*The bottom line is that it* (standing at matches) *is illegal under the legislation that was brought in after Hillsborough. We can't have standing in the Premier League and the Championship and it's not a situation we would like to see change.*'

In January 2012 *The Daily Record* reported that Glasgow City Council had given its blessing for clubs to install the SPL - sanctioned safe standing areas. Calling for FIFA to relax their rules on international matches, Tartan Army spokesman Hamish Husband told the paper, '*I would love to go back to the old terraces as it creates a better atmosphere. If you go to the North Stand at Hampden on any international date you will find that most of the Tartan Army stand up anyway.*'

Arrest figures for the 2010/11 season again showed no evidence to link disorder with standing. A total of 3,089 supporters were arrested inside and outside grounds, a drop of 9% on the previous year and an average of less than one per match. No arrests were made at 71% of matches and 51% of games were police free. The rate of 8.2 arrests per 100,000 spectators showed that despite additional offences being introduced, the arrest rate had halved since Taylor's deadline for the top two divisions to be all-seated. Comparison of arrests in Leagues One and Two showed that over the four seasons 2007/8 to 2010/11 the average rate was approximately 14% higher at all-seated clubs than those with terraces.

Liverpool FC announced that 6,000 tickets would be allocated to Manchester United supporters for their FA Cup 4th round tie at Anfield, but that the end two seats on each row would not be sold, to prevent supporters spreading into the gangways. It seems that there was an acceptance that fans would stand, but at last a common sense action to keep aisles clear rather than an unnecessary and arbitrary allocation cut.

A report commissioned by the Premier League, by Crowd Dynamics (CD), a consultancy specialist in safety and crowd behaviour, concluded that, *'standing in seated areas alone may be considered to carry a negligible statistical likelihood of spontaneous progressive crowd collapse'*.

CD highlighted that, *'safety issues are not related to the persistency of standing in seated areas by itself; in many respects the level of risk will be greater at times of excitement, especially when fans suddenly leap to their feet, rush forward or jump up and down'*.

The report stated that supporters will stand at moments of excitement and highlighted the increased risk in steeper areas. It stated that, *'Although standing in seated areas with shallow rakes may be considered as low risk, if it is tolerated by safety management it may be more challenging to influence those in steeper areas to sit'*.

The report recommended actions such as avoiding steep areas, leaving seats at ends of rows and at the front of upper tiers empty, and introduction of strategically placed barriers to seated areas. These actions and the comments on safety were broadly in line with those proposed in Chapter Twenty One, and the last seemed to be suggesting a similar principle to the rail seats proposed by the FSF.

In January 2011 Aston Villa announced that they were exploring the possibility of installing a standing area of rail seating in the corner of Villa Park; (under the scoreboard where the Holte End and Trinity Road stands meet). Chief Executive Paul Faulkner told the Birmingham Mail that the plans had been unanimously backed by both male and female members of the Supporters Consultation

Group. Villa bosses said that they hoped the scheme would improve atmosphere and bring back fans, and that if successful could be extended to other areas of the ground. Other Premier League and Championship clubs were also showing serious interest in installing rail seats, but were yet to make this public.

THE FOOTBALL SUPPORTERS' FEDERATION

The Football Supporters' Federation (FSF) is the national supporters' organisation for all football fans. It comprises more than 180,000 individual fans and members of local supporters' organisations from every club in the professional structure and many from the pyramid.

The FSF is a democratically run members' organisation which was formed in 2002 from a merger between the Football Supporters' Association and the National Federation of Football Supporters Clubs. Membership is free to all football supporters. It has regular meetings with the football authorities and the Department of Culture Media and Sport, discussing a wide range of issues, to take forward policies or in response to concerns raised by supporters.

The FSF has detailed meetings on specific topics with the relevant authorities or other bodies such as the Independent Football Commission and the Police Match Commanders. It also meets with Government and the all-party football group of MPs when necessary. The FSF regularly takes up specific complaints and cases which are raised with it by individual members or affiliated organisations and encourages the participation of all supporters in this process.

The Football Supporters' Federation believes that all supporters should have the choice to either stand or sit at football matches.

www.fsf.org.uk

ALSO BY PETER CATON

NO BOAT REQUIRED
– EXPLORING TIDAL ISLANDS

When is an island not an island? Peter Caton takes us to all four corners of England, Scotland and Wales to find out.

Sharing our nation's fascination with islands, Peter sets out to be the first person to visit all 43 tidal islands which can be walked to from the UK mainland. Along the way he faces many challenges: precipitous cliffs, vicious dogs, disappearing footpaths, lost bus drivers, fast tides, quicksand and enormous quantities of mud, but also experiences wonderfully scenic journeys by road, rail and on foot. He contrasts the friendly welcome from most islanders and owners with the reluctance of others to permit visits, and tells how he was thrown off one secret island.

An entertaining narrative illustrated with colour photographs, *No Boat Required* contains a wealth of information as the author unearths many little known facts and stories. It tells of the solitude of the many remote islands and the difficulties of balancing the needs of people and wildlife. We learn of the islands' varied histories – stories of pirates, smugglers, murder and ghosts, of battles with Vikings, an island claimed by punks and another with its own king. He writes of the beauty of the islands and our coast, and reflects on how these may be affected by climate change.

In *No Boat Required* Peter Caton takes us to explore islands, some familiar but most which few of us know exist and even fewer have visited. He finds that our tidal islands are special places, many with fascinating and amusing stories and each one of them different. It adds up to a unique journey around Britain.

£12.99   343 Pages   ISBN 9781848767010 **Published by Matador**

ALSO BY PETER CATON

ESSEX COAST WALK

When Peter Caton set out to walk the Essex coast he had no idea of the beauty, wildlife and stories that he would find on the way. He takes the reader up and down the many creeks and estuaries of the longest coastline of any English county, through nature reserves, seaside resorts, unspoilt villages, sailing centres and alongside industry past and present. On the way we read of tales of witchcraft, ghosts, smuggling, bigamy and incest. We learn of the county's varied history – stories of battles with Vikings, of invading Romans bringing elephants, a fort where the only casualty occurred in a cricket match, burning Zeppelins and of Jack the Ripper.

Whilst an entertaining narrative, not a guidebook, *Essex Coast Walk* contains a wealth of information, including many little-known facts and stories. With gentle humour to match the coastline's gentle beauty, and illustrated with photographs and maps, the book makes for easy reading.

The book highlights how climate change may alter our coast and looks at new methods of coping with rising sea levels. It tells us how tiny settlements grew into large holiday resorts and how other villages have remained as unspoilt and isolated communities. The author's thought provoking final reflections consider how the coast has changed over the centuries and what its future may be.

Written in an accessible style, *Essex Coast Walk* has been enjoyed not only by those living in the county, but by others who have been surprised to read of the beauty and history of this little known part of our coast.

£9.99 376 PAGES   ISBN 9781848761162   Published by Matador